De-Centring Western Sexualities
Central and Eastern European Perspectives

Edited by

ROBERT KULPA
Birkbeck College, London

and

JOANNA MIZIELIŃSKA
Warsaw School of Social Sciences and Humanities, Poland

Routledge
Taylor & Francis Group

LONDON AND NEW YORK

First published 2011 by Ashgate Publishing

Published 2016 by Routledge
2 Park Square, Milton Park, Abingdon, Oxfordshire OX14 4RN
711 Third Avenue, New York, NY 10017, USA

First issued in paperback 2016

Routledge is an imprint of the Taylor & Francis Group, an informa business

British Library Cataloguing in Publication Data
De-centring Western sexualities : Central and Eastern European perspectives.
 1. Sexual orientation–Europe, Central. 2. Sexual orientation–Europe, Eastern. 3. Sexual minorities–Europe, Central. 4. Sexual minorities–Europe, Eastern. 5. Sexual minorities–Legal status, laws, etc.–Europe, Central. 6. Sexual minorities–Legal status, laws, etc.–Europe, Eastern. 7. Sexual orientation–Cross-cultural studies. 8. Sexual minorities–Cross-cultural studies.
 I. Kulpa, Robert. II. Mizielinska, Joanna.
 306.7'6'0943–dc22

Library of Congress Cataloging-in-Publication Data
Kulpa, Robert
 De-centring western sexualities : Central and Eastern European perspectives / by Robert Kulpa and Joanna Mizielinska.
  p. cm.
Includes bibliographical references and index.
ISBN 978-1-4094-0242-8   ISBN 978-1-4094-0243-5
 1. Sex–Europe, Central. 2. Sex–Europe, Eastern. 3. Sexual minorities–Europe, Central. 4. Sexual minorities–Europe, Eastern. I. Mizielinska, Joanna. II. Title.
HQ18.C36K85 2010
306.76'60943–dc22

2010036370

ISBN 13: 978-1-138-24690-4 (pbk)
ISBN 13: 978-1-4094-0242-8 (hbk)

Contents

Acknowledgements

As with many other projects, we feel that this book would not have been possible without the support of many people. First of all – the authors, who helped to shape our vision with flesh of their insight and expertise. Then our reviewers who encouraged us to think through some of the threads in our chapter. Our thanks go also to Judith Halberstam and Gavin Brown. We would also like to thank Agata Stasińska, Lynne Segal, Sasha Roseneil, Jonathan Kemp, Caroline Walters and Katherine Ludwin for their inspiration and help.

Always already Judith Butler, for constant and timeless inspiration.

Finally, our deepest gratitude goes to our 'chosen families' – friends, partners, and relatives who were with and next to us in time of need. Thank you.

Notes on Contributors

Jon Binnie is reader in human geography and director of the Manchester Institute of Social and Spatial Transformations at Manchester Metropolitan University. His research interests focus on sexuality and urban space, particularly in a transnational context, as well as the spatial politics of cosmopolitanism, citizenship and everyday life. He is the author of *The Globalization of Sexuality* (Sage 2004) and co-author of *The Sexual Citizen: Queer Politics and Beyond* (Polity Press 2000) and *Pleasure Zones: Bodies, Cities, Spaces* (Syracuse University Press 2001). He is also the co-editor of *Cosmopolitan Urbanism* (Routledge 2006).

Jelisaveta Blagojević received her PhD in Gender Studies at the University of Novi Sad, Association of the Centers for Interdisciplinary and Multidisciplinary Studies and Researches. She holds the M.Phil Diploma in Gender&Culture Studies at Open University. Since 2001 she has been working at the Belgrade Women's Studies and Gender Research Center, and she is a Associated Lecturer at the Gender and Politics program at the Political Science Faculty, Belgrade University. Since 2006 she has been a Professor and Dean for Academic Affairs at the Faculty for Media and Communications, University Singidunum in Belgrade. She works as a Lecturer at different universities in South East Europe. Selected publications include: 'Culture to Come' in *Culture, Others, Women*, ed. Jasenka Kodrnja (Zagreb 2010), *Media/ Power* (Belgrade 2010), *Hieroglyphs of Jealousy* (Euro-Balkan Institute Skopje 2008), *Zajednica onih koji nemaju zajednicu* (Community Without Community) (Belgrade 2008), and *Gender and Identity* (Skopje, Ljubljana, Belgrade 2006).

Christian Klesse is a lecturer in cultural studies at Manchester Metropolitan University. Christian's research interests are in the fields of the body, sexualities, intimacies, race/racism and sexual politics. He is author of *The Spectre of Promiscuity: Gay Male and Bisexual Non-Monogamies and Polyamories* (Ashgate 2007).

Roman Kuhar is an assistant professor in the Department of Sociology at the Faculty of Arts, University of Ljubljana. He was also a guest lecturer in gay rights at the European Inter-University Centre in Venice. He holds a PhD in sociology and works as a researcher at the Peace Institute, Ljubljana. He is the author of two books: *Mi, drugi* [*We, the Others*] (Škuc-Lambda 2001) and *Media Construction of Homosexuality* (Mediawatch, 2003), co-author (with A. Švab) of *The Unbearable Comfort of Privacy: Everyday Life of Gays and Lesbians* (Politike, 2006) and co-editor (with J. Takács) of *Beyond the Pink Curtain: Everyday Life of LGBT People in Eastern Europe* (Politike Symposion 2007). He is also co-editor of the annual Intolerance Monitor Report, published by the Peace Institute, and an editor of LGBT magazine *Narobe*.

Robert Kulpa is a PhD candidate in the Department of Psychosocial Studies, Birkbeck College, University of London, UK. He is interested in queer studies, post-communist transformations, non-normative identities, post-colonial studies and nationalism. His recent publications include articles in journals (*Europe-Asia Studies*, *Slavonic and East European Review*) and books: *Sage Encyclopedia of Gender and Society* (2009) and *The EU and Central & Eastern Europe: Successes and Failures of Europeanization in Politics and Society* (2009). He is a guest editor of the 'Queer Studies: Methodological Approaches' Special Issue of the *Graduate Journal of Social Science*, Amsterdam University Press.

Alexander Lambevski is the founding editor and publisher of *Sextures.net* – a new Central and Eastern European online academic journal of sexualities, cultures and politics. He lives in Macedonia and Australia. He is affiliated to the National Centre for HIV Social Research at the University of New South Wales, Sydney. His main research interests are: the interface between gender, ethnicity, class and sexuality; queer ethnography; queer theory; and the history, anthropology and sociology of emotions. He has published in *Sexualities*, *Social Semiotics*, *International Journal for Critical Psychology*, *Gay and Lesbian Quarterly (GLQ)* and *Journal of Homosexuality*, among others. He is a joint author of *Living as Men – Masculinities in Contemporary Urban Australia* (NCHSR 2001), and author of chapters published in *Sexualities: Critical Concepts in Sociology* (Routledge 2002) and *Here Comes the Rain Again: The World about Milcho Manchevski's Before the Rain* (Skopje 2004).

Joanna Mizielińska is an associate professor at the Warsaw School of Social Sciences and Humanities, Poland. In the academic year 2001/2002 she was a Fulbright scholar at Princeton University, where she conducted her research under the auspices of Prof. Judith Butler. She also teaches gender and queer studies at Warsaw University. In the academic year 2004/2005 she was a CIMO researcher at the Christina Institute in Helsinki University. In 2004 she published her book *(De)Konstruckje kobiecości* [*(De)Constructions of Femininity*] (Słowo/Obraz Terytoria). In 2007 her second book was published, called *Płeć/Ciało/Seksualność: Od feminizmu do teorii queer* [*Gender/body/sexuality: From Feminism to Queer Theory*] (Universitas). Her academic interests include: sex, gender and sexuality in culture; social construction of sexualities/genders/bodies; gender performativity; the problem of exclusion of the Other in culture; society and feminist thoughts; new concepts/models of family, 'families we choose'; representation of femininity and masculinity in global culture; feminist philosophy and queer theory.

Kateřina Nedbálková is an assistant professor in sociology at the Masaryk University in Brno, Czech Republic. She teaches sociological theories of gender, and methodology in social sciences. She also works at the Institute for Research of Social Reproduction and Integration. Her academic and research interests focus on gender and sexuality, imprisonment and methodology of qualitative research. She has published extensively in Czech academic journals.

Sasha Roseneil is Professor of Sociology and Social Theory and director of the Birkbeck Institute for Social Research at Birkbeck College, University of London. Sasha is one of the founding editors of the journal *Feminist Theory*, and is the author of *Disarming Patriarchy* (Open University Press, 1995) and *Common Women, Uncommon Practices: The Queer Feminisms of Greenham* (Cassell 2000). She is editor or co-editor of *Stirring It: Challenges for Feminism* (Taylor and Francis 1994), *Practising Identities* (Macmillan 1999), *Consuming Cultures* (Macmillan 1999), *Globalization and Social Movements* (Palgrave 2000) and special issues of the journals *Citizenship Studies*, *Feminist Theory*, *Current Sociology* and *Social Politics*. Her latest book is Sociability, Sexuality, Self: Relationality and Individualization (Routledge 2008).

Mariya Stoilova is a research fellow at the Birkbeck Institute for Social Research, University of London. She has completed doctoral research on 'Gender and Generation: Women's Experiences of the Transition from Socialism in Bulgaria' in the School of Sociology and Social Policy at the University of Leeds (2004–2009). At present Mariya is working on an EU FP6 Integrated Project, FEMCIT. As part of FEMCIT, Mariya is researching transformations in intimate citizenship in Bulgaria.

Shannon Woodcock is a specialist in Romani, Romanian and Albanian history. Her forthcoming monographs document Romanian deportations of Roma during the Holocaust, and everyday life experiences of Romani, Vlach and ethnic Albanians under the communist dictatorship of Enver Hoxha in Albania. She teaches at La Trobe University, Australia. Her work has been published in anthologies – *The Politics and Aesthetics of Refusal* (Cambridge Scholars Press 2007), *Living Gender after Communism* (Indiana University Press 2007) – and journals: *Anthropology of East Europe Review* (26/1, 2008) and *Patterns of Prejudice* (44/5, 2010).

Introduction:
Why Study Sexualities in Central and Eastern Europe?

Robert Kulpa and Joanna Mizielińska

Although homosexuality in its many manifestations has been a significant factor in societies throughout the ages and across cultures, the real explosion of its politics and visibility has taken place after World War II and, arguably, in the 'West'. The vast amount of academic literature about sexuality is written from and in a Western (Anglo-American) context. However, even when considering the recent shift in queer studies towards embracing the margins and outskirts, de-centring the politics of geolocation, the growing amount of literature on non-Western cultures continues to concern mostly post-colonial 'far-flung' regions (Asia, Africa). There is still noticeably less work done about the West's 'neighbouring' countries of Central and Eastern Europe (CEE).

By introducing CEE as a 'European context' (somehow 'Western-ish' since 'European' tends to equal 'Western') we would like to pluralise and problematise the notion of 'Western/non-Western' sexualities (because of the stress on 'Central and Eastern' denotation). We do so because we believe that the dichotomy 'West/non-West' is mainly constructed on the basis of Anglo-American ways of experiencing sexuality, making the 'Western experience' the normative one, placed at the centre of narratives. The most straightforward aim of this book is, thus, to critically assess the current state of knowledge about sexualities outside the all-pervasive framings of the 'West', and to focus on their expressions in the 'nearby' and still underexplored region of Central and Eastern Europe. By doing so, we consider both categories, West and CEE, and show that it is virtually impossible to foreclose and homogenise them as any sort of coherent entity.

Sexuality and Post-Communist Studies

The 20 years after the fall of communism produced a vast amount of literature about the CEE region (among many others, see Rupnik 1999; Drulák 2001; Kymlicka and Opalski 2005; Shiraev and Shlapentokh 2002; Ekiert, Kubik and Vachudova 2007; Pleines and Fischer 2009). However, we feel that post-communist studies are still predominantly political science studies, interested in transformations of political systems in the region; together with economics, these two disciplines form the dominant perspective. There is, however, a growing body of work about cultural and social re-evaluation of everyday life experiences in CEE, written from cultural studies perspectives; yet it still remains relatively small in comparison with economics and politics.

When focusing specifically on CEE, one needs to acknowledge the existing and well-developed body of literature about women and feminism (e.g. Funk and Mueller 1993; Gal and Kligman 2000a, 2000b; Jähnert and et al. 2001; Johnson and Robinson 2007). However, hardly any of these positions undertakes the effort of scrutinising non-heterosexuality. It can be said that, contrary to the existing literature on gender and sexuality in the Western cultural context, the field of sexuality studies in (and about) CEE is in its infancy. The scarcity of work is clear. So far only a couple of publications (e.g. Štulhofer and Sandfort 2004; Kuhar and Takács 2007) have directly targeted the issue of homosexuality in the post-communist countries. There are a few other books that contain entries on a single country (e.g. Eder, Hall and Hekma 1999), books about CEE (or a particular country) that have a chapter on sexuality, among other issues (e.g. Flam 2001), or gender and lesbian and gay studies journals that occasionally publish articles concerning the region. It is not much, although of all the regions, Russia seems to stand out, with a fast growing scholarship (e.g. Essig 1999; Baer 2002, 2009; Stella 2007). However it is not our aim here to present a comprehensive bibliography because this is well covered through the references at the end of each chapter.

CEE and Sexuality Studies

By introducing CEE as the geopolitical framework, we bring a 'new' area of examination into queer/sexuality studies. The epistemological focus on the hierarchies and dynamics of exchange between West and CEE highlights power as one of the main categories, together with wider structural inequalities in the organisation of the world (the macro level). At the same time, the chapters explore the hegemonies of everyday life, e.g. lived experience of 'globalised/localised gay identities' (the micro level). In the spirit of an intersectional approach, we are convinced that by grouping chapters that deal with different national settings, both theoretically and empirically, we open up the platform for further study by constantly refocusing attention on different categories and issues, specific to each context.

Consequently, this book highlights some underlying hierarchisations present within queer studies, and contributes to the discussion about the notion and meaning of 'queer'. In doing so, we join other voices calling for the de-centralisation and de-Westernisation of 'queer theory'. If, in a Western context, 'queer' is to somehow relate to (and presumably reject) identitarian politics of the 'Stonewall era', this volume asks what is left of 'queer' in the CEE context, where Stonewall never happened; where it stands as an empty signifier, a meaningless figure, and yet is still a pervasive and monumental reference.

We hope that this book will help to unsettle Western perspectives in queer studies by providing new insights in discussions about what constitutes 'queer'. It brings together macro- and micro-level analysis, providing conceptual and empirical tools and arguments. It probes the boundaries of geographical regions, cultural practices, temporal narratives, discursive concepts and imagined locations. The chapters collected in the book offer a perspective (or rather a range of perspectives) on non-normative sexualities that are relational and performative, temporal and 'geohistorical'. These sexualities remain in wider economies of global exchange of capital (cultural, social, financial, spatial and historical). We look at them at particular moments of 'post-communist transformation' and 'democratisation' as a site of tussles between hegemonic discourses in a transnational context of negotiation and resistance.

Outline of Chapters

The chapters are grouped into two areas. The first consists of theoretical writings focusing on the transnational circulation of homosexualities and identities, and on lesbian, gay, bisexual and transsexual/transgender (LGBT) politics in CEE. The second focuses on issues of intimacy, practising queer citizenship and kinship in CEE. All chapters question the relation of CEE to the West on various levels, and so proliferate the debate about 'transnational sexualities', 'global LGBT activism' and 'locality'.

Joanna Mizielińska and Robert Kulpa's chapter, '"Contemporary Peripheries": Queer Studies, Circulation of Knowledge and East/West Divide', creates a larger theoretical framework for the whole book. By undertaking issues of the hegemony of time and space – as reflected in the Anglo-American production of knowledge, globalisation, post-socialist transformation and lesbian and gay studies – the chapter provides critical engagement with current trends in queer studies, especially of a post-colonial provenance. The authors aim to problematise and pluralise the notion of 'Western' sexuality and indicate its 'contemporal periphery' – i.e. mechanisms of 'Othering' CEE (e.g. by rendering it 'permanently transitional'/'post-communist'). The authors try to visualise their ideas of time by providing a graphical representation as two separate geopolitical-temporal modalities running parallel, where in 1989 one of them finishes and the other becomes universal for both. However, the authors contrast the Western 'time of sequence' with the Eastern 'time of coincidence' represented as a 'knotting' and 'looping' of time(s). Mizielińska and Kulpa use as an example sexual politics in CEE and try to organise the 'knotted temporality of CEE' into familiar stages and inscribe it into a particular history (here into a Western history of LGBTQ (queer) movements), simplifying it in order to make sense of it. However, they also ask a set of important questions:

- Does such 'unknotting' make sense, and for whom?
- What are the prerequisites to be able to understand it in either form?
- Why are certain models familiar to 'all'?
- Why will local narrations of lesbian and gay emancipation be seen as precisely 'local' and not 'universally' recognised?

With this chapter, they want to undertake the task of questioning the power relations between 'West' and 'CEE', between Western queer academic scholarship and CEE theoretical insights, calling not only for the 'de-centralisation of queer theory', but also for greater attentiveness to spatial and temporal choices in doing so.

Jelisaveta Blagojević, in her chapter 'Between Walls: Provincionalism, Human Rights, Sexualities and Serbian Public Discourse on EU Integration', recalls the recent debate about the second national gay parade in Belgrade in 2009. What prevailed in the arguments of the local authorities, and also those who declare themselves in favour of 'Europe, EU integration and human rights', was the conviction that sexual orientation is a private matter and 'should be kept behind the [four] walls'. Accordingly, there are no reasons to demonstrate one's sexual preferences in public. The metaphor of 'the wall' helps Blagojević in analysing public discourse on human rights and sexuality in contemporary Serbian society. Additionally, she refers to the notion of the 'provincial mind', introduced by the Serbian philosopher Radomir Konstantinovic in *Filosofija palanke/Philosophy of the Provincial* (1981). Although predominantly targeting Serbian nationalism, Konstantinovic's criticism may equally be applied to any geopolitical location. 'Provincial mind' is a state of consciousness that may, and indeed does, occur everywhere. So by asking questions about sexuality, provincialism, the Balkans, the European Union (EU), Gay Pride, nation and nationalism, and homosexuality Blagojević explores some deeply intertwined, and thus not obvious and not much analysed connections between them. This chapter can be said to deal with provincialisms of every identitarian logic (of thinking and politics) that continue to haunt, like Marx's spectre, every idea of a 'community' (be it sexual, national or pan-national).

In the third chapter, 'Nations and Sexualities – "West" and "East"', Robert Kulpa reflects on the recent flourishing of works about nations, nationalism and national identities in relation to homosexuality. Although recently there have been more attempts at discussing homosexuality and nationality (mainly within the domain of 'sexual citizenship'), overall surprisingly little has been written about the sexual underpinnings of nationalistic politics and about the nationalist dimension of gay politics. Thus, the chapter's goal is to build up the theoretical relation between the literature on sexuality and on nationalism, reflect on their intrinsic connections and analyse any possible conjectural foundations on which further analytical work could be done. The author uses examples from CEE to round up his writing with empirical flesh and probing questions. Kulpa traces these relations of nation/al and sexual in the emerging discourses and uses of the geotemporal categories of 'progress', 'West' and 'East' and 'transition'. By doing so, he critically engages with some recent writings on the topic, and shows how neo-imperial politics of the 'West' may operate not only as a 'civilising' (and annihilating) mission but also as a 'pedagogical' (profiteering) one.

The fourth chapter – 'A Short History of the Queer Time of "Post-Socialist" Romania, or Are We There Yet? Let's Ask Madonna!', by Shannon Woodcock – maps the turbulent decades of contested activism and the practice of 'sexual rights' in Romania. By confronting rather underground and radical Romanian youth queering politics, she highlights and critiques the pervasive EUropean hegemonies of 'modernisation'. By the use of a simple term, 'EUropeanisation', Woodcock manages to draw a sharp and uncompromising picture of powerful hegemonies and inequalities in relations between Romania and the EU. She shows how Western donors have continued to set the agenda for the funded development of an LGBT community in Romania, irrespective of the local cultural and historical context. The author uses recent queer writings about the processes of 'racialisation' of Otherness – at the expense of which the 'gay progressive' agenda of Western societies is funded – to analyse Romanian relations between sexual and ethnic minorities. In particular she shows how 'Western-like' 'pro-gay politics' is established through the exclusion and degradation of the Roma minority.

In the chapter 'Travelling Ideas, Travelling Times: On the Temporalities of LGBT and Queer Politics in Poland and the "West"' Joanna Mizielińska writes on the translation of 'Western' ideas of LGBT and queer politics into a Polish context, and tries to show what is lost/gained throughout this process. First, she presents the recent Polish political scene and other examples of sexual politics in Poland. By doing so she aims to describe the limitations of queer (in) politics in Poland, but also to show some of the resistance actions performed by LGBT and feminist circles in Poland. She argues that queering politics can mean different things locally and that what can be described as an identity approach from a US perspective can have its queer face on the local level. Therefore, she expands upon the already introduced concepts of the Western 'time of sequence' and the Eastern 'time of coincidence' and suggests that Polish LGBT activism cannot be categorised simply as 'identitarian' or 'queer' because it exists in a different geotemporality compared to the 'West'. She focuses on the Campaign Against Homophobia (CAH), the largest and best-known Polish LGBT organisation, and shows that in their choice of strategies and discourses one can see the queer mixture of ideas that represent various historical stages of Western LGBT activism. She suggests that one of the reasons is the 'temporal disjunction', a historical void, in which the CAH works. The 1990s mark the beginning of LGBT activism in Poland but not in the West. During that period Western ideas were unanimously applied without much attempt at understanding their cultural and historical context and functioning. At the end she reflects upon Anglo-American knowledge production and presents critical queer stances towards primarily American 'queer theory'. She points to the recent developments in the field of queer studies that show the need for greater 'localisation' of sexual politics, contextualising it within local historical, geographical, political and linguistic contexts. Her chapter thus contributes towards opening the debate about the shape and meaning of 'queer' and its potential outside the Western context.

Jon Binnie and Christian Klesse's chapter, 'Researching Transnational Activism around LGBTQ Activism in Central and Eastern Europe: Activist Solidarities and Spatial Imaginings', is based on an empirical research project on transnational activism around LGBT politics in Poland. Transnational activism has been a significant component of resistance against the banning of equality marches in 2005 and 2006, and against violent attacks by far-right groups and homophobic public discourse – all associated with the rise of the Law and Justice Party and the League of Polish Families. The chapter considers the different understandings and conceptions of solidarity that motivate and inform transnational actions. For instance they discuss how notions of sameness and difference are articulated within these conceptions of solidarity, and are particularly concerned with exploring the affective dimensions of what Carol Gould has termed 'networked solidarities'. Finally the authors consider how sexuality can be theorised in relation to alternative conceptions of (transnational) solidarity within social and political theory.

The next chapter, 'Rendering Gender in Lesbian Families: A Czech Case', by Kateřina Nedbálková, focuses on methods and strategies used by lesbian parents to construct and rework concepts of gender in their everyday practices. Considering still present social stigma and many instances of culturally sanctioned homophobia, the author examines how these redoings are used for political legitimisation, social restriction, cultural stigmatisation or personal empowerment. Another focus of this chapter concerns the academic scholarship about 'queer kinship' – in particular how concepts are 'framed' by social scientists re/searching lesbian and gay families. Nedbálková is especially interested in the interplay between regimes of knowledge, both at the level of personal lives and their academic theoretisation, and between Western 'non-normative kinship' scholarship and Czech realities. The chapter is based on ethnographic research of lesbian couples with children in the Czech Republic.

Roman Kuhar, in the chapter 'The Heteronormative Panopticon and the Transparent Closet of the Public Space in Slovenia', writes about the heteronormativity of public space in Slovenia and its repercussions in the everyday life of gays and lesbians. In the heteronormative geography of public space, where images of heterosexuality are omnipresent, and thus 'invisible', signs of homosexuality automatically present a disturbance to the system. The omnipresence/invisibility of heterosexual codes 'magnifies' homosexual ones, which are then immediately accompanied by potential threats of homophobic violence. This chapter is also based on empirical results of the author's earlier research. The author suggests that the experiences of gays and lesbians in public space can be interpreted in the context of Foucault's elucidation of Bentham's panopticon and Hannah Arendt's 'Pariah/Parvenu' dichotomy. The panopticon, as Foucault explains, establishes self-surveillance whereby power is actually exercised by prisoners themselves. Similarly, the sense of 'being watched' experienced by Slovenian lesbians and gays in public spaces leads them to a self-performed surveillance of their own homosexuality; they 'abolish' their own expressions of sexuality during the time of being 'imprisoned' in the panopticon of public space (the 'transparent closet').

In their chapter 'Heteronormativity, Intimate Citizenship and the Regulation of Same-Sex Sexualities in Bulgaria', Sasha Roseneil and Mariya Stoilova aim to expand the theorisation of heteronormativity in Central and Eastern Europe by exploring the regulation of intimate citizenship in Bulgaria since the late 1960s. Their central argument is that the institutionalisation and regulation of intimacy in Bulgaria has been both implicitly and explicitly heteronormative. They also trace a number of shifts in legislation and policy, and the emergence of lesbian and gay activism, during the post-socialist period, which indicate an emergent challenge to the heteronormative framing of intimate citizenship. So, for example, they discuss how the socialist state regulated an individual's sexuality and reproductive behaviour through the promotion of marriage and procreation, and the penalising of those who did not have children. Further, they discuss the relaxation of state policing of intimate lives after 1989, the final revoking of laws criminalising homosexual acts, and the establishment of rights to non-discrimination and protection from violence. The authors explore two cases and argue that their importance goes beyond the protection of individuals concerned with discrimination; they had a larger cultural and symbolic importance in a situation of rapid social change. Finally, the investigation goes into how LGBT groups are seeking to challenge the heteronormative regulation of intimacy.

Alexander Lambevski, in his chapter 'Situating Intimate Citizenship in Macedonia: Emotional Navigation and Everyday Queer/*Kvar* Grounded Moralities', explores the 'democratisation' of intimate spheres of life in post-socialist Macedonia – from the difficult democratisation of intimate relationships and development of new sexual subjectivities, to the increased visibility of new intimate and sexual stories and ways of existence contesting traditional heterosexist and patriarchal models of sexual object choice. These new arrangements are linked by membership in various complex and competing groups and communities, and thus marked by various degrees of solidarity, conflict and tension. Theoretically situated at the lesbian and gay/queer/feminist border, the chapter examines the fragile creation of multiple and overlapping intimate queer public spheres which single mothers, gays, lesbians, bisexuals, sexually liberated women and non-traditional heterosexual men occupy, and where they practise the politics of affinity and emancipation. By paying very close attention to actual lived situations of a small group of people, the chapter attempts to ground the rather abstract current debates on intimate and sexual citizenship by focusing on how these Macedonians confront ethical dilemmas arising from their non-normative sexuality and how they deal with them practically.

References

Baer, Brian James. 2009. *Other Russias: Homosexuality and the Crisis of Post-Soviet Identity*. Basingstoke: Palgrave Macmillan.

———. 2002. 'Russian Gays/Western Gaze: Mapping (Homo)Sexual Desire in Post-Soviet Russia'. *GLQ: A Journal of Lesbian and Gay Studies* 8(4): 499–521.

Drulák, Petr. 2001. *National and European Identities in EU Enlargement: Views from Central and Eastern Europe*. Prague: Institute of International Relations.

Eder, Franz, Lesley A. Hall and Gert Hekma, eds. 1999. *Sexual Cultures in Europe: Themes In Sexuality*. Manchester: Manchester University Press.

Ekiert, Grzegorz, Jan Kubik and Milada Anna Vachudova. 2007. 'Democracy in the Post-Communist World: An Unending Quest?'. *East European Politics and Societies* 21(1): 7–30.

Essig, Laurie. 1999. *Queer in Russia: A Story of Sex, Self, and the Other*. Durham, NC: Duke University Press.

Flam, Helena. 2001. *Pink, Purple, Green: Women's, Religious, Environmental and Gay/Lesbian Movements in Central Europe Today*. East European Monographs, no. 577. Boulder, CO/New York: East European Monographs/Columbia University Press.

Funk, Nanette and Magda Mueller. 1993. *Gender Politics and Post-Communism: Reflections from Eastern Europe and the Former Soviet Union*. London/NY: Routledge.

Gal, Susan and Gail Kligman. 2000a. *The Politics of Gender after Socialism: A Comparative-Historical Essay*. Princeton: Princeton University Press.

———, eds. 2000b. *Reproducing Gender: Politics, Publics, and Everyday Life after Socialism*. Princeton: Princeton University Press.

Jähnert, Gabriele et al., eds. 2001. *Gender in Transition in Eastern and Central Europe: Proceedings*. Berlin: Trafo.

Johnson, Janet Elise and Jean C. Robinson, eds. 2007. *Living Gender after Communism*. Bloomington: Indiana University Press.

Konstantinović, Radomir. 1981. *Filosofija palanke/Philosophy of the Provincial*. Belgrade: Nolit.

Kuhar, R. and J. Magić. 2008. *Experiences and Perceptions of Homophobic Violence and Discrimination (Research Report)*. Ljubljana: Legebitra.

Kuhar, Roman and Judit Takács, eds. 2007. *Beyond the Pink Curtain*. Ljubljana: Peace Institute, http://www.policy.hu/takacs/books/isbn9616455459/#content.

Kymlicka, Will and Magdalena Opalski, eds. 2005. *Can Liberal Pluralism Be Exported? Western Political Theory and Ethnic Relations in Eastern Europe*. Oxford: Oxford Scholarship Online.

Pleines, Heiko and Sabine Fischer, eds. 2009. *The EU and Central and Eastern Europe: Successes and Failures of Europeanization in Politics and Society*. Changing Europe. Stuttgart: Ibidem-Verlag.

Rupnik, Jacques. 1999. 'The Postcommunist Divide'. *Journal of Democracy* 10(1): 57–62.

Shiraev, Eric and Vladimir Shlapentokh, eds. 2002. *Fears in Post-Communist Society*. Basingstoke: Palgrave Macmillan.

Stella, Francesca. 2007. The Right to Be Different? Sexual Citizenship and its Politics in Post-Soviet Russia. In *Gender, Equality and Difference During and After State Socialism*, ed. Rebecca Kay. Studies in Central and Eastern Europe. Basingstoke: Palgrave Macmillan.

Štulhofer, Aleksandar and Theo Sandfort, eds. 2004. *Sexuality and Gender in Post-Communist Eastern Europe and Russia*. Binghamton, NY: Haworth Press.

Švab, A. and R. Kuhar. 2005. *The Unbearable Comfort of Privacy: Everyday Life of Gays and Lesbians*. Ljubljana: Peace Institute, http://www.mirovni-institut. si/Publikacija/Detail/en/publikacija/The-Unbearable-Confort-of-Privacy-The-Everyday-Life-of-Gays-and-Lesbians.

Chapter 1

'Contemporary Peripheries': Queer Studies, Circulation of Knowledge and East/West Divide

Joanna Mizielińska and Robert Kulpa

Hurley: Let me get this straight. All this already happened?

Miles: Yes.

H: So this conversation we're having right now, we already had it?

M: Yes.

H: Then, what I am going to say next?

M: I don't know.

H: Ha! Then your theory is wrong.

M: For the thousandth time, you dingbat, the conversation already happened, but not for you and me. For you and me, it's happening right now.

H: OK, answer me this. If all this already happened to me then why don't I remember any of it?

M: Because once Ben turned that wheel, time isn't a straight line for us anymore. Our experience is in the past, and the future occurred before this experience right now.

H: [silence] Say that again.

M: Shoot me! Please? Please!

H: Aha! I can't shoot you because if you die in 1977 then you'll never come back on the island on the freighter thirty years from now.

M: I can die! Because I've already come to the island on the freighter. Any of us can die, because this is our present.

H: But you said that Ben couldn't die because he still needs to grow up and become the leader of the Others.

M: Because this is his past.

H: But when we first captured Ben, and Sayid, like, tortured him, then why wouldn't he remember getting shot by the same guy, when he was a kid?

M: [silence] Huh ... I haven't thought of that.

H: Huh!

('Time travel' conversation between Hurley and Miles,
Lost, season 5, episode 11.)

Hurley and Miles end their dialogue in confusion and uncertainty. The perplexity is caused not only by the heroes' current condition (i.e. travel in time from 2007 to 1977, with some short breaks at different times), but also by the usual way we conceptualise, theorise and memorise time. At the end of the conversation, Miles, who seems to have understood the workings and mechanisms of time, admits otherwise. For a short moment we believe in his explanation/construction of temporality, but then again we get lost – lost in time, lost in translation of time, lost in time construction, lost in space …?

We all live 'here and now', but what do 'here' and 'now' mean – for you, for me, for us? How do we (re)construct them? What elements of a past are persistent in the present? In what form will the present survive into a future? What does it mean to live a certain time in the West?[1] What marks this time? What kind of expectations does it produce for/on its subjects? Everybody has their time, but is this time the same for all? And how is the common perception of time achieved? How is it constructed? What will become history, and what will remain forgotten forever? Unspoken? Unwritten?

These are not new questions, and the reflection on time is perhaps one of the most persistant, troublesome topics, accompanying humankind throughout centuries of civilisation. But in this chapter we want to ponder about the time in a specific context of Central and Eastern Europe (CEE), and its historical and current developments of lesbian, gay, bisexual, transgender and queer (LGBTQ) movements and sexuality/queer studies. What is important is to ask whether CEE's LGBTQ's 'now and here' is only a reflection of a much broader and older Western narrative. Do the movements develop along the same trajectories? And why does it matter to know?

Protagonists of the *Lost* series find themselves not only lost in time, but also in space. The mysterious island on which they found themselves after the plane crash is a no-where no-place. As the narrative develops, we learn that it is somewhere – but the island's 'here' placement is in fact its temporal 'now' harbouring. Time and space, in other words, are inseparable. Therefore, we also feel it is important to ask: if time of CEE is a little queer (a joy of word-play), where is CEE? Where is the West? How does 'here' of one of these myriad geo-referents correspond to/is translated on to '(t)here' of the other? Are the geographical boundaries of regions as fixed as their enclosed countries? Is it possible to establish a relation between 'West' and 'CEE', as between (respectively) 'metropolis/centre' and 'colony/periphery' (popular in post-colonial writings)? And considering that CEE is not (so far) a region of much interest to post-colonial theorists,[2] what would be the implications of such a juxtaposition of geographical regions and academic theories?

---

1   We will reflect on the construction and meaning of the 'West' and 'Central and Eastern Europe' later in this chapter.

2   That is not to say that there is no interest at all. We discuss this issue later.

In this chapter we would like to outline a general theoretical framework for the whole book. Its primary goal (though one of many) is to question the construction and conceptualisation of sexuality and LGBTQ activism in contemporary Central and Eastern European countries. We consider how Western discourses/theories influence this process. How (as we suggest) does Western hegemonic imposition/dominance work in local contexts? Therefore, the question of *CEE locality* (local translation of politics and theories) plays a significant role in gathered analyses. This local geotemporal dimension of sexual politics problematises, usually taken for granted, the Western/(post-)colonial dichotomy and also the unified notion of 'Western activism', dominated by the Anglo-American model. Therefore, we want to scrutinise it and see to what extent it forecloses, marginalises and separates histories of LGBT movement and sexuality studies in CEE. This stance is obviously a particular enactment of reflection present in the field of 'queer studies' and, as we like to connect our work with this body of literature, we will begin by outlining our relation to queer studies. As we progress, we expand our analysis of time and space, as introduced above. While doing so, we also take up the question of relations between post-colonial and post-communist studies, showing (with the ultimate example of the whole book) how the 'cross-contamination' of theories is one of the best queer studies practices we can think of.

Geographies of Queer Studies

There are many uses of the word 'queer', varying from context to context, within academic and activist circles. It may be an umbrella term for 'LGBT', or opposition to 'lesbian' and 'gay'; queer may be predominantly concerted with sexuality, or may stand for an intersectional approach; it may be another term for 'homo', or a non-identitarian category. The word might be meaningless in a non-English speaking context, or its notion may be differently shaped according to needs and conditions.

In the Western context the history of queer is rooted in AIDS politics and in the opposition to the gay liberation of the 'Stonewall era' (e.g. Jagose 1996; Phelan 1997). In CEE countries, and also in some Nordic (Rosenberg 2008) and perhaps other non-Western countries, the term 'queer' is often used to express identity politics, and becomes a bone of contention/battle between local queer theorists (who know the academic narrative of 'queer vs LGBT' and are willing to preserve it) on the one hand, and on the other local communities and activists, who use the term as another, 'new' name for 'lesbian and gay' or often use it in the commercial context (e.g. TV series as *Queer As Folk* or *Queer Eye For a Straight Guy*).

This volume shows localised meanings of these categories in CEE. Consequently, the authors will use the words 'queer', 'lesbian', 'gay', 'homosexual' or 'LGBT' differently, according to their specific needs and cultural uses. However, each author specifies the way they use these labels. As such, this is already one of the ways this book contributes to queer studies – it offers the proliferation of perspectives on the meaning and application of the 'queer' category.

If one evaluates this volume from the Western/Anglo-American queer perspective, one can rightly question the lack of articles dealing with transsexuality, bisexuality and its representation of non-normative sexualities outside homosexuality. There are many reasons for this. For example, a primary reason for not dealing with bisexuality and transsexuality relates to what we call a 'temporal disjunction'. Transgender activism in CEE only began to emerge since around 2007–2008. This might be one reason for the general lack of scholarship about transgender issues in/about the region. However, it also must be noted that unlike in the West – where transgender groups had a long history of struggle for inclusion and widening of lesbian and gay politics to 'LGBT politics' (Meyerowitz 2002; Stryker and Whittle 2006) – 'transgender' was included in lesbian and gay politics in CEE almost from the very beginning of these movements. Homosexual activism was self-labelled as 'LGBT', even if 'B' and 'T' were purely discursive invocations. This 'inclusion before coming into being' occurred because of different temporalities of West and CEE. As in many other spheres of life, activists in CEE adopted labels already in use in the West, even if these markers did not denote their new reality. So when the first lesbian and gay groups began to self-organise in the early 1990s, they looked at the Western models and their categories (LGBT), rather than trying to figure out their own terminology.

Another issue to be raised is the substitution of 'sexualities' from the title of the book with the primary focus on 'homosexuality' in its content. Actually, we believe that the book's content develops and builds around the concept of 'heteronormativity' rather than 'homosexuality'. Heteronormativity is not only an object of direct examination in some chapters (e.g. Roseneil and Stoilova, Lambevski) but also forms a viable and crucial backdrop of analysis in others (e.g. Blagojevic, Kuhar). This is already another way (focusing on heteronormativity as one of the major categories organising our contemporary lives, irrespective of geopolitical locations) in which this book contributes to the field of queer studies.

Our Time Which Is Not Yours Is Not Ours: Sequence, Coincidence and Temporal Disjunction

After the collapse of the 'Iron Curtain', CEE countries quite unanimously adopted a Western style of political and social engagement, without much questioning of its historical particularism and suitability for their context. When lesbian and gay activism began to emerge in CEE, the West was already at the 'queer' stage, with a long history and plurality of models, forms of engagement, goals and structures. Conversely, the communist past of CEE built completely different social structures and modalities. This could be represented graphically as two separate geopolitical-temporal modalities (communism and capitalism) running parallel, where in 1989 one of them finishes (communism), and the other one becomes universal for both regions (capitalism).

This is what Francis Fukuyama (1992) once called 'the end of history' – (neo-)liberal democracy and capitalism triumphing over decades of long struggle for dominance in world ideologies and politics. However, for the West the continuity was preserved and the 'end of communism'/1989 may be placed as another event in the sequence of events. For CEE, this change was much sharper and more abrupt, literally bring the collapse of one world and the promise of a '(brave?) new world' much more coincidentally than sequentially – 'everything at once'. Indeed, it should be even more complicated, and represented as a constant 'knotting' and 'looping' of time(s) after 1989. This Western 'time of sequence' and CEE's 'time of coincidence' might, therefore, look as shown in Figure 1.1.[3]

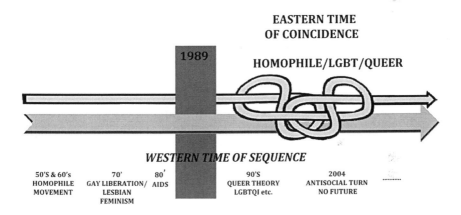

WESTERN AND EASTERN GEO-TEMPORAL MODALITIES?

Figure 1.1   Western 'time of sequence' and Eastern 'time of coincidence'

---

3   We are fully aware that this drawing is a simplification or even a process of strengthening of what we call 'Western time'. The way people in Western countries live/experience/perceive their time differs (within countries, but also in the way time is theorised). Also, as we want to show in this book 'Western/Eastern' division is highly problematic. In our opinion what is perceived as Western is dominated by Anglo-American, or even just American thinking/theories. Therefore, our aim is not only to recognise particularities of the CEE countries, usually 'put into one box', in this Americanised model, but we also want to problematise the notion of the 'West', which barely touches/reflects the experiences of the non-English speaking countries.

Figure 1.1 may seem familiar to some. This might be because we have intended this representation of CEE time-knotting to resemble the 'figure-eight knot' or 'four knot' from the cover of Diana Fuss's seminal *Inside/Out* (1991). At the end of her introduction, she addresses this figure and writes about it in these words:

> This three-dimension geometrical domain, constituted by rings and matrices, loops and linkages, is nonetheless embodied, sexualized. The undecidability of this simple topology may be its greatest appeal, for it seems to signify at once an anal, a vaginal, a clitoral, a penile, and a testicular topography. The knot interlaces many orifices, many sites of pleasure, many libidinal economies. It visualises for us in the very simplicity of its openings and closures, its overs and unders, its ins and outs, the contortions and convolutions of any sexual identity formation. (Fuss 1991: 7)

So the 'knotted time' not only represents the queer experience of CEE, but it is also an embodiment of sexual desires and pleasures. Thus, when we use the term 'queer time' for CEE, as opposed to 'straight time' of the West, it is not only a linguistic game we play upon various meanings of 'queer' and 'straight'. We also intend to highlight the erotic dimension of time, the oddly erotic experience of identity formation in CEE.

When in 1989 'the communist time' ended and the physical borders began to dismantle, the flow and exchange of material products and ideas really took over. The protuberance of clutching ideas, into which CEE was 'thrown', was far from a linear and progressively accumulative vision of time, which continued (exactly: continued!) to unfold in the West (or at least in its academic representation). Sexual politics in CEE may serve as an example. The strong assimilationist model of activism currently present in CEE, as some authors in this book show, could be read as 'stepping back in time' to 'Western homophile times' of the 1950s and 1960s. Yet this 'going backward' is actually 'stepping forward' for lesbian and gay activists in CEE, if only because they can self-organise, which was not possible before 1989. Additionally, these 'homophile-like' claims of acceptance and assimilation may be attempted by 'jumping into the 1970s' and using some contestation strategies predominant at the time in America (and a handful of other countries). At the same time, other groups in CEE label themselves 'queer' and draw directly on 1990s Queer Nation events such as 'kiss-ins' in public spaces. Therefore, the beginning of the 1990s for LGBT activists in CEE is truly a 'queer time': a time of mismatched models and realities, strategies and possibilities, understandings and uses, 'all at once'. It is the time when 'real' and 'fake', 'the original' and 'the copy' collapse into 'the same'/'the one'; and yet, nothing is the same, nothing is straight any more. (Had it ever been?)

However, what we have just presented is already an attempt to 'untie the knot' and 'linearise' the present 'here and now' reality of CEE. It is done by categorising various activities, attitudes and approaches present all at once, as belonging to certain historical, sequential narratives. Thus in organising the 'knotted temporality of CEE' into stages and inscribing it into a particular 'familiar' history (of Western history of LGBTQ movements) we already simplify it in order to make sense of it. But do we actually succeed? Does such 'unknotting' make sense, and for whom? And what are the prerequisites to be able to understand it in either form? In other words, we feel it is important to ask why certain models (notably Western/ American) are familiar to 'all' and perceived as 'The One' and not one of many; and why 'local' narrations of lesbian and gay emancipation will be seen as, precisely, 'local' and not 'universally' recognised. We follow postmodern historians who see history as a discursive narrative activity, a strongly (and irreversibly?) (non)linear process that shapes cultures, political customs and social attitudes, and serves to maintain particular power relations (White 1990; Carr 1991; Jenkins 1991, 1997). Thus, 'another stage in development' from the Western perspective, knots the time, as from the CEE perspective it is 'just a beginning'. Consequently, this disjunction/crossover has to become problematic for both Western and CEE people. It is troublesome for the latter, who are trying to 'catch up' with the West (although living in the 'common present', the feeling is of being sort of 'retarded', in the 'past'); but also for Western communities, who see CEE as 'lagging behind' or 'dragging the progress down' (equally here, CEE is seen as 'contemporary', but somehow 'hindered' and 'behind').

Discursively, it is forcing the 'Western present' as a 'CEE future' to be achieved. Consequently, the 'CEE present' is coerced as 'past', although since 1989, the 'CEE present' and 'Western present' are one. Paradoxically then, 'Western progressive narrative' unfolds into its own aporia. But since this would annihilate the very idea of 'Western progress', something else needs to be done; some mechanism needs to be deployed to differentiate the 'West' and 'CEE' as 'not at the same time'. So although the 'communist time' 'collapsed' into the Western narration, making it 'The One', CEE (or former 'communist time') and West are still discursively maintained as 'parallel' and separate. This may seem paradoxical, but as Foucault (1998) noted, the use of opposite and apparently contradictory discourses by one discursive instance may not have to be that unusual. In his own words: 'Discourses are tactical elements or blocks operating in the field of force relations; there can exist different and even contradictory discourses within the same strategy; they can, on the contrary, circulate without changing their form from one strategy to another, opposing strategy' (Foucault 1998: 101–2).

What is at stake here is power and hegemonic strategies of subordination. How then is the difference between CEE and West kept alive, while at the same time the smokescreen of its lack is deployed? Our proposition is to understand the constant reference to CEE as 'post-communist' as a technique aimed at rendering CEE as the 'other'. It is this constant 'transformation' through which CEE supposedly 'has been going' (present perfect continuous is much at home here) that allows the West to place itself 'above'/'before', as the mentoring force which CEE should look up to. How and who is to decide when the 'transition' ends? When the CEE will no longer have to 'transform' anything; when will it join the Western club?[4] Of course there is no single instance, yet we somehow feel under the skin that the agency here is not belonging to CEE, that authority lies elsewhere. In a sense the West is always already 'post'. In this construction, whatever CEE became/is/will be, West had become/has already been/will have been.

Central and Eastern Europe is a 'contemporary periphery' because it is 'European enough' (geographically), 'yet not enough advanced' to become 'Western' (temporally). This 'temporal disjunction' and the meaning of 'time'/'temporality' and 'history'/'History' are shaped by economic and political conditions. These, in turn, have clear gender and sexual underpinnings (Friedman 1997; Young 1997). The 'hegemonic temporality of West' is constructed as continuous and linear, progressive and 'accumulative' (from 'old-primitive' to 'new-advanced'). As such it becomes clear that the contemporary Western notion of 'time' has underpinnings in classical liberal ideology of the individual in a progressive, future-oriented world (Adam 1995, 2004). Following Lee Edelman's (2004) queer polemic that sparked discussions about queer rejecting such a temporal trajectory ('anti-social turn'), this collection problematises this perspective. Edelman claims that queer should reject the hetero- and homonormative trajectory of a progressive future-oriented world symbolised by the figure of a child. However, he does not take into account that this turn for 'no future' has some *raison d'être* only in cultures that *have* 'future', are 'future-oriented', and in the privileged position of being able to 'waste' it.[5]

The notion of 'future' in CEE was shaped differently and its vector does not have the same direction as the 'Western future'. In the context of post-communist CEE, where people have just released themselves from the dominance of the USSR, that call of Western queer theory to 'reject future' and 'embrace the negativity' does not resonate with the needs, positions and opportunities of queer people in CEE. In fact it would be a kind of suicidal move to embrace the position that the majority of homophobic society has always already seen as the most appropriate for queers. Thus, by engaging with the discussion about temporality and the 'anti-social turn' in queer studies, this volume provides new insights about the other possible shapes of 'queer temporalities'.

So, in summary, we would like to ask whether it is possible to do 'queer' politics without the historical baggage. Is it possible to do non-identitarian politics (the Western model of queer) without first going through a stage of identity politics?

---

4 Please note that Shannon Woodcock makes the similar claim in this volume. We were not aware of each other's work before, hence this 'coincidence' of almost identical thoughts is even more telling and interesting.

5 This is why the book was criticised by lesbians, feminists and people of colour – for representing the privileged position of the white, middle-class man, who could afford to 'fuck the future'. For a summary of this critique see Elizabeth Freeman's Introduction to the *GLQ* special issue on time (Freeman 2007: 166–7; see also Halberstam 2008; Muñoz 2009).

As much as these are open questions without definite answers, what we want to suggest is that perhaps more important is the need to contextualise meanings and focus more on the 'cultural translation' of queer, conceptualising it each and every time anew. So, as Joanna Mizielińska argues in her chapter in this collection, we may realise that what is called 'essentialist politics of identity' in the Western context may very well function to bring close results to those of 'Western queer', if present or used in a non-Western (here CEE) context.

East and West: Post-Colonial Relations of (Dis)placement

There is an ongoing debate about what constitutes 'colonialism', 'post-colonialism', 'neo-imperialism' etc. (Loomba 1998; Chakrabarty 2007). There is also a growing body of work about queer post-colonial subjects (Patton and Sánchez-Eppler 2000; Hawley 2001a, 2001b; Cruz-Malavé and Manalansan 2002; Pitcher and Gunkel 2009) and sexuality and globalisation (Hennessy 2000; Altman 2001; Binnie 2004; Padilla 2007). It has become clear by now that post-colonial scholarship is an important field of reference for this book. Indeed, we are influenced by this body of work and use some of the key concepts in our own formulation of ideas and analyses. In a sense, we would like to see this project as an effect of merging post-communist and post-colonial studies.

This volume is an exploration of sexual politics in CEE ('contemporary periphery') in relation to the West ('metropolis'). It contributes to post-colonial studies by problematising the category of 'centre/metropolis/West' by showing it as a relational and unstable concept. However, we have also noted that many works of post-colonial scholarship tend to bipolarise the centre–periphery relation. Often unintentionally 'metropolitan centre' is constructed as more or less unified and coherent, against which the pluralisation and diversification of 'post-colonial periphery' is done.

Therefore, we join voices calling for wider coverage and scrutinisation of the metropolis, and not only of the colony (Mishra and Hodge 1991; Hulme 1995; Loomba 1998; Janion 2007). In particular, this collection shows how some geographical locations are under-theorised in post-colonial studies. The obsolete communist 'Second World' (contemporary Western relations with China, Korea and Cuba have developed more individualistic discourses) – remnants of which fall in CEE, located somewhere between the 'developed countries' of the 'First World' and 'developing countries' of the 'Third World' – disrupts the dyad centre–periphery. As we have shown above, geographical, political, economic and temporal status of CEE puts it at times in either the first or the third class, and at times in both simultaneously. Consequently, we need to ask: where exactly does 'Central and Eastern Europe' locate itself? And where is 'West'? Does (geographical) being in 'Europe' automatically grants the privilege of belonging to the first-class 'Global North' club? Or does the process of 'catching up with (the idea of) West' make CEE more a part of the 'Global South'? How global is

'Global'? The terms 'Global North/South' are relatively new and their use is just spreading; but do they really solve the problems imposed by previous hegemonic categories? What is the role of homosexuality and lesbian and gay activism in making, sustaining and transcending those divisions – especially in light of the resurgence of nationalist movements after 1989 and post '9/11'? As more and more scholars highlight (Duggan 1994; Beverley 2004; Puar 2007; Butler 2009), cultural attitudes and legal provisions for lesbian and gay people are becoming important factors in creating and maintaining modern divisions of 'Us' ('West', 'civilised', 'secular', 'liberal' and supposedly 'pro-gay') and 'Them' ('Orient', 'primitive', 'religious', 'fanatical' and consequently 'anti-gay'). This volume joins this discussion and shows another dimension of how this process works, not only in relation to 'West/Orient', but also 'West/CEE', which in our eyes is a much more problematic relation, not easily classifiable along the 'Us/Them', 'insider/ outsider' lines.

Additionally, the context of 'democratisation' of CEE, which in practice denotes installing some type of modern, liberal, democratic regime in politics and neo-liberal capitalism in economics, evokes recent works about consumerism, 'mercantilisation of sexuality' and the neo-liberal economy of sexual identities (e.g. D'Emilio 1993; Chasin 2000; Hennessy 2000; Duggan 2004; Woltersdorff 2007). This book contributes therefore to the some of the hottest debates in today's queer scholarship, offering new perspectives on the influence of market organisation and political regime for the formation of non-normative sexual identities and activism in the transnational context.

What is 'Central and Eastern Europe'?[6]

There are many labels in use, denoting, describing and indicating what 'CEE' might be. There are geographical ones: East, Central Europe, Eastern Europe, Central and Eastern Europe, Balkans, Southern and Eastern Europe, or just Southern Europe. There are historical ones: post-communist/former communist, post-Soviet/former Soviet, communist/Soviet satellite countries, former communist bloc, countries behind the former Iron Curtain. There are also political ones: post-authoritarian, emerging democracies, new democracies, transitional/transforming countries, developing democracies, consolidating democracies. There is also a set of terms relating to the EU only: new members, second-wave enlargement countries, aspiring countries. And of course the use of these names is neither systematic nor consequential; they are all being used as parallels and as synonyms. The three types under which we have grouped them are only to highlight how geography, history, politics and time are the fabric of these categories. And since the labels are

---

6   What we present here is just a brief exercise. More comprehensive and in-depth analysis is to be found in a handful of works that attempt a post-colonially inspired analysis of 'CEE' and its relations to/with 'West' (see Todorova 1997; Moore 2001; Buchowski 2004; Kelertas 2006; Melegh 2006; Chari and Verdery 2009; Owczarzak 2009; Korek 2009).

highly contested and conflated, intention, meaning and understanding rely heavily on the user rather than on the label itself.

Let us briefly discuss two examples. First: is Germany a part of CEE? Most people would say no. But eastern Germany, a former communist republic, is without doubt in a similar state of 'transition' as other former communist countries. Facing similar problems of unemployment, slow economy, social disappointment and intensified migration to big cities and western parts of the country, the only difference is that it is now officially part of 'one Germany', the 'correct one' (Western), and not a independent state. The process of 'unification of Germany' thus somehow erased the difference, erased the memory of Germany being a 'former communist' country, setting the boundaries of a 'post-communist world' east of Germany.

There is no doubt that 'former communist bloc' was not a bloc at all, that there were significant differences between the USSR, Poland, Hungary, Romania, Yugoslavia and East Germany; and that there are equally significant differences between what they have become now. Yet still, these and all other countries in the region are thrown into one bag (with the discussed exception of 'Germany'), and often referred to as coherent, 'out there'.

Second example: is Poland an 'Eastern European' country? The answer depends on who is asked. For Poles themselves, no; Poland is either simply a 'European' or a 'Central European' country. 'Eastern Europe' is outside Poland's eastern borders. In the UK and other Western European countries, 'Central and Eastern Europe' and 'Eastern Europe' are interchangeable, denoting the same. Thus, Poland is an 'Eastern European' country. But is it 'post-Soviet'? No – neither for Poles, nor for Western Europeans. But yes, from American point of view, where it is more common to use the 'post-Soviet/former Soviet' label; whereas in Europe 'post-communist/former communist' would be more popular. Also the geographical designation 'CEE' seems to be more popular in a European rather than American context, where the historical/political categories prevail. (But then again, all of these are only our, the editors', perceptions. And these are shaped by the fact that we share a Polish cultural upbringing, although Robert has chosen the UK as a place to live, and Joanna maintains relations with Nordic countries while working and living in Warsaw.)

What is 'West'?

Similarly, it is important to ask: where is the 'West' to which we (and other authors in this book) refer? The answer is (not so) simple. 'West' is a myriad constellation, floating in a time-space of individual perceptions and 'CEE' idealisations. It is at times synonymous with 'Europe', sometimes more precisely to 'European Union', sometimes 'Western Europe'; it denotes 'Europe and America' or only 'America' (and this in turn means solely the USA, although at times a shadowy and weak hint of Canada beams from underneath the colossal USA) or 'Anglo-America'. 'West' is 'liberalism and progress', 'West' was 'a promise of freedom', 'El Dorado' –

a dreamland of colourful prosperity; 'here' and 'there', perhaps (t)here; 'West' was/is where 'we' (CEE) want to be. Finally, 'West' is a normative ideal of 'how things should be'. How to make sense of what is actually meant each time 'West' as a category is invoked – we do not know. As much as we want to rationalise and categorically understand/understand through existing categories, we also *feel* (and it is precisely the *feeling* that we want to stress here) that none of the above explanatory terms ever fills the vessel of 'West' completely. We *feel* that even the most 'precise' denotation of 'West' (e.g. 'EU') always carries a suitcase (or just a small handbag, or even perhaps only a pocket) full of other labels, always echoing something else, in a never-ending chain of equivalence and relationality.

What does it mean in the context of queer studies, knowledge production and LGBT activism? Possibly, that for us 'Western' means 'English', 'Anglo-American'. In fact, it should be narrowed even more to denote just 'American'. During various presentations and discussions, we became increasingly aware of how much more our perception of English-speaking academy ('Anglo-American', as we used to call it) was persistently 'Americanised' than we initially thought ourselves. So for example, while exploring 'CEE's temporal knotting' in the earlier part of this chapter, we constructed a linear narrative of the lesbian and gay movement, calling it 'Western narrative' – it has to be noted and acknowledged that, for example, British scholars working in the field of histories of non-normative sexualities may not necessarily agree with it,[7] and rightly so. However, what this situation of us, 'non-Westerners', labelling English literature about sexuality as 'Anglo-American' (yet more American than British, and not even trying to think through the case of Australia) highlights is the actual workings of the hegemonic position of 'America'/United States in the production and circulation of knowledge. And we, although critically engaged and presumably more aware of it, are not exempt from its conditioning – unfortunately and unwillingly, yet perhaps necessarily, reproducing at times these mechanisms of inequality ourselves.

*   *   *

We are fully aware that the processes and mechanisms we criticise here are partially recreated in our own analysis when we make certain generalisations or, conversely, when being very particular, perhaps too much so to make sustainable claims. This seems an inevitable process of approaching own aporia in trying to 'see behind' (if it is possible at all). Self-reflection thus needs to be an indispensable element of any research dealing with discourse and power. We particularly owe a debt to a number of significant feminist works, all dealing with 'new' epistemologies of 'situated knowledge(s)' (e.g. Alarcon 1990; Minh-ha 1990; Haraway 1997; Applebaum 2001; Presser 2005). However, we also feel that although risking some over- and

---

7   We would like to thank participants (especially Prof. Lynne Segal and Prof. Sasha Roseneil) of the 'Beyond the Pink Curtain?' seminar organised at Birkbeck Institute for Social Research, University of London, 22 January 2010, for drawing our attention to this issue.

understatements, it is important to not be afraid of them. Only by pushing the boundaries one can approach what is set aside of the core in hegemonic discursive practices, sparking discussion and enabling more diversified exchange of ideas and insights.

Keeping all this in mind, what possible lesson one can draw from exercises we have carried out with 'West' and 'CEE'? Perhaps the conclusion is that since none of the markers can be perceived as stable, the 'West' and 'Central and Eastern Europe' are ultimately a phantasmagorical '(t)here and now'; two regions impossible to enclose within fixed boundaries, neither geographical, nor temporal-historical, nor political. 'West' and 'CEE' are thus relational concepts, and as such entail hierarchies of power, subversion, resistance and hope. Referring to 'CEE', as in the case of any other discursive practice, is not a value-free, or 'neutral', 'objective' practice. It already designates 'self' ('West'), policing and distinguishing it from the 'other' ('CEE'). Yet still, thanks to the variety of uses, flexibility and permeability, the opposite may occur. By using and exchanging 'West' with 'European' and 'American', blurring of communities and cultures is intended, subverting established power hierarchies (West over CEE), carving a space for 'Central and East Europeans' to become part of the 'First World', 'just Europeans', club. Such practices subvert the core and re-render CEE as part of the 'European' 'self', and not its 'other'.[8]

Conclusion

To summarise, we would like to repeat that this volume offers a new perspective on some crucial contemporary issues raised in queer studies. These are globalisation of sexual identities, circulation and power(s) of knowledge, strategies of acculturation and the translation of dominant approaches to a local (country-specific) level. We offer the theoretical figures of 'contemporary periphery', 'temporal disjunction/knotting' and 'time of sequence vs time of coincidence' as perhaps useful ways of thinking about CEE – 'European enough' (geographically), but 'not yet Western' (temporarily). Thus, we take a geotemporal rather than only a geopolitical approach, which we believe offers wider possibilities of understanding the current process of transmission of sexual identities and models of activism. We further try to problematise the very categories of 'West', 'CEE', 'centre/ metropolis', 'periphery/colony', 'First, Second and Third Worlds', and 'Global North or South', 'homo- and heterosexuality', 'queer', 'lesbian and gay', 'local and global', 'democratisation' and 'post-communist transformation', and lay the general framework for all other chapters gathered in this book.

---

8 And we leave aside the case of Russia, whose relation to the 'West' has its own, equally complicated, narrative.

References

Adam, Barbara. 1995. *Timewatch: The Social Analysis of Time*. Cambridge: Polity Press.

————. 2004. *Time*. Cambridge/Malden, MA: Polity Press.

Alarcon, Linda. 1990. 'The Theoretical Subjects of That Bridge Called My Back and Anglo-American Feminism'. In *Making Face, Making Soul = Haciendo Caras: Creative And Critical Perspectives by Feminists Of Color*, ed. Gloria Anzaldúa. San Francisco: Aunt Lute Foundation Books.

Altman, Dennis. 2001. 'Global Gaze/Global Gays'. In *Sexual Identities, Queer Politics*, ed. Mark Blasius. Princeton: Princeton University Press.

Applebaum, Barbara. 2001. 'Locating Onself, Self 'I'-dentification and the Trouble with Moral Agency'. *Philosophy of Education Yearbook*. http://www.ed.uiuc. edu/EPS/PES-Yearbook/2001/applebaum%2001.pdf.

Beverley, John. 2004. 'Queering the Nation: Same Thoughts on Empire, Nationalism, and Multiculturalism Today'. In *Empire & Terror: Nationalism/ Postnationalism in the New Millennium*, ed. Begoña Aretxaga. Center for Basque Studies Conference Papers, series no. 1. Reno: Center for Basque Studies, University of Nevada.

Binnie, Jon. 2004. *The Globalization of Sexuality*. London: Sage.

Buchowski, Michał. 2004. 'Hierarchies of Knowledge in Central-Eastern European Anthropology'. *Anthropology of East Europe Review* 22, no. 2. http://condor. depaul.edu/~rrotenbe/aeer/aeer22_2.html.

Butler, Judith. 2009. *Frames of War: When is Life Grievable?* London: Verso.

Carr, David. 1991. *Time, Narrative, and History*. Bloomington: Indiana University Press.

Chakrabarty, Dipesh. 2007. *Provincializing Europe: Postcolonial Thought and Historical Difference* (new edition). Princeton: Princeton University Press.

Chari, Sharad and Katherine Verdery. 2009. 'Thinking Between the Posts: Postcolonialism, Postsocialism, and Ethnography After the Cold War'. *Comparative Studies in Society and History* 51, no. 1: 6–34.

Chasin, Alexandra. 2000. *Selling Out: The Gay and Lesbian Movement Goes to Market*. New York: St Martin's Press.

Cruz-Malavé, Arnaldo and Martin Manalansan, eds. 2002. *Queer Globalizations: Citizenship and the Afterlife of Colonialism*. New York: New York University Press.

D'Emilio, John. 1993. 'Capitalism and Gay Identity'. In *The Lesbian and Gay Studies Reader*, eds Henry Abelove, Michele Aina Barale and David M. Halperin. London: Routledge.

Duggan, Lisa. 1994. 'Queering the State'. *Social Text*, no. 39 (summer): 1–14.

————. 2004. *The Twilight of Equality: Neoliberalism, Cultural Politics, and the Attack on Democracy*. Boston, MA: Beacon Press.

Edelman, Lee. 2004. *No Future: Queer Theory and the Death Drive*. Series Q. Durham, NC: Duke University Press.

Foucault, Michael. 1998. *The History of Sexuality. Vol. 1: The Will to Knowledge.* London: Penguin.

Freeman, Elizabeth. 2007. 'Introduction'. *GLQ: A Journal of Lesbian and Gay Studies* 13, no. 2: 159–76.

Friedman, Susan Stanford. 1997. 'Making History: Reflections on Feminism, Narrative, and Desire'. In *The Postmodern History Reader*, ed. Keith Jenkins. London: Routledge.

Fukuyama, Francis. 1992. *The End of History and the Last Man.* Harmondsworth: Penguin.

Fuss, Diana, ed. 1991. *Inside/Out: Lesbian Theories, Gay Theories.* New York: Routledge, Chapman and Hall.

Halberstam, Judith. 2008. 'The Anti-Social Turn in Queer Studies'. *Graduate Journal of Social Science* 5, no. 2. Queer Methodologies (December): 140–56.

Haraway, Donna Jeanne. 1997. *ModestWitness@SecondMillennium.FemaleMan-MeetsOncoMouse: Feminism and Technoscience.* New York: Routledge.

Hawley, John C., ed. 2001a. *Postcolonial and Queer Theories: Intersections and Essays.* Contributions to the Study of World Literature, no. 101. Westport, CT: Greenwood Press.

———, ed. 2001b. *Postcolonial, Queer: Theoretical Intersections.* SUNY series, Explorations in Postcolonial Studies. Albany: State University of New York Press.

Hennessy, Rosema. 2000. *Profit and Pleasure: Sexual Identities in Late Capitalism.* London: Routledge.

Hulme, Peter. 1995. 'Including America'. *Ariel*, no. 26(1): 117–23.

Jagose, Annamarie. 1996. *Queer Theory: An Introduction.* New York: New York University Press.

Janion, Maria. 2007. *Niesamowita Słowiańszczyzna: Fantazmaty Literatury.* Krakow: Wydawnictwo Literackie.

Jenkins, Keith. 1991. *Re-thinking History* (2nd edn). London: Routledge.

———, ed. 1997. *The Postmodern History Reader.* London: Routledge.

Kelertas, Violeta, ed. 2006. *Baltic Postcolonialism.* Amsterdam/New York: Rodopi.

Korek, Janusz. 2009. 'Central and Eastern Europe from a Postcolonial Perspective'. *The Postcolonial Europe.* http://postcolonial-europe.eu/index. php?option=com_content&view=article&id=60%3A-central-and-eastern-europe-from-a-postcolonial-perspective&catid=35%3Aessays&Itemid=54&l ang=en.

Loomba, Ania. 1998. *Colonialism-Postcolonialism.* London; New York: Routledge.

Melegh, Attila. 2006. *On the East-West Slope: Globalization, Nationalism, Racism and Discourses on Central and Eastern Europe.* Budapest: Central European University Press.

Meyerowitz, Joanne J. 2002. *How Sex Changed: A History of Transsexuality in the United States.* Cambridge, MA: Harvard University Press.

Minh-ha, Trinh T. 1990. 'Not You/Like You: Post-Colonial Women and the Interlocking Questions of Identity and Difference'. In *Making Face, Making Soul = Haciendo Caras: Creative and Critical Perspectives by Feminists of Color*, ed. Gloria Anzaldúa. San Francisco: Aunt Lute Foundation Books.

Mishra, Vijay and Bob Hodge. 1991. 'What is Post(-)Colonialism?' *Textual Practice* 5, no. 3: 399.

Moore, David Chioni. 2001. 'Is the Post- in Postcolonial the Post- in Post-Soviet? Toward a Global Postcolonial Critique'. *PMLA* 116, no. 1: 111–28.

Muñoz, José Esteban. 2009. *Cruising Utopia: The Then and There of Queer Futurity*. New York: New York University Press.

Owczarzak, Jill. 2009. 'Introduction: Postcolonial Studies and Postsocialism in Eastern Europe'. *Focaal* 2009 (spring): 3–19.

Padilla, Mark, ed. 2007. *Love and Globalization: Transformations of Intimacy in the Contemporary World*. Nashville: Vanderbilt University Press.

Patton, Cindy and Benigno Sánchez-Eppler, eds. 2000. *Queer Diasporas*. Durham, NC: Duke University Press.

Phelan, Shane, ed. 1997. *Playing with Fire: Queer Politics, Queer Theories*. New York: Routledge.

Pitcher, Ben and Henriette Gunkel. 2009. 'Editorial: Racism in the Closet – Interrogating Postcolonial Sexuality'. *Darkmatter Journal* (6 May). http://www.darkmatter101.org/site/2008/05/02/racism-in-the-closet-interrogating-postcolonial-sexuality/.

Presser, Lois. 2005. 'Negotiating Power and Narrative in Research: Implications for Feminist Methodology'. *Signs: Journal of Women in Culture and Society* 30, no. 4 (1 June): 2067–90. doi:10.1086/428424.

Puar, Jasbir K. 2007. *Terrorist Assemblages: Homonationalism in Queer Times*. Durham, NC: Duke University Press.

Rosenberg, Tiina. 2008. 'Locally Queer. A Note on the Feminist Genealogy of Queer Theory'. *Graduate Journal of Social Science* 5, no. 2. Queer Methodologies (December). http://gjss.org/images/stories/volumes/5/2/0805.2a02rosenberg.pdf.

Stryker, Susan and Stephen Whittle, eds. 2006. *The Transgender Studies Reader*. New York: Routledge.

Todorova, Mariia Nikolaeva. 1997. *Imagining the Balkans*. New York: Oxford University Press.

White, Hayden. 1990. *The Content of the Form: Narrative Discourse and Historical Representation*. Baltimore, MD: The Johns Hopkins University Press.

Woltersdorff, Volker. 2007. 'Neoliberalism and its Homophobic Discontents'. *InterAlia: A Journal of Queer Studies*, no. 2. http://www.interalia.org.pl/en/artykuly/2007_2/06_neoliberalism_and_its_homophobic_discontents_1.htm.

Young, Robert. 1997. 'White Mythologies: Writing History and the West'. In *The Postmodern History Reader*, ed. Keith Jenkins. London/New York: Routledge.

Chapter 2

Between Walls: Provincialisms, Human Rights, Sexualities and Serbian Public Discourses on EU Integration

Jelisaveta Blagojević

In both, political and academic debates, globalisation as one of the key features of our contemporary world is one of the major topics (today), in discussion concerning various paradoxes characteristic of the global, networked and ever more connected world today. Some of these paradoxes are related to the fluid status of the contemporary world in terms of tensions in/between the logics of local (nation-state) and global (inter-/transnational), between barricading and opening, and between inclusion and exclusion.[1]

It is the metaphor of the Wall, one of the most striking political metaphors, which symbolises some of those tensions, the metaphor that is all too familiar to us all. The face of contemporary political and ideological cartography changed significantly when the in/famous Berlin Wall fell, and the division between East/ socialist and West/capitalist political spaces of the Cold War era symbolically collapsed. Similarly, the wall between Israel and Palestine has come to symbolise hostility, violence and fear between communities. The Chinese Wall symbolised a demarcation line between different cultures and ideologies for centuries. In any case, millions of lives were invested in building, rebuilding and maintaining these walls over time. Questions we need to face are: how can one understand this constructing and maintaining of walls in the globalised world? Are these concrete walls more solid and impenetrable than the invisible walls we are bouncing off in our daily experiences? And, finally, whose property are all those walls, both visible and invisible? Who actually needs them?

In this chapter I will first outline a Serbian context of national and sexual politics, recalling some key facts from recent Serbian history which I think are crucial for a better understanding of its cultural specificity. Then I will elaborate more theoretically on the concept of the provincial mind, which I find useful in answering the questions about Serbian and European Union (EU) relations, power relations and dualistic thinking.

---

1   When using the notions of *inclusion* and *exclusion*, I refer mostly to Giorgio Agamben (1995, 1998, 1999, 2000) and to Wendy Brown (1995, 2004, 2009).

National Pride vs Gay Pride: the Case of Serbia

Since the (re)formation of the Socialist Federal Republic of Yugoslavia (SFRJ), with Serbia as one of the founding constituents, the country has passed through very difficult and different cultural, political and ideological challenges and changes. While the dominant socialist ideology in the former Yugoslavia was organised around Tito's ideas of 'brotherhood and unity', helping to pacify and diminish differences between various ethnic and religious groups, Serbian society during the period of Slobodan Milošević's rule (of Serbia 1989–97, Yugoslavia 1997–2000) deployed different ideological patterns. These are mainly national pride, territorial integrity and 'all Serbs in one country' politics etc. – all under the banner of securing national and cultural identity as well as territorial integrity. Although those ideological values are not commonly considered to be a part of socialist ideology, this so-called 'Milošević's Serbia' was also self-labelled as a socialist project. However, as it turned out, this 'socialist project' maintained its values through bloody ethnic wars.

In dominant political and ideological discourses, contemporary Serbian society is most often characterised as a society 'in transition', colloquially named as 'Serbia after democratic changes'. In those discourses, everything in Serbia in the last 15 years was in transition: justice system, economy, culture, but also people's lives, freedoms and rights. Its recent historical trans-experience generally refers to the path from communism and socialism to capitalism and liberal democracy, recognised as the other name for EU integration. At the same time, while 'transiting' from one ideology to another, Serbian society is carrying a heavy burden of recent historical events: wars, ethnic cleansing, isolation, collapse of all institutions among others. Only the Orthodox Church did not experience any transition: more then ever, it has played and continues to play the role of moral authority in Serbia, thus influencing and shaping social and political life.

Lesbian, Gay, Bisexual and Transgender (LGBT) Communities in Serbia

In such a political, cultural and economic environment national pride came into deep conflict with gay pride. Thus Serbia is one of the last countries in Europe to adopt general anti-discriminatory laws.[2] In spite of continuous and enormous efforts of various LGBTIQ (intersex, queer),[3] human rights, peace and other civil

---

2   From the editors: Although the author seems to be rather critical about this advancement of Serbia as 'late', it has to be noted that such laws are not yet standard, and in fact some of the supposedly 'more advanced' countries of the EU (such as Poland) still do not have them, which actually puts Serbia at the forefront of change.

3   I will use the LGBTIQ abbreviation for it circulates as such in Serbian non-heterosexual communities. However, it has to be noted that the actual politics is only about lesbian and gay people, rendering BTIQ empty signifiers; custom of use is not a real denotation of politics.

organisations and groups, different social groups and individuals are facing various kinds of discrimination, sometimes expressed in radically violent ways. In recent research entitled 'Prejudices Exposed – Homophobia in Serbia', conducted for Gay Straight Alliance by the Centre for Free Elections and Democracy (CeSID) in 2008, 70 per cent of the population in Serbia thought that homosexuality was a disease.[4]

In order to try to understand all the complexities and specificities of the LGBTIQ population and its positioning within larger cultural, ideological and political context in Serbia I have conducted interviews with representatives of two LGBTIQ organisations in Serbia: Labris and Queeria Center. Labris is a lesbian, feminist, non-governmental and non-profit organisation, founded in Belgrade in 1995 with the aim of promoting lesbian rights and visibility in Serbian society. It emerged out of the lesbian and gay lobby, Arkadija, founded in 1990 in Belgrade as a result of social, legal and other invisibility, marginalisation and discrimination against lesbians at that time. At the present time, Labris is a part of the women's movement, the human rights movement and the LGBTIQ movement and collaborates with different civil organisations; it is also a member of different networks and coalitions (e.g. Coalition against Discrimination, Coalition of Women's Rights Defenders etc.) employing women regardless of their sexual orientation. Queeria Centre for the Promotion of Culture of Nonviolence and Equality is Belgrade's gay organisation, existing since 2000. The focus of Queeria Center is on strengthening and building the LGBT community in Serbia through media, cultural and artistic activities.

According to Labris, the LGBTIQ community in Serbia is still invisible, afraid to report violence and discrimination suffered and to advocate for their rights. As a Labris survey in 2006[5] indicates, two-thirds of LGBTIQ people suffered some kind of violence, yet less than 10 per cent reported violence to the police, and less than 3 per cent reported violence to the court. The reasons for not reporting violence are fear of further victimisation in the public institutions (e.g. police, hospitals, courts). Labris has also conducted a needs assessment of lesbian beneficiaries of Labris and other LGBTIQ organisations, according to which more than 90 per cent of people are not open about their sexuality with their family, and feel it should not be disclosed to others.[6] LGBTIQ activism in Serbia is quite limited, since LGBTIQ activists are afraid to work in such homophobic surroundings, especially after the violent confrontations during the Pride parade in 2001. The so-called 'democratic changes' after 2000 did not bring any improvement in LGBTIQ human rights though: violence against queers continues to be tolerated by the majority of the population, affecting LGBTIQ activism and activists and

---

4 See more: http://www.gsa.org.rs/cms-run/.

5 'Let's Do Something Together for Ourselves', http://labris.org.rs/en/research/research/violence-upon-same-sex-oriented-persons.html (accessed: 1 February 2010).

6 http://labris.org.rs/en/images/stories/razno_2008/istrazivanjepotreba_eng.pdf (accessed: 1 February 2010).

others, preventing them from actively participating in social and political processes. And although Serbia ratified most of the international human rights resolutions and conventions, including the International Covenant on Civil and Political Rights and the European Convention on Human Rights, Serbian society is still characterised by strong prejudices and ignorance towards LGBTIQ people, and a general xenophobic lack of tolerance towards all 'otherness'. By 2009, the Serbian Parliament adopted five laws that specifically ban discrimination based on sexual orientation: Labour Law, Higher Education Law and two media laws – Public Information Law and Broadcasting Law; and, in March 2009, the Anti-Discrimination Law was adopted. Still, none of those laws are adequately implemented in practice, and any implementation is significantly decreased by the low readiness of the LGBTIQ population to report violence and discrimination, (as stated earlier, because of the fear of further institutional victimisation – which closes the vicious circle).

Gay Pride

Speaking about the already mentioned Pride parade in 2001, Maja Savić[7] from Labris stressed that it was organised just after the 'democratic changes' in Serbia and the fall of the authoritarian regime of Slobodan Milošević. LGBTIQ activists were then quite enthusiastic and organised the parade without allowing time for the newly established political structures to improve their democratic aspirations. Human rights were not deployed, or their idea properly rooted in the social imagination, and EU negotiations were still miles away. Homophobia was not only a social problem, but also a highly systematic, deeply established institutional practice. For example, judging by the extremes of violence that took place during the 2001 Pride parade in Belgrade, it is clear that the organisers did not take into consideration the lack of political will and administrative support for holding the parade in Belgrade. The result was more than 40 injured people, and police refusal to protect the participants of the event.

In contrast, the Pride parade in 2009 was initiated after the adoption of the Anti-Discrimination Law. This initiative came as a consequence of the changes regarding the position of LGBTIQ people in Serbia in 2009. After five years of lobbying and advocacy efforts, the Anti-Discrimination Law was adopted in April 2009; visibility of LGBTIQ people and issues related to LGBTIQ human rights increased, both in the media and the political agenda; LGBTIQ activists were more often sources of information in print and electronic media and there was improved cooperation between LGBTIQ organisations. Finally, according to Maja Savić and Labris, cooperation with democratic political parties, the Ministry of the Interior and the Ministry of Human and Minority Rights was on a much higher level than ever before. All of these changes resulted in several public protests by LGBTIQ and human rights non-governmental organisations (NGOs). For example, LGBTIQ organisations took a visible part in the October 2008 anti-fascist March; a

---

7   (Personal interview with Maja Savić, 10 April 2010.

proposed demonstration by fascists and other right-wing organisations was banned and police protection for the LGBTIQ organisations was significantly improved. Moreover, police protection of the LGBTIQ protesters was also well organised and executed during the first solely LGBTIQ manifestation since 2001, in front of the Sava Congress Centre.[8] And finally, during the International Women's Day protest march in the centre of Belgrade in 2009, there was the second public protest by LGBTIQ people, together with women's and human rights organisations, which were also adequately protected by the police. Taking all of these changes into consideration, Labris and other LGBTIQ organisations decided to organise the second Pride parade in Belgrade in 2009. They estimated that this was the crucial political moment in Serbia to start organising the parade and to demand the freedom of movement, peaceful protest and gathering for the LGBTIQ community. This time, the important issue of visible violence against LGBTIQ people in Serbia was raised during preparations and organisation of the Parade.

Diversity at Wake

However, the organisation of the second Pride has proved to be more problematic, in part because of the possible threat from neo-fascist and nationalist groups. It was also the rising diversity of expectations and approaches within LGBTIQ activists in Serbia that led Boban Stojanović from Queeria to withdraw from the Pride organising committee. Stojanović's starting point is that there is no such a thing as LGBTIQ community in Serbia. There are some people/places/actions that mark a community, but it does not exist, since it does not have its own voice in Serbian public discourse. Even if we say that there is LGBTIQ community in Serbia, one has to say that that community lacks self-awareness, education, information and self-affirmation, says Boban.[9]

According to Queeria, what was then problematic was the focus of the organizers on dominant Institutions instead of on the needs of queer people. Boban believes that the adopted strategy was inappropriate (a futile belief that the state will recognise queers only because they organise a public march). According to him, there was no 'life impulse' and the focus was on 'negatives': fascism, nationalism and violence. The organisers' strategy was more about adverse conditions for the LGBTIQ community in Serbia than about understanding the ways in which we could live better. Generally speaking, he believes that the efforts made by LGBTIQ and other human rights activists in Serbia have a tendency to follow and reflect the logic of 'Western' models of cultural and political agency. Even among alternative and/or underground organisations, there is a strong tendency to copy other

---

8   The protest was spontaneously organised against Sava's new management and their ideological decision to ban a Gay Straight Alliance conference (although it had been held at their premises before).

9   Personal interview with Boban Stojanović, 15 April 2010.

Western European scenes, without taking into account the local context and its specificities. It is a similar situation with the so-called 'mainstream' human rights organisations, Boban claims, since they are simply trying to apply so-called 'European standards' dressed in the frocks of 'universality' to Serbian society. Therefore during the last two years, Queeria Center – in cooperation with experts in applied psychology, PR and marketing – has prepared and implemented a new strategy in the promotion of LGBTIQ human rights in Serbia. The main idea is that ratification of various human rights oriented laws cannot produce results without wider individual and cultural changes in society.

It is rather obvious that one of the most important debates around the organisation of Pride 2009 in Belgrade was between different LGBTIQ groups and concerned their strategies. This reflects a wider political and organisational diversity of LGBTIQ groups, informing us about the 'internal' heterogeneity and complexity of LGBTIQ activism in Serbia. On the other hand, precisely those differences were manipulated and used against LGBTIQ activists by their opponents wanting to weaken and dismiss them from the Serbian public space, or at least from the possibility of appearing there. Even though one could think of political heterogeneity as a mature and responsible way of approaching the instance of political agency, it appears to be a sign of weakness whenever and wherever the other partner in dialogue – in this case the Serbian political establishment – is homogeneous, uniform and consistent in its ideology (and in this case, in its homophobic approach to the politics of human rights).

I will clarify my argument through the statement of Dragan Djilas, the mayor of Belgrade. He made an official statement in which he suggested that sexual orientation, as a private matter, 'should be kept behind the [four] walls'. Accordingly, there are no reasons to demonstrate one's sexual preferences in public. Interestingly enough, Mayor Djilas is a representative of the Democratic Party (DS), which declares itself to be in favour of european values, EU integration and human rights. It is also a ruling party in the government that has a dominant role in public political discourses in Serbia.

In such a context, Mayor Djilas's words bear a dangerous dimension that cannot be silenced and go unnoticed. This metaphor suggests that different sexual orientations are acceptable only if they are invisible, distant, silenced, barricaded and finally controlled – behind walls. They have to remain in a domain of what is unacceptable, thus reinforcing social stratification – that is to say production of differences. It is this walled-up situation that reminds me of the notion of the provincial mind which I shall elaborate in the following sections.

Provincial Mind

Our experience is provincial, writes Radomir Konstantinović in his book *Filosofija palanke* (*Philosophy of the Provincial*), first published in Belgrade in 1969. Province is our destiny, our evil fate, he continues, using the metaphor of the provincial in order to describe the way of life and thinking typical of the small-town mentality.

Every reading of Konstantinović's book is actually a re-reading and re-opening of one and the same problem – the problem of the dual and ambiguous nature of the provincial mind. Although predominantly targeting Serbian nationalism, Konstantinović's criticism does not primarily refer to any particular territorial or geopolitical location, but rather to the provincial mind in the way as 'there is no country where it [the mind] is impossible, since it is equally possible everywhere in its demand to be ideally barricaded' (Konstantinović 1981: 8–9, my translation).

By invoking Konstantinović's work, I would like to pose a question about new, contemporary provincialisms, local and global, Balkans provincialism as well as European provincialism, 'Eastern' provincialism as well as 'Western' provincialism. I want to probe the provincialism of every identitarian logic of thinking and politics that continues to haunt – like a ghost, like a spectre – every idea of community. Or, to put it differently, what is provincial in the concept of the provincial mind is not constituted within any particular position, but rather through denying the exposition towards the difference and otherness. Therefore, what is provincial is the very relation, not the position as such.

Provincial mind is constituted by its uniform and unified way of thinking, by the various procedures of community homogenisation and thus by the exclusion of what is different and other. However, in some cases these strategies of excluding differences and otherness operate precisely through the processes of inclusion. For example, in the domain of contemporary EU integration, discourses that eventually result in annihilation, assimilation and absorption of every difference and every otherness. As Rodolphe Gasché claims in his recently published book Europe, or the Infinite Task (2009: 6) '[n]ot only has Europe lost much of its economic and political clout, but the history of its relations to non-European world, as well as its relation to the others within its own borders, has cast a seemingly final verdict on the superiority and integrity of European "values".' The politics of inclusive exclusion operates through various procedures of assimilation and integration. This means that it is politics that embraces cultural, political, sexual, national and all other differences only through erasing them.

It seems that both discourses of exclusion and inclusion – as it is with the example of applying politics of human rights as a 'European value' in the Serbian political context – mark the other, re-mark the marginalisation of those who are already marginal, point to the 'other' as to the possible danger for the infantile world of the provincial. In return, the *provincial mind* has to protect its own uniformity through denying any possibility of change, and through rejecting any kind of uncertainty and risk that unavoidably go together with the kind of thinking that is always already the other thinking, the different way of thinking. Within a province, within a small town (where it is important to underline that its smallness is constituted by the very fact that it is closed off), thinking always becomes one thinking, same thinking, certain thinking.

Provincial mind is the mind of ready-made solutions, the mind of life patterns and life routines – 'values' if you will, with ready answers to all possible questions; it is about the constant re-establishing of tradition, perpetual renewal of inner and outer walls that serve as safeguards, and does nothing but repeats the provincial past. Thus, it is the refusal of the provincial mind to look into the future that appears to be the origin of every aspiration to turn the world into a provincial place, i.e. a small town.

'We Must Be Part of the European Union'

In Serbia, the idea of EU integration has the logic of a normative discourse. The unquestionable nature of this '*we must be part of the European Union*' attitude has its performative effects and serves as an argument which is to be repeated and cited whenever decision-makers in Serbia become unwilling to actually confront the majority and so-called 'traditional values'.

For example, in March 2009 the Serbian Parliament debated an anti-discrimination law that bans any kind of discrimination on grounds of race, religion, sexual orientation, gender or any other basis. It was strongly opposed by the Serbian Orthodox Church and other conservatives, but the legislation was part of reforms to align the nation with EU policies, and was crucial if Serbian citizens were to become EU citizens and gain – what is seen as *the* major advantage of EU integration – the right to travel without visas. Finally, the law was passed.

However, the religious communities continued to actively oppose it. The Serbian Orthodox Church, supported by other religious communities (including Belgrade's archbishopric of the Catholic Church, the Islamic community of Serbia and the Evangelical Church), issued a letter to the Ministry of Human and Minority Rights requesting withdrawal of the draft law proposal. The church was particularly 'dissatisfied' with Articles 18 and 21 of the Anti-Discrimination Law, which deal with possibilities of altering religious beliefs and expression of gender identity and sexual orientation. Church representatives argued that the law might be liable to misinterpretation and misuse. Other critics have said it runs counter to Serbian tradition.[10] The Prime Minister's office issued a lapidary statement that changes were to be dealt with urgently, 'since we are dealing with a law in a set which represents a precondition to include Serbia into the white Schengen list'.[11]

Serbian Women and the EU

Another interesting example of the relation of some Serbian discourses towards EU integration that bounces off issues of gender and sexuality is a speech given

---

10   The Associated Press, http://www.google.com/hostednews/ap/article/ALeqM5h-vdO5u-DRbjfP8eGSRbIF0difZvAD975P6PG1 (accessed: 9 April 2009).

11   Peščanik.net, http://www.pescanik.net/content/view/2793/158/ (accessed: 20 March 2010).

by Dragan Markovic Palma, the current mayor of the small town of Jagodina. As a member of the Serbian Parliament and leader of the United Serbia Party, he offered a rather twisted (at least for non-Serbs) way of argumentation: 'In Serbia, there are over 3,700,000 women. Out of 3,700,000 women, we might say 3,650,000 are very beautiful women. If this [anti-discrimination] law passes, given that a large number of women are already finding it hard to cope with the global financial crisis, if we vote for this law, then these women will surely have a problem.' He also claimed 'If we are to proceed towards Europe in the company of homosexuals, it would be better not to go at all.'[12]

Now, let us try to understand what message the mayor of a small Serbian town is actually trying to convey. First, a vast majority of Serbian women are very beautiful (out of 3,700,000 only 50,000 are not); second, most of these very beautiful women are in financial crisis. (Still remaining is the question of what kind of financial status is facing those 50,000 not very beautiful women.) Further, if one is a very beautiful woman who lives in Serbia in the midst of a world financial crisis, one can/should certainly count on financially successful heterosexual men. (Is there any other possible way?) And finally, if the anti-discrimination law is approved, there is an obvious danger that heterosexual men will become homosexuals, and thus financially less capable of supporting (no longer willing to support?) 3,650,000 very beautiful women who live in Serbia. We can only assume that, in consequence, Serbia will eventually collapse.

Besides the fact that this argument is absolutely homophobic and operates in accordance with extremely patriarchal logic, it also shows fear: fear that financially capable, heterosexual men in Serbia will somehow become homosexual (read: less masculine and powerful) if they lose the ability to discriminate against homosexual people (as well as against 3,650,000 very beautiful Serbian women and 50,000 not very beautiful women).

Let us now return to the other effects of the law itself. Due to intentional chronology and to the way these laws were presented by the decision-makers, it turned out that those who voted 'yes' to the anti-discriminatory law voted, in fact, for travelling around Europe without visas (of course, if they had the money). However, since the vast majority of Serbian citizens cannot afford to travel due to the economic situation, they will also have to vote 'yes' to a law that introduces extra taxes for Serbian citizens in order to fill holes in the government's budget. Furthermore, given that most of the people struggle in their day-to-day existence, they would vote 'yes' for everything that promises money and investment – for example the Universiade (International Student Games), a huge sports competition in Belgrade. But then, in order to have the Universiade in Belgrade, Serbians will have to vote 'yes' to the 'reallocation' of Roma citizens so that Belgrade's city government can present it as a modern city of the twenty-first century. This will mean a 'Roma free' (read: problem free, since it is 'them' – Roma minority, not

---

12 See http://rapidscan.me/video/KQdtxhCrEus/Dragan-Markovi%C4%87-Palma-Bolje-da-%C4%8Duvamo-ovce.html (accessed: 1 April 2010).

'us', ethnic Serbs, a problem) future capital of the Balkans and, of course, a great opportunity for foreign investment.

In this ideological vicious circle, the line of argumentation and political decision-making does not really go along with any kind of thinking that advocates human lives and quality of life in certain communites; this line of argumentation has the same trajectory as the neo-liberal logic of money and/or ideology circulation. Consequently, it is neither about our lives nor about the lives of others; it is neither about the others right to have rights, nor about our right to have rights. It is all about re-establishing the dominant ideological patterns; that is to say, it is all about keeping the status quo and its provincial conservative effects as if they were neutral, objective and non-political.

Searching for Alternatives and Political Possibilities

One of the best possible examples of how the Anti-Discrimination Law has explicitly unravelled this logic of status quo as a political formation per se would be everything that followed and happened around the already mentioned Pride parade 2009.

It was the first attempt to organise such a gathering after the devastating parade organised in 2001. One of the explanations circulating for such a decision after eight years was that the Anti-Discrimination Law gave hope and motivation to the LGBTIQ community in Serbia that, this time, it would make a difference.

On 20 September 2009, after months of media attention, strong arguments were laid both on political and social levels. Hence the end result of this socio-political action was the following: according to officials, the parade was cancelled for security reasons. At the same time, the organising committee of Pride officially announced that the parade was *de facto* banned by the political forefront, yet not *de jure*.[13]

How did this happen? Learning lessons from the past, the organising committee tried to cooperate closely with the political and state officials. By engaging the Ministry of Internal Affairs, together with police forces, various ministries and political figures, foreign officers etc., the organisers wanted to ensure the safety of Pride supporters as well as to gain approval as a minority with newly 'recognised' and 'gained' rights. Symbolically, this meant to signify a radical turn from the traditional, patriarchal and conservative ideological patterns to some liberalised sphere of socio-political action of change. However, this action backfired not only on the Serbian LGBTIQ community as a 'specific/special' social group, but also on the whole society which, all of a sudden, found itself stranded in/between an invisible border: a wall that separated one Serbia from 'the other Serbia' (as it is usually expressed), and that set a off chain reaction which resulted in a series of grave (re)interpretations, criticisms and discussions on both sides.

---

13   http://www.balkaninsight.com/en/main/analysis/22369/ (accessed: 1 April 2010).

Assessing the role of political actors, media and the influence of public discourses in Serbia in the context of organising the Pride Parade in 2009, Labris activists claim that the state proved its inability and incompetence in dealing with the hooligans and violators. After 20 September, it became irrefutable that government representatives, through their meek, unconvincing statements and lack of clear dismissal of hate speeches, had contributed to the general permissiveness of hate violence against LGBTIQ people. And even though a certain degree of cooperation existed between the Pride organisers and state officials,[14] at the same time most of them used every opportunity to distance themselves from this protest (which actually represented the implementation of a basic human right – the freedom of public gathering).

In fact, a pattern became evident whenever government representatives were asked to comment on Belgrade's Pride Parade. It inevitably consisted of an 'I don't share their beliefs or values' interlude. Besides the fact that politicians confused 'beliefs and values' with sexual orientation, government representatives also acted as urged to distance themselves from or to rebuild the walls between them and Pride supporters. It is this kind of behaviour that actually reveals a number of things. First, a lack of understanding of the importance of human rights politics – for which the government is actually advocating in the name of EU integration and implementation of the so-called 'European values'. Second, it also shows politicians' inability to act in the interest of the citizens of Serbia as a whole. And finally, it shows their readiness to use their privileged position of public figures to manipulate public opinion. Consequently, instead of representing Serbian citizens who voted for them and the seemingly liberal and 'European' system of values they advocated for during the electoral campaigns, government officials actually represented themselves and their personal and provincial homophobic attitudes.

In this overview of the responses and attitudes of the institutional representatives, one of the most symptomatic statements was the one made by the Public Prosecutor, Slobodan Radovanović, who commented on the right-wing threats 'quoted' in various newspapers:

> We can't react to what the newspapers are writing, we can react only if there are consequences of all of that. I think that, as far as the media goes, I don't really see much in that, we have opposing views, those are just polemic tones. Let's not comment on that now, but let's create the preconditions so all of this can end well.[15]

---

14   Although support for the Pride Parade came only from the State Secretary at the Ministry for Human and Minority Rights, Marko Karadžić, and the offices of the Republic and Regional Ombudspersons.

15   'Right-wing threats before the Pride Parade', *B92*, 16 September 2009: Republic Prosecutor, Mr Slobodan Radovanović.

If one reads this statement carefully, the Public Prosecutor is suggesting that only the consequences of death threats are important enough for launching any kind of reaction. But, what could be the consequence of a death threat? It seems as if neither Public Prosecutor nor any other state representative has witnessed and experienced the devastating consequences of death threats received during the Pride Parade in 2001. Even more so, it is not only about providing a safe environment for Pride parades in Serbia; it is also about the frightening logic that only casualties are worthy of institutional care and action.

In this case, the Public Prosecutor shows not only a very superficial understanding of how the media in general produces their own consequences but, in the same manner as all the other state representatives, he is avoiding facing the problem and taking any kind of responsibility for possible violence. He actually tries to neutralise it by using euphemistic phrases such as 'opposing views' and 'polemic tones'. This statement, according to Labris, represents the behavioural pattern of government officials regarding the protection of the parade. Politicians state that all citizens should enjoy equal protection; yet, at the same time, they do not take any measures to ensure that.

As a summary, I would suggest that the way in which the Anti-Discrimination Law was debated, motivated and presented in Serbia does nothing other than produce subjects in need of protection, without political possibilities and alternatives. Yet even if it is based on the best possible EU practices and values, this particular law – without considerable changes in Serbian society and political culture – in fact does nothing else but reinforce the infantile provincial mind, which is again (through the very 'strategy of inclusion') exclusive not only in respect to marginalised individuals and groups but also in terms of searching for alternatives and political possibilities.

At the end of the day, those who criticised the Anti-Discrimination Law and were worried that it 'runs counter to Serbian tradition' could rest easy. Serbian provincialism and its traditions remained intact since the real debate on human rights politics and anti-discriminatory policy has been almost completely silenced. In any case, it did not even touch upon those most important issues which such a public debate could bring to a particular community: the search for alternatives to the politics of exclusion as well as to the political culture and ideology based on war, violence and discrimination.

It seems that the most serious 'benefit' of the anti-discriminatory law will be that discrimination, human suffering, misery and violence against the citizens of Serbia will be better controlled and institutionalised from now on. Thus, once again the most vulnerable ones will be time marked and reproduced in their otherness, since human rights discourse and anti-discriminatory policies are producing a certain kind of subject who needs protection. They are removed from politics; they are made passive and consequently someone else got the mandate to act in order to help or protect – e.g. to intervene. It is this constant recreation of the need for protection that leads to a kind of interventionism, which is not necessarily an aspect of emancipatory politics.

Through its conventions, the EU has already established procedures in which for the first time in history made it possible for individuals, citizens, to come out on to the international stage, into the field of international law that used to be reserved solely for sovereign states. The tendency towards internationalisation of human rights indicates the increasing willingness to take into account the sovereignty of individuals and minority groups, not just institutional actors. On the other hand, the process of visible globalisation of human rights testifies to how the 'Western' insistence on the universality of human rights can function virtually as a diplomatic and political alibi for neo-colonial interventionism (Savic 1995–1996).

By Way of Conclusion ...

Described above is the kind of politics that actually depoliticises the power relations and historical and cultural contextualisation of the existing conditions that had produced social stratification and differentiation on a local level. If supposedly depoliticised humanitarian politics of human rights were really depoliticised, it would not create any normative or subject-producing dimensions. It would not carry any cultural assumptions or aims; it would not prescribe or proscribe anything. It would simply expand possibilities, alternatives, possible freedoms and more inventions in our future.

However, the very matrix of Europeanisation of the Balkans understood as inclusive exclusion is being constantly repeated within the Balkans itself. Thus, we have to depart from the world of what is 'ideally closed' – that is to say, the world that resides in the mind or spirit that resists opening and struggles to reify its resistance (by building all sorts of visible and invisible walls). We have to move towards openness, fusion, transparency and deterritorialisation. We should leave behind 'our province', 'our past', 'our provincial barricaded mind', our maps and borders, our whole fetishistic world; we should break down all the walls and step forward into the yet unknown exploit of inventing, discovering and opening.

It might appear that this is a rather enthusiastic view concerning the ways in which one should overcome the whole logic of provincialism. One of the main arguments of this chapter is the very necessity to question the concept of identity whenever it appears as a site of what is normative, secure and familiar. This means that we should take a risk and at least try to remain open to the unknown; to make an effort and allow changes, transformations and mistakes to happen and reinvent ourselves in yet unknown ways. The very fact that this is difficult to perform does not mean that it is impossible. On the contrary, our resistance to changing ourselves is marked by the fact that we are always already exposed to what is different and other – that we are *other*.

One of the most significant tasks in today's world is to re-define, re-construct, re-read and re-write the very concept of politics and/or the political. And it should be (in) plural because it is about life in all its complexities; it is about some hard decisions that need to be made; it is about the absence of certainty; it is at stake whenever and wherever the 'I' and 'The Other' are (ex)posed to each other. It contains in itself, paradoxically, inclusion and exclusion, transcendence and belonging, absolute external appearance of somebody and something unknown and strange as well as intimacy of the familiar and close: in other words, distance and intimacy at the same time.

Who is then this other who is constitutive for the political, the other who is both a stranger/foreigner and someone closest – both 'I' and 'The Other'? In the spirit of Heidegger's terminology, Derrida offers the following answer:

> [it] has no shape. No sex. No name. It is neither a man nor a woman. It is not selfhood, not 'I', not a subject, nor a particular person. It is another *Dasein* that every *Dasein has, through the voice*, a voice it hears … At a distance which is neither absolute – or, absolutely infinite – nor worthless in the absolute closeness of one's ownership … This range of voice, to-be-in-the-range-of-voice … makes the other someone of a different kind. (Derrida 2001: 465)

Thus, the political requires an *ear* for the other, listening to the other; thus, politics is always the other's politics; it requires the other, demands the other and is responsible to the other. Every relation to the other would be, said Derrida, before and after anything else, *an adieu*.

In this sense, an adieu to Europe invokes the gesture of hospitality towards the moment of separation, of departure; sometimes forever (this can never, in fact, be excluded), with no return. In this sense, and precisely in this sense, it is a gesture of welcoming the unknown, foreign and strange, of what is new and different, of breaking the walls. An act of responsibility for the others, as much as a response to the others, must be thus an *Adieu to Europe*.

Bibliography

Agamben, Giorgio. 1995. 'We Refugees'. *Symposium* 49 (2): 114–20.
———. 1998. *Homo Sacer: Sovereign Power and Bare Life*. Stanford: University of Stanford Press.
———. 1999. *Potentialities*. Stanford: Stanford University Press.
———. 2000. *Means Without Ends: Notes on Politics*. Minneapolis and London: University of Minnesota Press.
Arendt, Hannah. 2004 [1958]. *Origins of Totalitarianism*. New York: Meridian.
Brown, Wendy. 1995. *States of Injury: Power and Freedom in Late Modernity*. Princeton: Princeton University Press.
———. 2004. '"The Most We Can Hope For …": Human Rights and the Politics of Fatalism'. *South Atlantic Quarterly* 103 (2/3): 451–63.
———. 2009. 'Walled States, Waning Sovereignty: Professor Wendy Brown Keynote Lecture', The Centre for Citizenship, Identities and Governance

(CCIG), Open University, http://www.open.ac.uk/ccig/media/walled-states-waning-sovereignty-by-wendy-brown (accessed: 1 February 2010).

Chakrabarty, Dipesh. 2000. *Provincializing Europe: Postcolonial Thought and Historical Difference*. Princeton: Princeton University Press.

———. 1993. 'Heidegger's Ear: Philopolemology (Geschlecht IV)'. In *Reading Heidegger: Commemorations*, ed. John Sallis. Bloomington and Indianapolis: Indiana University Press.

———. 1997. *Politics of Friendship*. London: Verso.

———. 1999. *Adieu to Emmanuel Levinas*. Stanford: Stanford University Press.

———. (Žak Derida). 2001. 'Geschlecht IV'. In *Politke prijateljstva* (*Politics of Friendship*). Belgrade: Beogradski krug.

Foucault, Michel. 1988. 'Truth, Power, Self: An Interview with Michel Foucault – October 25th, 1982'. In *Technologies of the Self: A Seminar with Michel Foucault*, eds Martin, L.H. et al. London: Tavistock.

Gasché, Rodolphe. 2009. *Europe, or the Infinite Task*. Stanford: Stanford University Press.

Konstantinović, Radomir. 1981. *Filosofija palanke*. Belgrade: Nolit.

Rancière, Jacques. 2004. 'Who is the Subject of Human Rights', *South Atlantic Quarterly* 103 (2/3): 297–310.

Savic, Obrad. 1995–96. 'Politics of Human Rights', *Belgrade Circle Journal* 3/4–1/2.

Chapter 3

Nations and Sexualities – 'West' and 'East'

Robert Kulpa

Although literature about nations and nationalisms on the one hand, and sexuality on the other are rich and profound in their fields, the crossroads still seem to be a rather neglected area of study, with a clear scarcity of work. However, a significant proliferation can be noticed in recent years, especially in relation to terrorism, fundamentalism and new (US) imperialism (e.g. Beverley 2004; Binnie 2004; Gabilondo 2004; Posel 2005; Puar 2007; Haritaworn, Tauqir and Erdem 2008; Kuntsman 2008; Butler 2009). This chapter aims at contributing to this discussion by undertaking a theoretical journey through, in my opinion, some of the most important issues sparking between nation/al/ism/s and sexualities. Where appropriate and useful, I will refer to Central and Eastern Europe (CEE) as the case study that, in my opinion, offers an interesting exemplification of discussed issues. I will also use this geographical, historical and political position – 'Central-and-Eastern-Europeness' – to question the relation between Western academic theories and non-Western realities. In doing so, I will try to highlight unequal power relations between the two regions, and better understand the workings of a hegemonic (neo-colonial perhaps?) 'West'. As such, this chapter is densely intertwined with some of the issues raised by the editors in their opening chapter, and remains in dialogue with other collected articles.

I will begin with a brief discussion of three seminal texts – George Mosse's *Nationalism and Sexuality* (1985), Andrew Parker et al. *Nationalisms and Sexualities* (1992) and Sam Pryke's 'Nationalism and Sexuality: What Are the Issues' (1998) – which directly address and theorise the issues of nationalism and sexuality together. I then proceed to unpack some of the key problem areas (modernities, identities, homo-assemblages and homonationalism), and characterise my own perspective on the emerging issues and contentions, especially relating to the study of Central and Eastern Europe.

Nation and Gender

As noted, the relationship between nation and sexuality is relatively new on the academic agenda, which has historically treated the two separately (Parker et al. 1992: 2). This newer focus was mainly conducted by feminist (-inspired) scholars, with a significant lack of interest from within 'mainstream' literature on nationalism (Pryke 1998: 530). More precisely, the interest is largely on gender and nationalism (Tolz and Booth 2005: 1–3), with questions of sexuality left marginal or evoked only in the context of gender roles – femininity and masculinity, within heterosexual framings – (e.g. Yuval-Davis and Anthias 1989; Nagel 1998; Mayer 1999). Moreover, the 'gender' aspect is often conflated with 'women' and their subordination to men, with significantly less attention paid to the formation of masculinities (Nagel 1998: 243), not to mention other dissident gender positions. Also some of the main works from the field of sexuality studies demonstrate a lack of interest in issues of nationalism (Pryke 1998: 530). In light of this, the pressing question is why – when certain elements of national ideologies and identities are so obviously gendered – was gender hardly ever examined in the 'classical' literature on nationalism? Tolz and Booth (2005) use the example of Benedict Anderson's *Imagined Communities* (1991). By quoting several passages from this canonical text, they show how Anderson (unconsciously?) acknowledges genders and their roles in the formation of national identities (e.g. through words such as camaraderie, fatherland, brotherhood etc.), but fails to address this relationship openly and clearly (Tolz and Booth 2005: 1–7).

Mosse, Parker and Pryke

Andrew Parker et al. open their collection of essays, *Nationalisms and Sexualities*, by writing on the very first page that '[w]henever the power of the nation is invoked ... we are more likely than not to find it couched as a love of country: an eroticized nationalism' (1992: 1). The authors acknowledge nationalism as one of the most powerful ideologies. They also identify sexualities as equally powerful sites of discourse creation, circulation and exercise. These considerations – taken together with the general lack of literature on these subjects – provide the primary motivation for their book, which is also a tribute to George L. Mosse's publication *Nationalism and Sexuality*. However, one of the main differences Parker et al. draw is an epistemological position. If Mosse tends to impose a vision of nationalism and sexuality as more or less stable and monolithic constructs, by adding the final 'ies' in the title of their book, Parker et al. argue that there is no 'one' nationalist ideology and/or identity; nor is there one formation of sexuality. Therefore they take a more poststructuralist position, implying the need for more work on these two (and other related) issues. Nonetheless, Mosse's book remains a landmark exploration of the worlds of nationalism and sexuality. One important observation he makes is that our modern notions of nationalism and 'respectable' sexuality emerge at the same time, with the Enlightenment and growth of capitalism. Mosse scrutinises the way nationalist ideas are inflected with a distinctive bourgeois politics of the body and sexual behaviour, and how this morality subsequently fed into the emergence of fascist nation-states in Europe in the twentieth century.

Also Sam Pryke's article attempts to theorise the link between the nation and sexuality in more general terms. In his hypothesis Pryke distinguishes three crucial problems: national sexual stereotypes, sexuality in national conflict and sex in nation-building (1998: 531). The first is about sexing 'Others' as a threat to the national ego (e.g. circulating stereotypes in 1930s Germany that teaching French to a girl will lead to her being trafficked into prostitution; or nationalist movements across CEE portraying the European Union (EU) as the 'Eurosodomy'). The second problem is the use of sex/uality in the time of war, as exemplified in interalia rape cases during Balkan War. The third and final problem is the exclusion of certain sexual practices/attitudes (such as homosexuality, masturbation or premarital sex) from the core of national ego (Pryke 1998: 535–41).

Time, Which Is Not the One[1]

George Mosse's work, however interesting and compelling, has also, from my perspective, some limitations. He focuses on the eighteenth and the nineteenth-century social and political changes, including industrialisation and a new social stratification (e.g. the emergence of new social classes, bourgeoisie and workers). On this premise, Mosse has built his theory of sexuality and nationality encapsulated in the idea of 'respectability' and bourgeois morality. From the perspective of a scholar interested in CEE, his historical study – which concerns only a handful of Western European countries (Germany and to a significantly lesser extent the United Kingdom, France and Italy) – is interesting, but may be less useful. Also important is to notice his rather too general use of 'modern Europe' as a denomination in the title and his claims that '[t]o be sure, respectability eventually spread thought Europe, a bourgeois movement at first, it soon encompassed all classes of the population' (Mosse 1985: 2). Mosse seems to forget that the populations and cultural make-up of (just constituting itself at the time) 'Germany' (in a more contemporary sense, as one federal state of current geographical boundaries) were extremely diverse (Prussians, French, Poles, Bohemians and Moravians, Italians). Hence the social processes were not necessarily spread equally among populations, and possibly occurred geographically unequally. We can also argue that in some cases of Central European countries (e.g. 'Poland'), whose territories were forcefully appropriated by 'Germany', this process of spreading 'respectable sexuality/morality' may not have taken place at all (or at least was severely restricted) – if only because of the specific cultural politics of 'Germanisation' deployed in the region, aimed more at the eradication of 'Polishness' rather than the acceptance/inclusion of Poles into the ongoing process of 'German' society. What we are dealing with here is then a need to historicise the idea of 'Europe' with particular interest in different and not overlapping boundaries of 'cultural' and '(geo)political'.

Today, Judith Butler (2009) and Jasbir Puar (2007) write about the proclaimed civilising mission of the West/Europe/USA. (The lack of precise denomination is not unproblematic in their writing, despite being supposedly acute on issues of difference and hegemony.) Butler, for example, analyses how US militarism creates the notion of the 'Arab mind' (savage) in order to pursue own 'civilising

---

1   For a more nuanced discussion of 'time' and 'space' in CEE, see Mizielińska and Kulpa's chapter in this volume.

mission' (legitimisation of its military attacks) (2009: 126). Accordingly, the construction suggests that the 'Arab mind' is fixed and cannot be altered; it has to remain 'uncivilised'. 'Our' (Western) modernity (advanced, secular, liberal, scientific) is counter-posed to 'their' premodernity (traditional, religious, non-liberal) (Butler 2009: 124–5). Similar framing of CEE can be observed in many Western-produced documentaries about 'homophobia in CEE'.

An example is in *Travel Queeries* (Graney-Saucke 2009), when Jenni, from Warsaw, suggests that Pride bans have had, overall and from today's point of view, a positive effect on the Polish reality. Why? Because they helped to mobilise society and built many important coalitions to support LGBT rights – but this observation is left completely unacknowledged or probed by filmmakers. Instead, what we see and hear is the image of Warsaw as in an 'old movie' and punk music about fascism. This can be read as if Poland were rather 'old-fashioned', still in the 'past', 'uncivilised' – where 'fascist' indoctrination moulds people's minds. Perhaps that is why the following comment comes from London-based Sally, reflecting on 'us' (Westerners) supporting 'countries like Poland' in their struggle 'because it really makes difference to them' (Easterners). This attitude is even more sharply present in *Rainbow's End* (2006) when Peter Tatchell talks about the ethical obligation 'we' (the West) have towards 'them' (Eastern LGBT people). In his words:

> Western lesbian and gay movement have the duty and responsibility to show the solidarity with the fledging gay and lesbian movement in those countries. And we also believe that we have the duty to help queers who are fleeing persecution in those countries, to bring them to a place of safety. (Hick and Jentsch 2006)

I remain uneasy about his and similar uses of 'we' and 'them', always demarcating a clear boundary between 'West' and 'non-West'. At the same time, the use remains vague and imprecise enough to be flexible and adaptive, if needed, according to changing situations and power configurations between the involved subjects, yet never losing sight of which subjects are proper 'We' and (improper) 'Them'. The hegemonic position of the 'West' in its supposed 'advancement' is taken for granted, a trajectory of modernist civilisation set up. All Eastern Europe needs to do is to 'catch up' with Western modernity, with the gracious help of the 'West'. As Tanja from Amsterdam's LGBT organisation COC states in the same film: 'We in Europe and [the] West have achieved tolerance, and maybe we can spread it, help them, so that they can accept it more easily.' There is, however, an unanswered question haunting such discourses of 'ethical obligation to help out'. How can we make sure that a good thing – to help others in need – will not become a manifestation of the 'moral superiority' of those capable of 'helping'? How can we make sure it will not become a hegemonic and 'orientalising' manifestation of power relations between the 'West' and 'the rest of the world'?

Postmodernity, Which Is Not the One

Puar and Butler write about the West's Radical Other – 'Middle East' (whatever is meant by this highly ambiguous and contentious term). But what about addressing the Time(s) and temporalities within the 'West', in the 'Europe' (which are no less contaminated terms)? I will ask again: Where is the 'West' and 'Western Europe'. And what about their (post)modernity?

If, according to Frederic Jameson's famous book *Postmodernism or, The Cultural Logic of Late Capitalism* (1991), we live in postmodern times – i.e. the times of 'late capitalism', or Anthony Giddens's 'late (high) modernity' or Zygmunt Bauman's 'liquid modernity' – what sort of modernity is lived in Central and Eastern Europe? If the West is characterised by 'late capitalism', then CEE could be thought of as being in its infancy, in 'baby capitalism'. Would that suggest that Poland and the CEE are not in postmodernity? Or is the highly temporal topsy-turvy twisting of applications here itself an example of postmodern gel, dissolving critical distinctions in its surface flux?

Perhaps, using some of the concepts deployed by Jonathan Kemp (2009: 1–2), Western modernity is already 'posthumous' and 'untimely' – rather than postmodern – because it ('late modernity') precedes (thus, in a way becoming actually 'premodern') itself (modernity) in CEE. It is 'old'/late, yet 'new'/early for the people of CEE, who only after 1989 joined the Western historical narrative (assuming its part therein no longer as a 'counter-narrative' of communism).

Furthermore, time in national narratives is often compounded, and is definitely not linear (which does not mean it is not teleological); it has more of a cyclical nature, even non-metric (Puar 2007: xvi). As shown in Mizielińska's and Kulpa's chapter in this collection, the three main categories of time – past, present and future – often collapse on to each other, making it difficult to mark the difference. In many national narratives, 'past' exists in the 'present', and only for the 'future'. Let us try again to find the way out of this labyrinth. The 'golden era' of past generations is a common (foundational) national myth (e.g. Hobsbawm and Ranger 1984; Smith 1991). It is, however, invoked performatively; it exists only in discourse and never 'in the reality' (because, as Jenkins (1991) insists, we cannot establish one past, one history). It is also one example of how the work of memory and constructing memories occurs. So the Past exists only Now, only in the present time/tense. The Past is nested/embedded in the Present. But the Present in any national narrative is important as long as it serves the Future. The Present is a way to achieve a 'golden future', when the 'golden past' will be reinstalled anew. It was (and continues to be) especially visible in the narratives of the first 'democratic' governments after the collapse of communism. Ewa Hauser (1995: 81) gives a Polish example:

> Self-consciously and with all pomp, today's Poland presents itself as a direct
> continuation of the Second Republic (1918–1939). Thus, at his inauguration,
> Lech Walesa chose to receive the insignia of presidential power from the Polish

president-in-Exile, while General Jaruzelski, the last communist president, was not invited to the ceremony.

As the conclusion to this discussion of 'national temporalities' in CEE and the West, the question still remains: which 'Time' is the 'Other Time'? I would suggest that if Western modernity is 'con-temporary/con-temporal', the temporal otherness is not necessarily 'a-temporal' (or 'pagan'/non-modern/barbarian). This would still imply the centrality of Western temporality, against which other ('a-')temporalities constitute themselves. Non-Western temporalities are rather parallel temporalities – 'para-temporalities' or 'alternative temporalities' – 'al-temporalities'. The case of CEE is a good example of parallel temporalities ('communism' as parallel to 'capitalism' from World War II until the fall of the Iron Curtain) and alternative temporalities ('post-communist transformation' as lived capitalism, or 'new democracies' as alternatives to 'simply' lived Western capitalism and 'simply' democracy).

Canon

These thoughts about Time(s) and temporal dimensions of (discursive) social existence also have something to do with a canon or 'The Canon'. Eve Kosofsky Sedgwick, in her seminal book *The Epistemology of the Closet* (1990), reflects on this issue under 'Axiom 6: The relation of gay studies to debates on the literary canon is, and had best be, tortuous'. On the one hand, the Western politics of greater sexual openness and inclusion of homosexual subjects into the state-controlled institutions (as, for example, in the case of 'sexual citizenship'), albeit at the expense of racialisation and Islamophobia, could be read as the reshaping of the social canon. The inclusion of a homosexual subject within Western nation-state narrative of own modernity is an instance of rethinking what it means to be Western, in relation to 'old' and 'new' Radical (outside) and constitutive (inside) Others. It may also be used to legitimise one's own imperialist politics, as Puar (2007) and Butler (2009) show. Clearly, this is only a case of selective Western countries, and seems a distanced future in CEE, still predominantly captured in the rather 'traditional' approaches to gender and sexuality roles, identities and embodiments (Stulhofer and Sandfort 2004).

There are, however, other attempts at reshaping the canon to include homosexual subjects. If the above could be characterised as 'canonising homosexuality' (writing homosexuality into an existing master narrative by dominant nation-state discourses), the other would be 'homosexualising the canon' (writing homosexuality into the existing national master canon of history by sexual dissidents – lesbian and gay subjects themselves). I think about 'reclaiming history', a popular strategy of lesbian and gay activism. To reclaim history is to rewrite it; it is to discursively invoke the 'al-temporality' of national discourse. After all, as Butler insists, lesbian and gay politics is about time (2009: 101). The mechanism is, however, the same as of the national narration. Reclaiming history is also a performative act of (re)creating the past in the present, which serves the (rainbow-coloured) future – a golden era of tolerance and non-existent discrimination. In other words, reclaiming history is rewriting the past in order to legitimise the present existence of lesbians and gays and the future perfect society. Lesbian and gay strategy of reclaiming the past not only operates according to the same logic as the national framing of time, but is also explicitly a national/ist practice. An example is the attempt at bringing to social attention not only world-famous 'gay' figures (Socrates, Michelangelo etc.) but also always figures from a particular national history (e.g. Shakespeare in the UK or the romantic poet and icon, Juliusz Słowacki, in Poland). When Krzysztof Tomasik in his book *Homografie* (2008) constantly 'rediscovers' famous Polish writers as 'gay' or 'lesbian', it is done precisely for the purpose of 'speaking out' for queer national voice by 'outing' Polish icons as 'les' or 'gay'. As such, this act is not only about building lesbian and gay identity, in a pursuit of its roots. It is also an act of rebuilding national identity, an attempt at strengthening bonds between lesbians and gays and their national community – especially as these bonds are most often denied to them, as in the common conservative pledge of homosexuality being a 'foreign' and 'alien' invention, non-existent in a given nation/community (see Hayes 2000: 10). So, reclaiming history by lesbian and gay people is the search for legitimisation for homosexuality within national parameters, an act of writing 'homosexual nationality' and 'national homosexuality'.

Pedagogy

Judith Butler analyses how the West and 'Europe' are discursively framed as a privileged sphere of Modernity, 'where sexual radicalism can and does take place. Often, but not always, the further claim is made that such a privileged site of radical freedom must be protected against the putative orthodoxies associated with new immigrant communities' (2009: 102). She then illustrates this with the case of the Netherlands, whose recent immigration policy confronts certain immigrants (notably those from the 'Middle East') with images of homosexual couples. Their reaction and attitude to these pictures is one of the measurements of their 'progress' and stage of Modernity, and hence acceptability for entry. For the same reason, immigrants from Europe or the USA do not have to take the same test, as presumably they are always already Modern (enough) (Butler 2009: 105). As written earlier, and as the above example illustrates, these are the discursive practices framing 'Arabs', the 'Middle East' and 'Islam' as 'pre-modern' and 'barbaric' that have to be 'civilised', even with the use of force and armed invasion.

But I would also like to add 'pedagogy' as another strategy of 'protecting' and 'promoting' western Modernity. Asking again, where is 'Europe' to suggest that there are at least two: 'Europe' (i.e. Western Europe) and '(Central and) Eastern Europe', I want to suggest that CEE is also one of the (Western) 'European' Others. This is perhaps because (although not as radically other as the 'Middle East', at least from the collapse of the Iron Curtain) CEE is an object of Western 'pedagogy' ('is being taken care of') rather than subject to any 'civilising mission'. After 1989 and the collapse of the Soviet bloc, some parts of the 'Second World' were recognised as 'European enough' to be upgraded/educated to the 'First World' club of (just) 'Europe'. This was done with the help of a 'carrot and stick' approach.

The 'carrot' represents maternal hospitality, invitation to reform, to return to the womb of Europe, to the 'European family' (i.e. to join the European Union). It is a discourse of 'common values', 'shared history', 'same Judeo-Christian roots', 'security' and 'cooperation'. The 'stick', on the other hand, represents the paternal side, with laws and regulations. Adapt yourself, and then you will be rewarded and granted privileges. If not, punishment will come: the court in Strasburg, or lack of financial support.

One recent example concerning homo/sexuality and 'homophobia in CEE', as 'taken care of' by Western European actors, is the European Parliament's resolution on homophobia in Europe (2007), in which MPs express their concern about the rise of homophobia in Europe (although given examples are almost exclusively from CEE). A screening of the *Beyond the Pink Curtain* documentary in the EU Parliament (2009) fits this bill; so too does the more legally binding Council of Europe's directive (2000) prohibiting discrimination in the workplace on grounds of sexual orientation. Within this framework we can also place the 2006 gay EuroPride, hosted in London, to which organisers invited a group of people from CEE (I leave the question of representation aside for the moment) and held a series of workshops about the rights of LGBT people (2006), and possibilities to come out (already visible in the West). Finally, the 'ethical obligation to help out', as discussed earlier in the case of temporality, found in many documentaries about homophobia in CEE (e.g. *Rainbow's End* or *Travel Queeries*) is also a fine example of Western 'pedagogy'.

Geography

According to Jon Binnie (2004), when studying sexual politics in modern times of globalisation, researchers need to be particularly aware of transnational power relations and local differences and particularities. A geographically acute perspective may also help us understand the workings of national sentiments. Geographical boundaries also maintain boundaries of Nation–State, of Self–Other. They ward off a Radical Other, the Other Nation, as much as they foreclose a particular nation-state on its neighbours – other nations. But as much as boundaries cordon off the Other, they also enclose the constitutive others within the body of the nation. Lesbian and gay people are examples of such enclosed (entrapped?) others. The strategy of coping with them, often deployed by the nationalist and conservative discourses, is to portray homosexuality as 'foreign' and 'alien' (Hayes 2000: 10).

For example, Polish LGBT groups were called 'eurosodomites' by members of the League of Polish Families Party, recalling the EU as the source of 'moral *dégringolade*' – a Sodom and Gomorrah polluting Polish national culture; or communist denial of the existence homosexuality in the Soviet bloc. To counter these discursive practices, lesbians and gay men are somehow interpolated to act upon the question of national belonging as homosexual subjects;[2] and so they embrace nationalism to prove their belonging to society (nation), thus gaining legitimisation of their life. 'We are the same/One' is used to show the 'normality' (here associated with the socially/nationally accepted norms) of a gay person, often played out as racialisation of other minorities[3] or conformity to stereotypes of gender. So 'butching up' and 'feminising down' is to act upon particular national, culture-specific norms of gendered behaviour – as in the case of the 'Let Them See Us' (2002/03) campaign organised by the Polish LGBT organisation Kampania Przeciw Homofobii (KPH)/Campaign Against Homophobia (CAH). It presented 30 lesbian and gay couples – 'just normal', 'ordinary' couples of 'feminine lesbians' and 'masculine gays'. As the organisers state in one of the articles:[4]

> Why have had they photographed? – As a duty – says Jacek, Arek's boyfriend. As sincerity – says Daria, Dominika's partner. Let them [society] see that a lesbian is not a butch woman, but a normal girl. ... No butch, masculine dykes. They take part in the 'Let Them See Us' campaign to show homosexuals as ordinary people. Just couples holding hands. Not villains, not perverts, nor bullied scapegoats. Not from gay parades, not in women's frocks, not bulldykes, as people imagine. But normal and ordinary, as next-door neighbour, or as shop assistant from the corner shop. As everybody. So on the posters they are slightly out of shape, slightly shy, without stylisation of posed gestures.

Acting up gender is to act up the nation; gender is always already national. In a sense it is about how the place/space is translated into psychological identifications; how the modern geographical delimitation of a particular nation-state gives rise to the 'imagined community' of the Nation, and how those geographical boundaries ward off Radical Other (Nations) and entrap others within its own body, somehow setting up a trap on itself, forcing itself to face those internal Others at some point. This leads Jarrod Hayes to the following conclusion:

> [o]ne cannot exclude someone from the Nation unless she is already there. ... If there must be such an effort to exclude the queer from the Nation ... and show

---

2   Not to mention that national sentiment could be embraced by the same people on many other occasions, not via their homosexual identification but as subjects of other identitarian categories. A good example is the anti-colonial struggle, or anti-communist struggle, when the 'common cause of liberation' becomes (or is imposed) as the overarching dominant organising idea of social life and cultural existence.

3   For an excellent example of the LGBT community's practices of racialisation of the Roma minority in Romania, see Shannon Woodcock's chapter in this volume.

4   Barbara Pietkiewicz, 'Niech Nas Zobacza', *Polityka* 19 March 2003, at: http://niechnaszobacza.queers.pl/strony/prasa/19.03.2003_a.htm (accessed: 27 February 2010).

she is an outsider trying to invade, the queer must always be inside already; that is, in some ways, the Nation is always already queer. (Hayes 2000: 15–16)

Performativity

If the nation exists, as long as it is being constantly evoked in the discursive and material practices of everyday lives, nationalism then is a process of calling a nation into being, practices and acts of bringing the 'imagined community' into life, into mass imaginary. In that sense, nationalism always precedes the nation, the nation become existent after a nationalist call (interpellation?), a point already made by Ernest Gellner (1983).

Now, taking inspiration from Bhabha (2004), writing about the nation as a performative act, let me recall Judith Butler's concept of the performative as another possible perspective on the relation between the two. It may be, perhaps, an obvious statement, but I still would like to make it: nation and nationalism work similarly to sex and gender (respectively), on which Butler elaborated in *Gender Trouble* (1990), *Bodies That Matter* (1993) and many other texts. As much as the notion of gender and sex is achieved thanks to the constant repetitive acts performing their phantasmatic existence, so is the imagined community of the nation also constituted performatively. Butler works on the examples of drag queens, analysing how they subvert hegemonic ideas of gender and sex by detaching masculinity from man and femininity from woman.

What I would like to suggest here is that drag queens do not only act out any women, any femininity; their shows always incorporate a reference and impersonation (to varying degrees) of a famous and iconic woman (in a specific cultural context), if only through the choice of songs from their repertoire. In other words, not just any gender, but rather a national gender is performed. For instance, when Polish drag queens perform songs of Violetta Villas (Polish singer), Halina Vondrackova (Czech singer) or Alla Pugacova (Russian singer), all 'superstars' of the communist period, there is something more than 'just a show' happening. These shows are untranslatable in any other than a 'post-communist' cultural context. They occupy the imagined space of 'Poland'; perhaps even an imagination spaced as 'Polish'. The 'communist nostalgia', dressed up and performed through the embodiment of iconic singers of communism, is what nationalises these performances of a culturally specific gender. And even if some singers come from other countries, they are still 'from the bloc'. And, as such, they partake as 'Polish' because 'communist Poland' – as much as any other 'communist country', except of its own national tradition – was strongly infused with the 'international communist culture' (shaped, contributed, distributed to/by each of the 'Soviet bloc' countries) that now forms an indistinguishable part of each national history.[5]

---

5   Another very interesting example of 'communist nostalgia' and the relation of 'post-1989 liberated gays' to 'pre-1989 homosexuals' is skilfully played out in the surprisingly successful book by Michal Witkowski, *Lubiewo* (2006)/*Lovetown* (2010).

So do we, in our everyday performative acts of gender, also always already act out the particular cultural/national regimes of gender. It does not necessarily mean that these embodiments are radically different from each other, from country to country; conversely it is perhaps their striking similarities, common features, motifs, tropes and icons across geographical (and temporal) boundaries of nation-states that are most gripping. So if not 'gender' but 'nation-specific gender', so is homo/sexuality always already national/ised.

Homo-Assemblage – Sociality, Eroticism, Sexuality

There are a significant number of texts discussing the relation of homosexuality to what is commonly referred to as 'homosociality' (e.g. Sedgwick 1985; Segal 1990; Britton 1990; Bird 1996). One of the most prominent figures who have written about this issue is Eve Kosofsky Sedgwick. In her book *Between Men* (1985), she elaborates on nineteenth-century English culture; more specifically, to use her own words from *Epistemology of the Closet* 'on the oppressive effects on women and men of a cultural system in which male–male desire became widely intelligible primarily by being routed thorough triangular relations involving a woman' (1990: 15). Similar observations are made by V. Spike Peterson (1999) in relation to nation and heterosexism. In her account, nationalist ideologies are heterosexist in that they foster 'fraternity' and male homosocial bonding, well extending its cultural rooting to political behaviour and institutional organisation. At the same time, national narrative of future generations and reproductive time imposes heterosexual family as the locus of attention. This, in turn, helps the prohibition and discouragement of homosexual practices (Peterson 1999). Similar observations about the homosocial cultures of Maghreb (Morocco, Algeria, Tunisia) and the post-colonial rise of national movements are made by Jarrod Hayes in his compelling book on Maghrebian literature, *Queer Nations: Marginal Sexualities in the Maghreb* (2000). Hayes also shows how the rise of nationalism in these three countries severely restricted and devalued homosexual practices, common among Maghrebian men, and elevated patriarchal Islamic visions of gender roles while still maintaining high levels of homosociality (Hayes 2000: especially Introduction and Part One).

Many other examples (USA: Allen 1999; Balkans: Lambevski 1999; France: Dean 2000; Germany: Heineman 2002; Indonesia: Boellstorff 2005; Ireland: Inglis 2005; Poland and Germany: Fischer 2007) show that the more homosocial a national culture, the fiercer the rejection of homosexuality (homophobia). But how is the tension produced by the contradictory vectoral orientations dealt with in homosocial, male-dominated institutions (such as the army, prisons, football teams etc.)? To answer this question, I want to bring back the concept of 'desire' and 'erotic', present in Sedgwick but less popular in the above-mentioned literature.

It has to be noted first that the rejection of homosexual desire by the homosocial culture of national institutions (e.g. army, prisons, sports teams) does not necessarily mean rejection of sexuality at all. On the contrary, I would suggest that the stronger the rejection of homosexuality, the stronger the perpetuation of the heterosexual fantasy. What is strikingly important, however, is the fact that fantasising and acting upon heterosexuality is group enacted, and done by, for and through other men – i.e. it is homoerotic. Let's unpack.

The homophobic rejection of homosexuality as a potential threat and aberration is enacted in national institutions by groups of men or through their assistance. Similarly, heterosexual actions and fantasies are group acts; for example watching pornography together, exchanging and commenting on pornography, group wanking, telling stories of (hetero)sexual conquers and (hetero)sexual adventures, up to the extreme of group ('heterosexual') rape of a 'sissy'/'pussy'. These are examples of perpetuating heterosexual fantasy done by men solely, for their pleasure, within enclosed male circles. They are about showing off, competing and (hyper)masculinising. The more a man needs to prove himself as not 'queer', in the eyes of other men, the more 'straight' and 'masculine' he needs to be for the acclamation of other men. Straight men play out what gay men describe as 'butch daddy top' type. And as much as this type of masculinity enacted in gay men's cultures is a form of performing 'attractiveness' for other (gay) men, so a similar type of attitude of straight men in national institutions is performed for other (straight) men. So if homosocial national institutions reinforce anti-homosexual attitudes (the use of homophobic language as the ultimate put-down) by perpetuating heterosexual fantasy (telling stories of sexual encounters) and practice (pin-ups from straight porn magazines), but for the pleasure and confirmation of other men (public displays of pin-ups, exchange of photos, put-downs performed in groups, not one-on-one), then I suggest calling it 'homoerotic desire'. 'Embodied presence' of homoeroticism is thus a medium of dealing with the tension created by 'absently present' homosexuality, a moment when men's desire for other men forecloses the possibility of own articulation in the act of sexual encounter.

This is one level of homosociality, eroticism and sexuality connecting and permanently inscribing them into the sphere of nation/al ('belonging to a nation'). But I believe we can also make this mechanism a more metaphorical condition of the relation between nationalists and the nation. First, we can recognise that national movements perpetuate homosocial bonding at the expense of women and their discursive and material subordination (Mosse 1985; Yuval-Davis 1997; Peterson 1999). Second, I have already discussed how national discourses reject homosexuality as a threatening Other to the national body (Hayes 2000: 10). So, third, national discourses are homoerotic because they are about the love of one's country. The country/nation is always represented as a woman (Yuval-Davis 1997), so in a sense nationalists perpetuate a heterosexual fantasy of the nation and envisage happily married life as a feature of a nation – family. Yet still it is a men-dominated, men-perpetuated, men-performed and, most importantly, men-for-men acted out homoerotic nation/alism.[6] Witness the case of Poland, idealised as a vital, reproductive woman, symbolised as 'Polish Mother'/'Mather the Pole' (Siemieńska 2000). Nationalists such as the League of Polish Families party, whose leaders are all men, constantly present themselves as guardians (husbands) of Polish culture/'(heterosexual) family' against the 'threat' of homosexuality, in the name of 'patriotism' – i.e. love of the country. At the same time, their fixation with homosexuality is striking.[7]

Homonationalism = Homonormative Nationalism?

There is no doubt that nationalism is, in most cases, a practice which grows and feeds back to heteronormativity, the concept which gained popularity after its use in Michael Warner's influential book *Fear of a Queer Planet* (1993). Now it seems, in queer, sexuality and gender studies, it is also one of those taken-for-granted concepts. Without entering nuanced discussions over its meaning, I will frame it here as used in Katherine Ludwin's thesis. For Ludwin, heteronormativity is about 'privileging of heterosexuality over all other sexualities'; it is 'defining a "normal way of life"' and 're-inscription of essentialist identity categories'; and it operates 'as part of a broader matrix of socially mediating systems' (Ludwin 2011). Heteronormativity is mediated and manoeuvred on a number of structural levels, most importantly institutional, discursive and in everyday practices (Ludwin 2011).

Recent writings, however, from the queer studies area focus much attention at homonormativity. What would it be? According to Lisa Duggan, who significantly helped to popularise the term:

> The new neoliberal sexual politics ... might be termed the new homonormativity – it is a politics that does not contest dominant heteronormative assumptions and institutions but upholds and sustains them while promising the possibility of a demobilized gay constituency and a privatized, depoliticized gay culture anchored in domesticity and consumption. (Duggan 2002: 179)

It is clear that the terms do not share much with each other on the conceptual level, and similarity is only verbatim. It is strengthened by Duggan's own statement that 'there is no structure for gay life, no matter how conservative or normalizing, that might compare with the institutions promoting and sustaining heterosexual coupling' (2002: 191, footnote 9). Also Berlant and Warner have stressed the

---

6   It should be acknowledged that of course women also participate in national/ist struggles; however, they are always only 'supporters' and hardly ever leaders, hence my insistance on nationalism as a male activity.

7   For a more nuanced discussion of Poland, see chapters by Mizielińska, and Binnie and Klesse in this volume.

impossibility of 'homonormativity' that would function as 'heteronormativity' does (1998: 7, endnote 2).

Even though Jasbir Puar is an acute reader of tensions and differences, various interlocked discourses and practices pervading everyday lives, her use of 'homonormativity' and 'homonationalism' is not unproblematic for me. For example, when she defines 'homonationalism' as a moment when 'certain homosexual bodies signify homonormative nationalism' (Puar 2007: 10), she is also aware of the limited scope of her referent. So she avers that writing on 'homonationalism' is not to disavow existing violence and discrimination, or to imply the cohesion and evenness of the very concept (Puar 2007: 10). However, her persistant use and invocation of 'homonormativity' creates the impression, I would suggest, that it is an overarching contemporary lesbian and gay politics, not leaving much space for alternatives. Surly it is not her point, yet still, when one reads '[c]oncomitantly, multicultural (and homonormative) subjects reorient their loyalty to the nation through market privileges, a remasculinisation that Heidi Nast terms 'market virility', that masquerade as forms of belonging to the nation and mediate the humiliation of waiting for national love' (Puar 2007: 26–7), one wonders why use rather derogatory (in this context) words such as 'masquerading' and 'humiliation', followed by the rejection of capitalism? What is so necessarily wrong with the willingness to be recognised as a part of the national community, to build one's own identification in relation to other nationals and not be left aside as encapsulated and self-contained, ab/sub/ob/ject? This passage also illustrates her rather tame perspective on nationalism, as negative, pervasive, militant and exclusionary. Even though she acknowledges that it can be flexible enough, as in her example of American nationalism, to reorient own internal dynamics to include (or rather swallow) those who were previously repulsive to it (i.e. homosexual abjects, now subjects).

In fact, as I have already suggested above, lesbian and gay communities in CEE and elsewhere may well embrace national ideas (reappropriation of nationalism?) as one of the methods of their struggle (e.g. reclaiming history, writing queer national history) and not be merely 'swallowed' by them. Moreover, Agnieszka Graff (2008) insists that in Poland (and perhaps in other CEE countries for that matter) – where xenophobic nationalist ideas seem to be the pre-eminent cultural sphere – winning back patriotism (love of country) may well be the best strategy overall. She insists that lesbian and gay people should not give up on their claims to 'national love' and leave this powerful social identification/imagination for ab/use by populists and xenophobes. After all, countries of Central and Eastern Europe are still 'transforming'; the potential for moulding and shaping is still warm and ready; and the future is by no means fixed, as in the rather pessimistic vision (of the West/America) painted by Puar. Finally, one should also reconsider the need of belonging to a national community, which Puar criticises as 'the humiliation of waiting for national love' (2007: 27).

Inclusiveness/Exclusiveness and Neo-Liberal Capitalism

One of the most widely held presumptions about nationalism and homosexuality is that the former is often exclusionary and negative towards the latter, an attitude well documented and analysed in the academic literature (e.g. Berlant and Freeman 1992; Hanna 1996; Lambevski 1999; Conrad 2001; Fischer 2007). But nationalism may also be an inclusive force, willing to accommodate (although not unproblematically and not without tensions) and 'swallow' – to use Bauman's metaphor (1997) – its constitutive 'inner' Other. Examples include French Canadian Quebecois nationalism (Stychin 1997; Dickinson 1999), post-apartheid nationalism in South Africa (Posel 2005) or recent nationalism in the USA, the UK and the Netherlands (Puar 2007; Kuntsman and Miyake 2008; Butler 2009). This shift was possible, among other reasons, thanks to the changing position of lesbian and gay people in the capitalist market, a 'success of states' biopolitics' and a shift from queers being figures of death to becoming figures of life (Puar 2007, xii). But Puar's unison rejection and critique of capitalism as an oppressive economic system, bound with 'homonormativity', and the rise of 'gay rights' as the mainstream LGBT politics need to be problematised. Following Binnie's (2004) call for greater 'geographical awareness' when theorising sexual politics, I would also call for greater acknowledgement of various 'capitalisms' and certainly not the-same-everywhere functioning of economics and politics. As stated early in this chapter, Western 'late capitalism' is not Polish 'baby capitalism'. But even within the West one needs to differentiate between (neo-liberal) capitalism of the USA or the UK and (social) capitalism of Germany or Sweden. One should also be aware of various forms of 'democratic' political systems, and how these influence economic spheres in the respective countries.

This leads me to the question of class, which is another factor linking nationalism and homosexuality, taking us back to part of the argument made by Mosse (1985) about the emergence of the bourgeoisie and 'respectability' as key formants of nationalism and policing homosexuality. This link between respected sexuality, aberrant homosexuality, class and capitalism is tightly connected to Western European history, privileging again 'Europe' (i.e. the West) as the Grand Narrative, presumably semi (if not fully) transparent universalisation. However, for somebody interested in non-Western European cultural logics of nationhood and homo/sexuality, the link might seem less pervasive, if only for reasons of lacking a 'capitalist, class-based society' (which is not to say that it is not stratified). The theme of neo-liberal capitalist logics, its Western queer criticism of recent years and the applicability of those criticisms and actual workings of the neo-liberal market in the CEE post-1989 context are recurring themes here. Let us look at the CEE examples.

Western queer critique of same-sex marriage/partnership highlights often that it is a claim of well-off, white, middle-class, urban gays and lesbians (e.g. Ettelbrick 1997). But recent study of Polish homosexuals (Krzemiński 2009) shows great, country-wide support for same-sex partnerships, across all social groups occupied by lesbians and gays. 'Pink Money' – implying more consumerist attitudes of lesbians and gays as potentially better educated, occupying better-paid jobs, without family obligations – is also controversial in the context of Central and Eastern Europe. One of the economic consequences of 'transformation' was a general pauperisation of society, independent of 'identity position'. In other words, CEE societies and social groups are for now too poor to develop marked-based ways of 'buying' into comforts of apolitical citizenship. This leads directly to another issue often criticised by Western queer scholars: 'gay tourism'/'sex tourism'. Again, scrutinising CEE, not only do we have to acknowledge that travelling abroad – especially to the 'Far East', South-East Asia, Indonesia ('sex paradises') – is very expensive and affordable only to a tiny minority of society, but also that the CEE gay community may actually be an object of such Western practices, as in the case of 'CEE boyz' in the Western porn industry (Radel 2001).

My own proposition is to talk about 'heteronormativity' of LGBT politics rather than using 'homonormativity' because, even if used with all those caveats, it still implies more than it actually refers to. Moreover, it creates an impression of mirroring heteronormativity, which it does not. The terms 'homonationalism' and 'homonormativity' seem to me rather too tricky and sleek to effectively deploy without falling into their own trap (as Puar does at times) and terminological confusion (Heinze 1995). It may be especially striking in the case of CEE, where terminological confusion and cross-contamination of notions often occur due to 'temporal disjunction'[8] between Western and CEE LGBT politics. It is also, in my opinion, far too early to talk about 'homonormativity' in the case of CEE LGBT communities, as all of them are still in the process of emerging and shaping. However, their practices along the way may normalise (and are normalising), but according to dominant social norms (as in the case of 'proper gendering' or racialisation described above). Thus it seems to me that talking of CEE lesbian and gay communities in terms of their 'heteronormativity' is a more suitable practice, helping to better understand their particularities, discontinuities and relations with hegemonic ideologies – be they 'own' (local, Central/East European) or 'theirs' (globalised and neo-colonial, Western).

Conclusions

In this chapter, I have tried to look at the mutual dependencies between nations, nationalisms and sexualities. I was particularly interested in the influence and 'cross-contamination' between the 'West' and Central and Eastern Europe. In my theoretical voyage, I have helped myself with CEE examples to better understand the dynamics between nation and sexuality, and also to highlight potential new areas of scrutiny, perhaps obscured without this geographically conscious lens. As often stated, we are dealing with processes, transformations and fluctuations.

---

8   For discussion of this concept, see Kulpa and Mizielińska's 'Introduction' in this volume.

Hence it seems important to stress again that this chapter is yet another voice in the discussion, but surely not the ultimate one; and I hope it will open a field of further enquiry and polemical dialogue.

Bibliography

Allen, Holly. 1999. 'Gender, Sexuality and the Military Model of U.S. National Community'. In *Gender Ironies of Nationalism: Sexing the Nation*, ed. Tamar Mayer. London: Routledge.

Anderson, Benedict. 1991. *Imagined Communities: Reflections on the Origin and Spread of Nationalism*. 2nd edn. London: Verso Books.

Bauman, Zygmunt. 1997. *Postmodernity and its Discontents*. New York: New York University Press.

Berlant, Laura and Michael Warner. 1998. 'Sex in Public'. *Critical Inquiry* 24, no. 2: 547–66.

Berlant, Lauren and Elizabeth Freeman. 1992. 'Queer Nationality'. *Boundary 2* 19, no. 1 (spring): 149–80.

Beverley, John. 2004. 'Queering the Nation: Same Thoughts on Empire, Nationalism, and Multiculturalism Today'. In *Empire & Terror: Nationalism/ Postnationalism in the New Millennium*, ed. Begoña Aretxaga. Center for Basque Studies conference papers series no. 1. Reno: Center for Basque Studies, University of Nevada.

Beyond the Pink Curtain. 2009. 'October Newsletter – Distribution News!' http:// www.ymlp181.com/pubarchive_show_message.php?matcharles+102.

Bhabha, Homi K. 2004. *Location of Culture*. 2nd edn. London: Routledge.

Binnie, Jon. 2004. *The Globalization of Sexuality*. London: Sage.

Bird, Sharon R. 1996. 'Welcome to the Men's Club: Homosociality and the Maintenance of Hegemonic Masculinity'. *Gender and Society* 10, no. 2 (April): 120–32.

Boellstorff, Tom. 2005. *The Gay Archipelago: Sexuality and Nation in Indonesia*. Princeton, NJ: Princeton University Press.

Britton, Dana M. 1990. 'Homophobia and Homosociality: An Analysis of Boundary Maintenance'. *The Sociological Quarterly* 31, no. 3 (summer): 423–39.

Butler, Judith. 1990. *Gender Trouble*. London/New York: Routledge.

———. 1993. *Bodies That Matter: On the Discursive Limits of Sex*. London: Routledge.

———. 2009. *Frames of War: When is Life Grievable?* London: Verso.

Conrad, Kathryn. 2001. 'Queer Treasons: Homosexuality and Irish National Identity'. *Cultural Studies* 15, no. 1 (1): 124–37.

Council of Europe. 2000. Council Directive 2000/78/EC of 27 November 2000 establishing a general framework for equal treatment in employment and occupation. http://eur-lex.europa.eu/smartapi/cgi/sga_doc?smartapi!celexapi! prod!CELEXnumdoc&lg=en&numdoc=32000L0078&model=guichett.

Dean, Carolyn J. 2000. *The Frail Social Body: Pornography, Homosexuality, and Other Fantasies in Interwar France*. Studies on the History of Society and Culture 36. Berkeley: University of California Press.

Dickinson, Peter. 1999. *Here Is Queer: Nationalisms, Sexualities, and the Literatures of Canada*. Toronto: University of Toronto Press.

Duggan, Lisa. 2002. 'The New Homonormativity: The Sexual Politics of Neoliberalism'. In *Materializing Democracy: Toward a Revitalized Cultural Politics*, eds Russ Castronovo and Dana D Nelson. New Americanists. Durham, NC: Duke University Press: 427.

Ettelbrick, Paula L. 1997. 'Since When is Marriage a Path to Liberation?' In *We Are Everywhere: A Historical Sourcebook of Gay and Lesbian Politics*, ed. Mark Blasius and Shane Phelan. New York; London: Routledge.

European Parliament. 2007. 'Motion for a Resolution on Homophobia in Europe – B6-0168/2007'. April 23. http://www.europarl.europa.eu/sides/getDoc.do?type=MOTION&reference=B6-2007-0168&language=EN.

EuropPride 2006. 'Gay Pride in the UK's Capital City'. http://www.europridelondon.org/en/.

Fischer, Henning. 2007. 'Straight Macho Nationalism'. *InterAlia: A Journal of Queer Studies*, no. 2. http://www.interalia.org.pl/en/artykuly/2007_2/12_straight_macho_nationalism.htm.

Gabilondo, Joseba. 2004. 'Performing Populism: A Queer Theory of Globalization, Terror, and Spectacle (on Lord of the Rings and 9/11/2001)'. In *Empire & Terror: Nationalism/Postnationalism in the New Millennium*, ed. Begoña Aretxaga. Center for Basque Studies conference papers series no. 1. Reno: Center for Basque Studies, University of Nevada.

Gellner, Ernest. 1983. *Nations and Nationalism* (2nd edn 2006). Basingstoke: Blackwell.

Graff, Agnieszka. 2008. *Rykoszetem: Rzecz o Płci, Seksualności i Narodzie*. Warszawa: Wydawnictwo WAB.

Graney-Saucke, Elliat. 2009. *Travel Queeries*. http://www.imdb.com/title/tt1454727/.

Hanna, Martha. 1996. 'Natalism, Homosexuality, and the Controversy over Corydon'. In *Homosexuality in Modern France*, eds Jeffrey Merrick and Bryant T. Ragan. New York: Oxford University Press.

Haritaworn, Jin, Tamsila Tauqir and Esra Erdem. 2008. 'Gay Imperialism: Gender and Sexuality Discourse in the "War on Terror"'. In *Out of Place: Interrogating Silences in Queerness Raciality*, eds Adi Kuntsman and Esperanza Miyake. York: Raw Nerve Books Ltd.

Hauser, Ewa. 1995. 'Traditions of Patriotism, Questions of Gender: The Case of Poland'. In *Postcommunism and the Body Politic*, ed. Ellen E. Berry. Genders 22. New York: New York University Press.

Hayes, Jarrod. 2000. *Queer Nations: Marginal Sexualities in the Maghreb*. Chicago: University of Chicago Press.

Heineman, Elizabeth D. 2002. 'Sexuality and Nazism: The Doubly Unspeakable?' *Journal of the History of Sexuality* 11, no. 1 (April): 22–66.

Heinze, Eric. 1995. S*exual Orientation: A Human Right: An Essay on International Human Rights Law*. Dordrecht: M. Nijhoff Publishers.

Hick, Jochen and Christian Jentzsch. 2006. *Rainbow's End*. http://www.imdb.com/title/tt0790738/.

Hobsbawm, Eric and Terence Ranger. 1984. *The Invention of Tradition*. Cambridge: Cambridge University Press.

Inglis, Tom. 2005. 'Origins and Legacies of Irish Prudery: Sexuality and Social Control in Modern Ireland'. *Éire-Ireland* 40, no. 3: 9–37.

Jameson, Fredric. 1991. *Postmodernism, or, the Cultural Logic of Late Capitalism*. London: Verso.

Jenkins, Keith. 1991. *Re-thinking History*. 2nd edn. London: Routledge.

Kemp, Jonathan. 2009. 'The Importance of Being Postmodern: Wilde, Nietzsche, Lyotard and "the Untimely"' (unpublished manuscript). London.

Krzemiński, Ireneusz, ed. 2009. *Naznaczeni: Mniejszości Seksualne W Polsce: Raport 2008*. Warsaw: Instytut Socjologii, Uniwersytet Warszawski.

Kuntsman, Adi. 2008. 'The Soldier and the Terrorist: Sexy Nationalism, Queer Violence'. *Sexualities* 11, no. 1–2 (1 February): 142–70.

Kuntsman, Adi and Esperanza Miyake, eds. 2008. *Out of Place: Interrogating Silences in Queerness Raciality*. York: Raw Nerve Books.

Lambevski, Sasho A. 1999. 'Suck My Nation – Masculinity, Ethnicity and the Politics of (Homo)sex'. *Sexualities* 2, no. 4 (1 November): 397–419.

Ludwin, Katherine. 2011. 'Women Negotiationg Heteronormativity' (working title). London: Birkbeck College, University of London (unpublished PhD thesis).

Mayer, Tamar, ed. 1999. *Gender Ironies of Nationalism: Sexing the Nation*. London: Routledge.

Mosse, George L. 1985. *Nationalism and Sexuality: Respectability and Abnormal Sexuality in Modern Europe*. New York: H. Fertig.

Nagel, Joane. 1998. 'Masculinity and Nationalism: Gender and Sexuality in the Making of Nations'. *Ethnic and Racial Studies* 21, no. 2 (March): 242–69.

Parker, Andrew, Mary Russo, Doris Sommer and Patricia Yaeger, eds. 1992. *Nationalisms & Sexualities*. London/New York: Routledge.

Peterson, V. Spike. 1999. 'Sexing Political Identity/Nationalism as Heterosexism'. International *Feminist Journal of Politics* 1, no. 1 (April): 34–65.

Posel, Deborah. 2005. 'Sex, Death and the Fate of the Nation: Reflections on the Politicization of Sexuality in Post-Apartheid South Africa'. *Africa: Journal of the International African Institute* 75, no. 2: 125–53.

Pryke, Sam. 1998. 'Nationalism and Sexuality: What are the Issues?' *Nations and Nationalism* 4, no. 4: 529–46.

Puar, Jasbir K. 2007. T*errorist Assemblages: Homonationalism in Queer Times*. Durham, NC: Duke University Press.

Radel, Nicholas F. 2001. 'The Transnational Ga(y)ze: Constructing the East European Object of Desire in Gay Film and Pornography after the Fall of the Wall'. *Cinema Journal* 41, no. 1 (autumn): 40–62.

Sedgwick, Eve Kosofsky. 1985. *Between Men: English Literature and Male Homosocial Desire*. New York: Columbia University Press.

————. 1990. *The Epistemology of the Closet*. Berkeley: University of California Press.

Segal, Lynne. 1990. *Slow Motion: Changing Masculinities, Changing Men*. London: Virago.

Siemieńska, Renata. 2000. 'Factors Shaping Conceptions of Women's and Men's Roles in Poland'. In *Reconciliation of Family and Work in Eastern European Countries*, eds Michel E. Domsch and Desiree H. Ladwig. Frankfurt/New York: Peter Lang.

Smith, Anthony D. 1991. *National Identity*. London: Penguin.

Stulhofer, Aleksandar and Theo Sandfort, eds. 2004. *Sexuality and Gender in Post-Communist Eastern Europe and Russia*. Binghamton, NY: Haworth Press.

Stychin, Carl. 1997. Queer Nations: Nationalism, Sexuality and the Discourse of Rights in Quebec. *Feminist Legal Studies* 5, no. 1 (February): 3–34.

Tolz, Vera and Stephenie Booth, eds. 2005. *Nation and Gender in Contemporary Europe*. Manchester: Manchester University Press.

Tomasik, Krzysztof. 2008. *Homobiografie: Pisarki i Pisarze Polscy XIX i XX Wieku*. Warsaw: Wydawnictwo Krytyki Politycznej.

Warner, Michael, ed. 1993. *Fear of a Queer Planet: Queer Politics and Social Theory*. Minneapolis: University of Minnesota Press.

Witkowski, Michał. 2006. *Lubiewo*. 4th edn. Krakow: Korporacja Ha!art.

————. 2010. *Lovetown*. London: Portobello Books.

Yuval-Davis, Nira. 1997. *Gender and Nation*. London: Sage.

Yuval-Davis, Nira and Floya Anthias, eds. 1989. *Woman – Nation – State*. Basingstoke: Macmillan.

Chapter 4

A Short History of the Queer Time of 'Post-Socialist' Romania, or Are We There Yet? Let's Ask Madonna!

Shannon Woodcock

In August 2009, Madonna performed in Bucharest as part of her European tour. Between songs, she said to the audience:

> Now, I've been paying attention to the news reports and it's been brought to my attention that there's a lot of discrimination against Romanies and Gypsies in general in Eastern Europe and that makes me feel very sad because we don't believe in discrimination against anyone; we believe in freedom and equal rights for everyone, right? Gypsies, homosexuals, people who are different, everyone is equal and should be treated with respect, ok, let's not forget that.[1]

The audience booed, and international headlines reported that Romanians had booed Madonna for her anti-racism comments. Indeed, Romanians swamped internet forums and discussion lists on media sites with overwhelmingly negative reactions to Madonna's comments. These comments repeated racist anti-Romani stereotypes *ad nauseam*, and only occasionally mentioned 'homosexuals', always in similarly pejorative terms. Discussion lists and blogs of Romanians who identify as gay and/or homosexual were similar to the mainstream racist opinions and dismissed Madonna as ignorant. Rather than supporting a stance against discrimination in general, many of these self-identifying gay bloggers rejected Madonna's equation of 'gypsies' and 'homosexuals', arguing that gay Romanians are valid recipients of 'respect', while Roma are not.

In the wake of recent theoretical scholarship highlighting the role of race as a catalyst in lesbian, gay, bisexual and transsexual/transgender (LGBT) rights movements, this chapter asks how nascent Romanian LGBT movements rely on racist discourses against Roma in order to claim a place for homosexuality in this heteronormative nation. As both the Romani and LGBT movements for human rights were introduced and developed only since the beginning of the 1990s, it

---

1 Transcribed by the author from the recording entitled 'Madonna Booed in Bucharest for Defending Gypsies!' posted on YouTube on 27 August 2009 by LostForces, http://www.youtube.com/watch?v=vMrk2PlFAKA (accessed: 10 January 2010).

is striking that in the debate over Madonna's words, LGBT claims to rights are explicitly staked over those of racial equality. The fact that this is occurring in the specific time of 'post-socialism' in Romania demands close engagement, just as Jasbir K. Puar's work (2007) is specifically situated in the Western time of post-9/11, and Henriette Gunkel's work in the time of post-apartheid South Africa (2010). The post-9/11 moment in time is significant to Romanian – and broader Central Eastern European (CEE) – national identity also as the cusp of EUropean accession, signifying the conditional acceptance of the poor 'Eastern' cousin 'back' into (albeit behind) European time.

This chapter is thus a primary exploration of how the LGBT movement in Romania relies on racial exclusion in the unique and dynamic space and time of post-socialist neo-liberalism. Drawing on a range of sources, we will trace the introduction of identity categories and politics in the temporal and political context of European Union (EU) accession, charting the creation of an LGBT movement in the model of Western LGBT movements, and the contestation of these categories on the ground at Pride parades. We will explore who is included in and excluded from the LGBT movement, and how this violent process of containment masquerading as liberation has been contested and scaffolded by individuals and institutions in the recent debates provoked by Madonna's observations.[2] But let us begin by questioning the temporality in which Romania is pinned through its status as a 'post-socialist' society and state.

What's in a Name? 'Post-Socialism' as Capitalist Belatedness

The East we name 'post-socialist' becomes fixed in time at the moment when socialism failed. After 1990, and looking back in time to the East that built socialism, the EUropean West dictated the terms by which it would drag its geographical and racial prodigal brothers 'back' to a EUrope that was in fact new itself. As Chari and Verdery (2009) argue, humanities scholars have used 'post-socialist' and 'transition' for CEE societies because the terms reflected the sense of chaotic liberalisation policies after specifically socialist regimes; but the

---

2   In this chapter I use the labels LGB or T only to refer to those who identify themselves thus. Many individuals in Romania who would not march under an LGBT banner or name themselves thus nevertheless recognise that their desires can be interpellated within these categories, but choose to reject and critique the LGBT label, as outlined in this chapter. These non-heteronormative sexual identities are often referred to as 'same-sex', and I use this terminology in this chapter because it is a widely supported concept in the community I am writing about, although I reject the binary construction of gender that enables it. The word 'queer' is very rarely used in Romania, and is not used as a publicly or even intellectually unifying identity category, and thus I use the aforementioned terms of same-sex and non-heteronormative to reference those who courageously question and problematise LGBT labels.

terms still function as the primary identification for CEE studies 20 years after the establishment of capitalist liberal democracies. The term 'post-socialist' plays a normative gatekeeping role for Western observers who, it is assumed, will be the ones to tell us when the East has actually arrived somewhere other than post-socialism. Just as the homosexual is born into his/her closet and needs to develop in order to 'come out' into the world of heterosexuals, the post-socialist East exists in Western capitalist discourse in order for EUrope to benevolently bestow recognition on its 'other'. Just as the closet metaphor naturalises heteronormativity and places homosexuality as originating in enclosure (Sedgwick 1990), the post-socialist title repeatedly situates CEE societies in a stagnant moment of time before capitalism and after socialism, lagging behind the singular trajectory of EUropean development. In both cases, the agency of the others is contained through articulation as closeted or lagging behind the (hetero)normative states.

As well as submitting to pervasive EU reform requirements, the system of governance in post-socialist states was reformed to exclude groups and sideline institutions that represented 'rights' in the new name of 'civil society'. In my personal interactions with Western civil society 'experts' in Bucharest and Tirana, they mostly ignored the fact that socialist governments had formal mechanisms to ensure parliamentary participation (albeit, for what that was worth) of women, ethnic and demographic groups. This new 'civil society' was a non-governmental sector that lobbied politicians for legislative change on behalf of socially disenfranchised communities, laws lacking in implementation support decried as too costly for the 'transition' period. Civil society was supposed to bring the stated categories of victims into the time of the nation, a task that formerly constituted the state. As if the represented and marginalised groups had excluded themselves from the sudden new liberal state, the struggle for inclusion in policy and society fell on their shoulders rather than on the government. In the new system, the same people sank (those without cultural or financial capital) or swam (those with capital) as in the West, but this new marginalisation of formerly included groups was not called 'neo-liberalism'; it was, and often still is, called 'post-socialism'.

For civil society to function, people have to identify and group themselves in specific ways to claim their 'human rights'. The first subjects of local non-governmental organisations (NGOs) in civil society were women, children in orphanages, ethnic minorities and, by 1998, lesbian, gay, bisexual and transsexual/transgendered (LGBT) communities.[3] NGOs were primarily funded by international (Western) donor organisations such as the Open Society Institute, United Nations Development Project (UNDP) and PHARE (Borza et al. 2006). Laura Grünberg (2008), the founder of the Society of Feminist Analysis (*AnA*), expressed frustration with the civil society model that in effect redirected women outside the sphere of government decision-making. NGOs are economically dependent on grants from

---

3　The 'T' was never clearly articulated in meaning – in the beginning it was written as transsexual, then later transgender, although the meaning seems to be understood overwhelmingly and disparagingly as 'transvestite'.

donors who set the agendas to which they ostensibly function, usually with short-term high rotation 'projects' leaving no time for staff development (Ghodsee 2006: 3). Activists are stretched too thin by structural requirements that do not support time for personal development, let alone the development of intergroup or extensive 'grassroots' networks. Grünberg (2008: 1) notes that the lack of clear long-term objectives marginalised the women's movement inside the Romanian civil society movement, and exacerbated 'tensions between the activist and academic sides or between generations'.

The naming of CEE countries as 'post-socialist' and 'transitional' meant not only that the failure of the system to provide 'rights' and protect vulnerable citizens was considered inevitable, but also dismissed practices from before 1989 along with the socialist system. Western donors and 'experts' drew a line between 1990 and the socialist period, the latter being erased as a world of its own although it was a political system that had also claimed to be a democratic representation of 'the people'. The formal (albeit controlled) incorporation of women in parliamentary structures under socialism in Romania was entirely dismantled, and the formal emphasis on rights of Romanian citizens as more important than ethnicity under socialism changed to the widespread scapegoating of Romani people through the pejorative and stereotypical name 'Ţigani' in post-socialism. Ţigani became the villains who could be blamed for everything from rising prices in the market (capitalism) to the fall of socialism itself (Cesereanu 1993: 11; PER 1997; Verdery 1996: 98; Zub 2002: 136). Finally, Western 'civil society' fought to have the rights of lesbian, gay, bisexual and transexual/transgender (LGBT) people represented, but only a tiny group of people came forward to stand under these names in the mid-1990s. Western LGBT donors and press took this as another sign of repression in the primitive East. Perhaps all the lesbians were hiding at home? Perhaps they did not know themselves as 'lesbians'? I do not know about other women, but I knew the words and I was watching and wondering what good could come of these new neon signs of sexual difference in such a hostile social environment, far from the context in which the identity terms were developed.

The Introduction of LGBT Identity Politics in Romania

Donor agendas, and thus NGO projects, are pinned to quantifiable identity groups and social changes; hence the formation of the first gay NGO, *ACCEPT* (formed from the Bucharest Acceptance Group) in 1996, staffed by a small, hardworking group of LGBT identifying activists. In 2001 *ACCEPT* was primarily funded by the United Nations Development Programme to run anti-HIV health projects – presenting homosexual health as disease containment in line with Western discourses before 2001. The Open Society Foundation and Western European Government Ministries funded *ACCEPT* to lobby for legislative change in line with pan-European LGBT movements for the decriminalisation of homosexuality. Article 200 (under which individuals were most often arrested in relation to alleged or actual sexual practice) was removed in 2001, after which *ACCEPT* continued to demand legislative changes concerning child adoption, civil union and marriage for LGBT identifying people (Human Rights Watch 1998). The work of *ACCEPT* to form and 'express' a local Romanian LGBT community has had to take place around these agendas, as the NGO itself exists on donor funding, as with the vast majority of 'civil (sponsored) society'.[4]

As recorded in the brief outline of the group's history on its website, *ACCEPT* was formed in a society where there were same-sex practices and underground 'communities' but no pre-existing LGBT identities in these Western categories. *ACCEPT* had to 'find, translate, store and distribute correct information about what homosexuality is and is not'.[5] The assumption implicit in 'post-socialist' funding is of course that once Romania standardises its identity categories and legislation with the European Union, this will assure 'rights' on the ground. This approach ignores and obfuscates the particular reality of decades of homophobic, racist and sexist legislation in Romanian social and legislative contexts. If there is ever to be real change on the ground, activists and scholars need to understand and untangle the specific matrix of sexuality discourse that already exists. New laws have been implemented in Romania despite strong local 'values' that are developed and socially policed today, whether the European Union flag flies or not and often primarily in reaction to the blatant neo-colonialism of EUrope. Romanians recognise ideological containment; they have seen it before.

Politicians across the spectrum saw Romania's 'return' to Europe as either or both an inevitable and a fraught utopian promise (Verdery 1996: 124). While EU accession requirements included human rights, scholars such as Böröcz and Kovacs (2001) outline how the process was unfavourably geared against accession countries, and Romanians knew from everyday experiences that some Europeans had more rights than others (Trandafoiu 2006: 7). The campaign to remove Article 200 was primarily perceived by conservative Romanian politicians as an external invasive pressure; and, ironically, the terms 'gay' and 'lesbian' were brought to Romanian media discussion only after the conservative pro-Article 200 'Homosexuality No No No' campaign in 2000–2001. Orthodox student groups protested in the street, and the patriarch himself and other religious figures made regular public speeches against homosexuality. Unsigned posters pasted along the major boulevards of Bucharest listed supposedly damaging effects lesbians and gay men would have on Romanian society. These posters articulated a vast range of signifiers of homosexuality, most showing continuity with discourses of degeneration from the socialist period. It was only after this poster campaign (and the largely uncritical media attention it received) that LGBT identities provided by the West were recognised by a larger portion of Romanian society as names

---

4   See the *ACCEPT* website for details of projects completed and financial support details, http://accept-romania.ro/proiecte/proiecte-incheiate/.

5   http://accept.ong.ro/foramoregayromania.html#chapter%201 (accessed: 9 December 2009).

for subjects who violate heterosexual norms, thus simultaneously constructing heteronormative signifiers. In Romania, the extended stereotypes attached to these new names were quickly and violently incorporated into the groundswell of anti-EUropean new Right parties, such as 'Romania Mare' (Greater Romania), so that there was a strong and well-funded political interest that ensured the Romanian public understood the new terminology in unique and violently exclusionary ways.

As the LGBT community did not yet exist as such – either as individuals self-identifying as one of the categories or as an LGBT community – many who did desire individuals of the 'same sex' also learnt these new names through the conservative anti-homosexual advertising. The vision statement of *ACCEPT* was to build 'a society in which sexual orientation is simply a human characteristic', not to build a politically active community primarily identified through sexual practice.[6] As I argue elsewhere, there is a gap between the way that Romanian LGBT activists saw their own identities as not just a sexual practice and the way that their identity was vitally positioned in the discourses of the legislative lobbying against Article 200 (Woodcock 2004). Romanian society had experienced horrific state intervention in private lives through sex – with Nicolae Ceauşescu's use of the entire bureaucratic structure to police an increase in childbirth through Decree 770 between 1966 and 1990 (Kligman 1998). This had damaging effects on how everyday people could talk about sex, as sex was claimed as a reproductive act in the name of the nation. In 1990, the legalisation of abortion and the availability of contraception were early and almost unanimously supported changes that vigorously reprivatised sex and the domestic space from under state control. For LGBT identity to be publicly asserted as a 'human right' when it had been previously punished as a public 'scandal' thus struck a discordant note in the Romanian context where sex was considered to be something properly privatised and out of state control after 1989. When the LGBT activists, with financial and professional support from the Western LGBT movement and in the name of EUropeanisation, were identified through lobbying against Article 200 (which claimed to be also against public sex scandals) this silenced what could have been an important local social discussion about the relationship between sex, personal identity, community and the state. Rather, Romanians learnt that accepting LGBT identity as a human right was one of the 'yardsticks of progress toward the Western model of modernity' vital for EU accession (Munro 2009: 404). Romanians also thus learnt that homosexuals had to fight for their rights from a heteronormative state able to bestow them in the name of 'the people'.

Of all the changes required by the European Union for Romania to join, politicians and clergy touted the changes to racial and gender order as primary threats to the Romanian people, and channelled the realistic anxieties of everyday Romanians into familiar prejudices. 'Post-socialist' governance simply reorganised the shared patriarchal and racial hierarchy, which both the West and the East relied

---

6   See http://www.accept-Romania.ro/despre.html (accessed: 5 September 2004).

on. But the new names and terminology, and the claims of groups for recognition under these new names, enabled the public to shift old stereotypes into new EUropean versions of racist discourse to maintain ethno-national identity. Even many conservative nationalist Romanian politicians realised in the early 1990s that they had little choice but to acquiesce to negotiations with the European Union that they saw as a neo-colonial process (Verdery 1996: 124). As Neville Hoad (2007: 9) has detailed in relation to post-colonial African legislative process, in this situation many governments take a stand against LGBT rights as 'a disavowable excess of the process of economic modernization that the state wishes to achieve'. This is true in Romania, as the majority of elected representatives argue against the LGBT campaigns for homonormative rights such as civil unions and adoption. Yet the very terms of this disavowal of gay rights as excessive modernisation rely on the state being made aware of its own claimed heteronormative position as reliant on the family, which ironically was made possible in 1990 through the pressure to recognise a homosexual movement.

The general argument of LGBT activists in Romania is that homonormative rights will enable Romania to catch up with EUropean time; that the West had its Pride parades and gay liberation movements in the 1970s and Romania 30 years later, but that legislative change in line with EUrope now will make Romania equal with the West. The responses from the other side are that, rather than accepting enforced EUropean teleology, Romanian politicians should take a stand in the name of the nation on this point and say that EUrope has gone too far and that Romania can choose to stay where it is.[7] This debate is between 'civil society' and powerholders and – as many bloggers and discussants in internet forums elaborate – it is happening despite a significant chorus from Romanian individuals who identify as 'gay' in various ways and do not perceive marriage and adoption rights as important in their lives.[8] There is no self-identified queer movement in intellectual or social Romanian circles, and the refusal of same-sex identifying Romanians to embrace the LGBT terminology and movement in public is evidenced by the lack of community publications, forums and even nightclubs. There have been no surveys of same-sex desiring individuals and their opinions in Romania because most of these individuals are not 'out' as LGBT, and they do not attend Gay Pride (which we will discuss later) or regularly go to the few gay clubs. There is, however, a blossoming internet-based gay dating scene, and blogs and internet forums are the best places to read the opinions of those who interpellate themselves under the LGBT identity, even if it is only to the point of using these

---

7   Realitatea TV – Da sau Nu, http://www.youtube.com/watch?v=glrg2R6UbcA&feat ure=related. Adrian Paunescu Remus Cernea is executive director of Solidarity for Freedom of Conscience (http://www.humanism.ro).

8   See the debate following Robert G.'s blog where he questions just how many gay men want children and why a 'piece of paper' (marriage) is the legislative goal of the LGBT movement GayFest 2008 – 'Un mars al jandarmilor', 16 May 2008, http://www.darkq. net/advertising/gayfest-2008-un-mars-al-jandarmilor/.

forums to argue for their right to remain outside the LGBT scene and movement. Gillian Whitlock (2007: 3) highlights that blogs are a form of life-writing that exemplify 'the synchronic connections between the virtual and material worlds'. Indeed, in a few active Romanian blogs, one can read the reflections of those people in whose name LGBT rights are being sought, where they relate their life experiences to these categories of identity and practice. Of course these blogs are not a representation of generalised or statistically reliable positions; but they are the only sources aside from personal communications in which the voices of individuals rather than a handful of activists speaking in the name of LGBT organisations can be heard.

Categorical Containment and Racial Scapegoats

While the term 'LGBT' has gained legislative and discursive ground since its introduction just a decade ago, the media and politicians have channelled the strongest tide of anti-EUropean anxiety into racial discourses against Romanian Roma through the established stereotypical projection of the Ţigan other. I have explored elsewhere the central role that the Ţigan other has played in Romania as a projected set of anxieties that changes depending on the social crises of the moment, and how these projected stereotypes are tethered as truth to Romani bodies (Woodcock 2007, 2008). Between the years 1385 and 1856, when all Roma in the Romanian territories were enslaved by law, and in the fledgling independent united Romanian state after this time, Roma were the internal others against which ethnic Romanians articulated their ethno-national independence. In the Holocaust, 26,000 Romani Romanians were deported to Transnistria alongside Romanian Jews, under the name Ţigan, stereotyped incorrectly as nomads, criminals and as of a different blood to ethnic Romanians (Woodcock 2007). Under socialism, Ţigani were not included in the socialist state's list of 'Co-inhabiting National Minorities', yet they continued to function as a phantom presence in Romanian society, often rumoured to be working in league with the mysterious and cruel actions of the dictatorship.

In the confusing and emotional days of the 1989 revolution, soldiers or mysterious assassins who killed protesters were rumoured to be Ţigani. The influx of consumer items for trade over suddenly opened borders that filled the streets of Bucharest was blamed on a Ţigani 'mafia' who not only supposedly 'stole' across borders but also stole the established social value of items in the sudden shocking mass of available goods. Anxiety about capitalist practice was displaced by media rhetoric on to supposed Ţigani 'mafia' who were blamed for the changes (Cesereanu 1993: 11; Gheorghe 1991: 837; Zub 2002: 136). Across political parties, politicians invoked ethnic stereotypes instead of naming capitalism as what it was, and physical and institutional violence against Romani Romanians dramatically increased. As a hurdle to European Union accession, EUrope required Romania to replace the term Ţigan, clearly pejorative, with the name Roma. This was widely articulated in popular and elite Romanian discourse as an attempt by Ţigani to hide their continual attacks on Romania, and was the point at which Romania was asked to relinquish its racial scapegoat. Yet Romania argued for the right to use the word 'Rroma', rather than Roma, in order to avoid possible confusion between Romanians and Roma – thereby inscribing both the meaning of the word Ţigan and the neo-colonialism of EUropean demands and Romanian resistance to this in the new word Rroma. As one Romanian political analyst entitled his editorial in 2000, 'Just between us – we say Rrom but we mean Ţigan' (Ghinea 2001: 3). In this way, Romanian resistance to EUropeanisation is inscribed in superficial capitulation; the survival of the Romanian state in the face of EUrope remains dependent on the Ţigan, even as Rroma.

Thus the existence of the racialised Ţigan stereotype enables Romanian ethno-national existence, which must remain in order for Romanian national uniqueness to survive EUropean accession. New LGBT identity relies on gendered identity as a binary, with heteronormativity in prime position, and is used by nationalists as the sign warning of excessive EUropean modernisation that threatens Romanian existence as such. Romani and same-sex attracted Romanians thus share a struggle against discrimination based primarily on the identity categories imported from EUrope for their supposed liberation. Do these groups support each other? Or is the LGBT movement racialised in order to claim its place in the nation on the basis of race over sexuality? Considering the primacy of public performance of LGBT identity – in 'coming out' discourses and in Gay Pride parades – in the next section we will examine who is called on to identify as an 'LGBT community', which individuals are interpellated and self-interpellate thus and how race functions in this process.

How Are Queer Practices Contained by LGBT Identities and Who is Excluded?

Those who seek out and participate in anonymous internet forums for LGBT people actively debate the usefulness of the term, even while acknowledging there is no rhetorical escape, that 'LGBT' is the dominant international paradigm of identity recognition. But of course, in that world and time before 'post-socialism', there certainly was a significant percentage of the community who identified themselves as 'homosexual' or as having same-sex desires and identities. While one could say that most 'homosexuals' were closeted or in prison before 1990, one Romanian gay blogger also wittily pointed out that in fact the Romanian gay scene could be called '100% bio-eco-powered', as queer men were the ones who most intimately knew the local parks.[9] There were always clubs, cafes, parks and beaches where same-sex desiring men and women could meet each other, although published

---

9   Gay in Romania, 'Gays in Romania: 100% bio-eco powered', http://www.darkq. net/advertising/gay-ii-din-romania-100-bio-eco-powered/.

reflections on this are thus far limited to the poetry of Dominic Brezianu (1996: 2000) and the novel by Constantin Popescu (2004). Brezianu, for example, knew of gay communities in other places, but in everyday life the most common term for homosexuality was to refer to someone as 'like that' (*aşa*).[10] More specifically, men identified other men as 'real men' (*barbaţi*) or 'girls' (*fetiţa*), which clearly plots a spectrum of sexual identity and practice between the two gendered binaries of identification. There were shifting visual signifiers of 'homosexuality', so that Romanian women who described meeting their lovers before they knew there were other women who also desired women (let alone that there was a word for this) of course recognised each other through the simple actuality of human attraction.

Common sense logic of both activists and everyday people of non-normative sexualities was that to 'come out' could be dangerous. The LGBT identity was a new Western identity that seemed useless/dangerous to many, but did offer a future community vision of utopia to Romanians who were white, tertiary educated and middle class – those with enough cultural capital to be employed in the sphere of 'civil society'. In the late 1990s, there were many actors moving between civil society, academia and new state institutions, where the category of 'women' meant ethnic Romanian middle-class women with a university education. Ethnic groups such as Romani Romanians were considered the subjects of specifically racial NGOs rather than taken as 'Romanian'. The hegemonic, white, middle-class activists did not mention the urban working classes either, which is not a specifically 'post-socialist' phenomenon but is undeniably a capitalist phenomenon and occurring here in a specific neo-liberal and post-socialist context. It is not just because socialism 'fell' that the new liberal democratic capitalist discourse does not include workers as humans who need specific rights as a group in 'civil society'. Rather, non-unionisation and the exploitation of workers increases profit margins for those who own the means of production, as Kideckel (2008) and Wiener (2005) have elaborated from the perspective of workers who themselves hopefully explain their own suffering as a 'transition' in neo-liberalist reform economies.

The gap between 'civil society' and lived experience for same-sex desiring Romanians was highlighted when the first Pride parade in May 2004 was cancelled because Stefan Iancu, the organiser, did not think he could 'convince gay people to come out into the streets ... They are too afraid of the repercussions (losing their jobs, shocking their parents etc.)' (Iancu, as quoted in *Ziarul* by Anon. 2004). The Pride parade was not organised in Romania as an expression of an existing gay community, even though donors assumed that self-identifying members of a united LGBT community would be the participants in a Gay Pride parade. Considering that Romanian anti-gay groups such as *Noua Dreaptă* stated they would physically attack marchers, the larger question is clearly the injustice of 'civil society' expectations that social change is to be implemented by the victims of violence

---

10   This information on naming is from a personal interview with Dominic Brezianu, 30 December 2009.

rather than through educating or punishing aggressors. Indeed, the funding and impetus for the event came under the civil society banner of 'diversity', and it was primarily NGO employed Romanian civil society employees and supporters who attended subsequent Gay Pride marches, regardless of their sexual orientation. This gap between the stated aim of the parade as a visibility of LGBT communities and the reality of Pride marchers – who were in fact straight folk, or non-straight folk disguised as journalists to avoid being beaten – highlighted the danger that still accompanies being out in Romania.

Gay Pride Romania – 'The March of Police'[11]

When the first Pride march took place in Bucharest on 29 May 2005 – as part of the 'diversity' festival and under the slogan 'I love who I want to love' – there was no reference to ethnic minorities, no formal representation of Romani or feminist NGOs and no banners linking anti-racism or anti-sexism to the fight for LGBT rights as 'diversity'. Romanian Orthodox students of the Faculty of Theology in Bucharest and the right-wing fascist group *Noua Dreaptă* physically intervened to stop the march, as they had announced they would, and there were over 1,000 violent protesters along the route throwing eggs, rocks and home-made bombs at the 300 Pride marchers from the sidelines.[12] *Noua Dreaptă* is a right-wing Romanian nationalist group primarily active in racist publicity against Roma (as Țigani) and also against 'homosexuality'.[13] The march lasted about an hour, without loud music or an abundance of rainbow flags and paraphernalia, which were not yet easily available in Romania (Miruna and Elena 2005).

In 2006, the Court of Bucharest, however, awarded *Noua Dreaptă* marchers a permit to hold their own parade, which they named 'The March for Normality', through central historic Bucharest on the same route that the Romanian fascist Iron Guard had used for parades in the 1930s.[14] The media and 'civil society' sector widely considered the government's reaction to the Pride parade a test of political readiness for integration in the European Union or, more specifically, a test of how EUropean values of tolerance would be enacted in the name of the Romanian state. Fifty-one anti-GayFest protesters were arrested and fined for provoking violence at the Pride march (Human Rights First 2007) and 'after the closing of the march six youths, amongst whom were two citizens of the European Union, were verbally and physically assaulted in the subway. The attackers shouted "Faggots, go to

---

11   Taken from the title of the blog, http://www.darkq.net/advertising/gayfest-2008-un-mars-al-jandarmilor/.

12   For information and images of GayPride 2005 see http://www.accept-romania. ro/fest/fest05EN2txt1.htm; http://romania.indymedia.org/en/2005/06/851.shtml; and the video posts at http://www.youtube.com/user/daraptii (accessed: 14 May 2008).

13   See http://www.nouadreapta.org (accessed: 18 January 2010).

14   See http://www.nouadreapta.org/actiuni_prezentare.php?idx=110 (accessed: 14 May 2008).

Holland" as they bestially beat the youths' (Accept 2006).[15] The severity of this violence influenced how members of the LGBT community and individuals who had chosen not to attend the march blogged about the parade in the following days, and stimulated discussion about how fears and experiences of violence affected individuals and the gay community. The violence that participants experienced was reconfigured as a baptism of fire (the Romanian Stonewall) by some and used to articulate divisions within the community between those who watched the parade from the sidelines or from home as lacking courage, and those who had paraded (Woodcock 2009).

The GayFest parades of 2005 and 2006 functioned as spaces of contestation. On one hand, the LGBT community 'came out' as a small group of overwhelmingly white, middle-class 'civil society' LGBT supporters rather than a grassroots gay community, many of whom actively refused to support the idea of parading under a sexual identity banner. Protesters against LGBT identity were granted institutional support in terms of public space and the freedom to attack Pride participants. Regardless of human rights issues, Romania was accepted as an EU Member in 2007 and the 2007 Pride Parade demonstrated how the Romanian state saw EUropean human rights in domestic space – the parade was violently corralled and policed by the state. The slogan of GayFest 2007 was 'Celebrate diversity! Respect rights!' and the media predictably peddled the two parades as 'diversity versus normality'. Only 400 people attended the parade, to which the Romanian government sent more than 800 regular, military and riot police, on horseback, with dogs, and backed up with water cannon trucks and military equipment.[16]

GayFest was given an entire half of the boulevard, traffic was redirected and the borders of the marching space were the police trucks on one side and the wide nature strip (for the media and those with cameras running alongside the march) and traffic on the other. Eggs and garbage were thrown at the marchers from open windows in apartment blocks along the route, and smoke bombs were lobbed into the parade from the margins. While Maxim Anmeghichean (2007), ILGA-Europe's Programme Director, considered the police cordon a success, Romanian marchers reflected on the effects of enclosing the parade in a heavily policed space with more ambivalence.[17] One participant, Romanian photographer

---

15   Press statement 5 June 2006 'Marşul Diversitaţii: Inca un pas spre toleranta', http://Accept-romania.ro/index2.php?option=com_content&task=view&id=52&pop=1 (accessed: 14 May 2008).

16   See photos at http://www.flickr.com/photos/rombaer/ tagged as 'law enforcement' and 'gay pride 2007'. See a wonderful series of photos and narratives about the day by a self-identified straight male American participant – who is also the only virtual narrator to say he was 'sadistically longing' for a confrontation with the protesters – at http://www.romerican.com/2007/06/14/gayfest-2007/ (accessed: 14 May 2008).

17   See Woodcock 2009 for a full exploration of how participants recorded their experiences of violence in the march

Andrei Namolosanu, nicknamed the event 'the march of the Police, with 30 police for every gay'.[18]

Those who marched in the GayFest parades in 2007, 2008 and 2009 were physically forced out of visibility in the name of protection – the parade was visible *as* the containment of EUropean 'diversity'. As Wendy Brown (2006: 96–9) points out, the state bestows tolerance on gay subjects on condition that they remain invisible in the public sphere. The Romanian state uses non-violent tolerance as the discursive rationalisation to physically prevent GayFest marchers from responding to anti-GayFest protesters who violently attack from the sphere of non-corralled public space in the name of 'normality'. The Romanian state claims it is acting in the name of Romanian adherence to EUropean values of freedom of expression, which throws into stark relief the ways that the rhetoric of liberalism and non-violence in democratic EUrope can be used as a form of violent containment.

In 2009, the discussion on 'gay' Romanian websites continued to ask what the point of the parade and legislation was when it is not in the interest of everyday people now identified as 'homosexual' regardless of their own identities. One blogger, Dan, suggested that instead of a Pride parade, there be a March of Silence, 'with men in everyday clothes, to show that we are not transvestites as most people in this country see us'.[19] This suggestion abandons the discursive constructions of gay identity thus far, actively removing the words that have been introduced on march banners and as identity categories, and draws hope for a future queer community based on the lived experiences of those who reject the agenda and practices of the homonormative EUropean LGBT community.

But what can we say about how this broader queer community sees their identity in relation to the dominant Romanian national identity as they claim to look like 'everyday' people – especially as Romanian ethno-national identity relies on the racialisation of Țigani as others? In Western Europe and America, Puar and Rai (2002) and Haritaworn (2008), among others, have detailed how the racialisation of Muslim men as terrorists relies upon the presentation of sexual liberation as a sign of progress, and depicting non-European ethnic groups as against progress because they are supposedly against homosexuality. Puar and Rai (2002: 124) also point out that this racialisation is only possible because of a long history of Europe constructing itself through monstrous others such as 'the vagrant, the Gypsy, the

18   Namolosanu posted his photographs on Flickr, accompanied by summaries of and comments on the event (http://www.flickr.com/photos/rombaer), tagged as 'law enforcement' and gay pride 2007' (accessed: 14 May 2008). Namolosanu has since moved his photos to http://namolosanu.tumblr.com, but these do not include the 2007 Gay Pride photos. Namolosanu's comments are referred to at greater length in Woodcock 2009.

19   Dan, 16 May 2008, http://www.darkq.net/advertising/gayfest-2008-un-mars-al-jandarmilor (accessed: 12 January 2010). Interestingly his comment was not seriously discussed; an active blogger and pro-LGBT activist, Robert G, replied that 'the idea of a march of men is great!', taking it in a different direction.

savage, the Hottentot Venus, or the sexual depravity of the Oriental torrid zone' without which the 'terrorist-monster' could not exist in this specific moment. Luckily for us scholars, Madonna chose this moment to publicly announce her views equating racism and homophobia in Romania and we can trace the various reactions to this announcement to better understand better the links between the LGBT identity movement and racism.

Madonna as Western Liberator and Romanian Responses

Madonna performed to a crowd of 60–70,000 people in Bucharest on 28 August 2009. Accompanied on the tour by Russian Romani band the Kolpakov Trio and Romani dancers, Madonna paused to speak to the audience in words recalled at the beginning of the chapter. The crowd's response was a lot of booing and a few cheers, which faded to silence as she then sang a watery rendition of a Romani song. This moment hit the international and Romanian press under headlines such as the *Guardian*'s 'Romanian fans boo Madonna for supporting Gypsies', and Reuters' 'Madonna booed in Bucharest over Gypsy remarks', both of which cut any mention of the word 'homosexuals' from Madonna's cited statement.[20] Only one of the 347 comments on the *Guardian* article, and none of the 42 comments on the Reuters article, notice that Madonna mentioned the rights of 'homosexuals' alongside Roma. The 231 comments on the most popular YouTube clip of the event gave the best outline of how Romanians reacted to the statement, and fewer than five of the comments refer to Madonna mentioning 'homosexuals' alongside Roma, all by linking their racist insults to anti-gay slurs.[21] While the *Guardian*'s web moderator has removed racist comments, participants on the YouTube chat site deleted anti-racist commentators – who were attacked as Western foreigners – distancing all pro-Romani and anti-racist comments as non-indigenous and therefore without the right to speak to Romanians.

The rage of Romanians against Madonna as gleaned from internet discussions covers many of the areas we have already discussed. Madonna's inclusion of Bucharest in her European tour, with tickets at Western European prices, was a powerful and rewarding symbol of Romanian access to European identity. Madonna's long statement to the audience – in simplified English and chastising, patronising grammatical structure ('let's not forget') – ruptured the ability of Romanians to enjoy the concert as consumers of entertainment on an equal level to Western European audiences. In this moment, Madonna spoke as a global,

---

20   http://blogs.reuters.com/fanfare/2009/08/27/madonna-booed-in-bucharest-over-gypsy-remarks/, 'Madonna booed in Bucharest over Gypsy remarks', 27 August 2009; http://www.guardian.co.uk/music/2009/aug/28/madonna-booed-at-romania-concert, 'Romanian fans boo Madonna for supporting Gypsies', Haroon Siddique, http://www.guardian.co.uk, Friday 28 August 2009.

21   http://Youtube.com/watch?v=AdDgcMsETDE.

progressive citizen embodying 'tolerance' for 'people who are different' (in itself scaffolding racialised heteronormativity) in a way that interpellated the audience as composed of Easterners yet to catch up with this global progressive time. Many comments expressed this in various ways, although the vast majority of responses were 'fuck Madonna, fuck the Gypsies' in various forms. In responses such as this, the Romanian speaker interpellated by the global progressive West (Madonna) as racist Romanian, talks back by embodying the Romanian ethno-nationalist identity (which relies on the Ṭigan other) against the EUropean discourses of tolerance.

One respondent commented, for example, 'So I AM A PROUND INTOLERANT ROMANIAN' (clementinebroken).[22] Another (BaiazidIX) wrote that 'we're discriminated all the time by Western Europe who calls us Romanians gypsys, and this bitch tells us not to discriminate? And why the fuck did she say "romanies and gypsys" like they are 2 different groups, what does that mean? That's like saying we romanians are romanies.' This is the post-accession discourse of deliberate confusion between Romanian and Romani ethnicities to maintain the Ṭigan other discussed earlier. DenisDMN presented another common argument dismissing the very concept of 'human rights' as universal when he wrote:

> gypsies ain't humans, they're animals ... y'all get this straight, you can't be a racist when it comes to a animal ... the gypsies she's talkin' about are not the kind of gypsies we hate ... the gypsies she's talkin' about are people ... the gypsies we hate are a virus, you wouldn't want them around ... get this straight ... respect humans but don't take everything, that stands on two legs and can think and talk, for a human being ... that's just insulting towards humans.

Finally, egoguitar's comment highlighted the way that dismissal of the universality of human rights draws on a complex range of Western and Romanian discourses when he sarcastically contributed '[e]veryone is created equal: Homosexual faggots, Romanians, Gypsies, 3 legged dogs, Nazi's, Mexicans, etc ... These are all equal. Please don't discriminate.'

Sadly, Romanian discussants on explicitly 'gay' and queer Romanian websites did not react much differently from these mainstream commentators. On the international gay news website Pink News (UK), the article 'Bucharest crowd boo Madonna's defense of gays and Roma' received 33 comments, beginning with Western European respondents who spoke in the name of EUropean progress, stating 'We need to start becoming tougher on these countries who are in, or wanting to be in, the EU, and making it a strong condition of membership that there is full equality for gay people' (Bentley, 28 August).[23] This tone is rebutted

---

22 All comments here and following taken from the previously cited YouTube clip 'Madonna Booed in Bucharest, Romania Concert' by Mikeyblogs2comments at http://www.Youtube.com/watch?v=AdDgcMsETDE.

23 Worldwide Gay Travel and Culture – Life, Sites and Insights: A Charitable Website Supporting Human Rights, http://www.globalgayz.com/country/Romania/view/

by a Romanian writing as SBV82 that 'gays should not be lumped together with the gipsyes, because gay and bisexual people are decent civilised people while the gipsyes are, for the most part, criminals that are incapable to live in a civilised society'; and this respondent foreclosed the right of non-Romanians to speak by writing that 'I bet you haven't met a gipsy in your life and if that is the case I politely ask you to SHUT UP.' After small rebuttals from non-Romanian readers, the Romanian argument that racism can only be critiqued by racists who have 'experienced' the (Ţigani) villain won, enabling all discussants to maintain the 'gay community' on the condition of silence about racist exclusion and practice.

On 31 August 2009, Robert G, a regular Romanian blogger and gay activist, posted a blog lambasting Madonna as 'stupid to mix music and other things', as 'probably imagining that Ţigani are some hippy bohemian people who travel with caravans and horses', and inviting Madonna to spend half an hour in a suburb with Ţigani and see if she comes back, probably without her watch.[24] One of the first responses to this post stated '[t]his article has no place here, it is totally disqualified. One minority attacking another. It is totally injust! We need to be an example of tolerance, acceptance, integration and Europeanism.'[25] Robert G replied that 'gays are one thing and Ţigani another' and from there other discussants such as Fireman posted messages saying that Ţigani are the reason he is ashamed whenever he leaves Romania. These gay male bloggers thus rely on the racialisation of Roma as Ţigani, the normative Romanian ethnonational identity claim to displace the reality and anxieties resulting from the fact that the West does discriminate against Romanians.

Numerous gay Romanians, however, did blog about their shame when their fellow Romanians booed what they saw as Madonna's stand against both racism and homophobia. Elements.de.Vie wrote that he was ashamed to be Romanian at the concert that night, and Wannabegay, who lives in Los Angeles, California, posted an open letter to Madonna thanking her for speaking out against discrimination against Roma. Wannabegay pointed out that the evidence of systemic discrimination is not only the plethora of blogs saying 'who cares if we discriminate against them', but also the fact that Romanians still refuse to use the self-appellation for Romani people.[26] One of the first respondents, Chris, said he believed it is 'improper to

---

ROM/gay-romania-news-and-reports-2009#article6, Gay Romania News & Reports 2009, 'Bucharest crowd boo Madonna's defence of gays and Roma'; http://www.365gay.com/ news/madonna-booed-in-bucharest-for-defending-gypsies, 'Madonna booed in Bucharest for defending Gypsies', The Associated Press, 27 August 2009 (1:30pm EDT), taken from associated press and elision of homosexuals comment, http://gaynews.pinknews.co.uk/ news/articles/2005-13846.html; video: 'Bucharest crowd boo Madonna's defence of gays and Roma', 28 August 2009, 11:26.

24   'Betty blue', http://www.darkq.net/romania/betty-blue/#comments.

25   Elements.de.Vie 20 September 2009, who on his own blog had written that he was ashamed to be Romanian at the concert that night, http://elementsdevie.blogspot.com/ search?updated-max=2009-10-01T19%3A33%3A00%2B03%3A00&max-results=10.

26   Draga Madonna, http://wannabegay.org/2009/09/03/draga-madonna/#comments.

speak in the same article of discrimination against both the Roma and against homosexuals, as they are not the same thing'. Subsequent comments included one asking whether this means the blogger is actually Țigan (as if this were an insult) and a general discussion where the majority of participants argued against the blogger that Roma really are criminals and hence the racism is warranted. Another website, 'Gay in Romania',[27] blogged that it was disappointing to hear Madonna booed at the concert, and again only one regular (and self-identified heterosexual woman) participant (Dak) on these websites wrote in support. The majority of the other 11 comments were against Țigani and against Madonna making 'propaganda' and 'political statements'. One discussant on this site also wrote that God is against gays and lesbians, highlighting the truly queer nature of communities online who are interested in discussing identity and 'human rights' outside formal forums.

Of course there are serious methodological issues with using even exhaustive blog and internet-based research to judge the opinions of any group of people, and far from all the same-sex identifying Romanians who are on internet dating sites write blogs. Nevertheless, in the same-sex and LGBT identifying blogs and discussions surrounding Madonna's comments we can read the same discourses against Roma that we find in the mainstream press and internet discussions. It is also a fact that the blogs posted by non-Romanian LGBT identified and internationally residing Romanian gay bloggers, such as wannabegay, were more open to the ways that anti-discrimination has to fight both racism and homophobia; while the bloggers who argued that anti-Țiganism was not discrimination because Roma were not civilised included LGBT 'civil society' activists from Romania, such as Robert G. In conclusion, the LGBT movement in Romania draws support from only a minority of individuals who consider themselves interpellated by the LGBT category, due to the obvious gap between the utopia it offers and the reality on the street; and many individuals are excluded by the racialised and middle-classed homonormativity of the movement itself. The queer communities that exist at and as the critical margins of the LGBT movement, however, also rely on racial discourses of the Țigan other in order to claim Romanian ethno-national identity in the face of specifically EUropean pressures, including economic and legislative reforms which are obscured by naming liberalisation 'post-socialism'.

Queering Containment in Post-Socialist Liberalism

I want a world where the queer reality of dynamic sexual identities is free to be muddled through and performed without fear of violence or the restrictions of categorical containment. I would like to share the utopian teleological homonormative vision of legislative reform – civil unions, marriage and gay

---

27   Gay in Romania – florin and Ionuti http://gayinromania.blogspot.com/2009/08/madonna-huiduita-la-bucuresti.html, 'Madonna huiduită la București', 27 August 2009.

adoption rights as the means of creating a world where everyone can enjoy a peaceful life, but I have only seen evidence to the contrary. The categories that were staked and won by Western activists for gay liberation are in the service of the capitalist state, and they contain us. In Romania, LGBT categories were introduced as an inevitable and singular sign of progress in the name of EUrope, within the 'post-socialist' liberalism that tethered identity politics to biology (gender, race, sexuality) and corralled the claims of individuals in these newly liberated categories to 'civil society'. Those who recognise that the massive police deployments required to 'tolerate' LGBT identity do not bode well for an everyday reality free of persecution in this generation refute state and 'civil' interpellation by this name. And yet the claims to both homonormative 'rights' and the queer search for new futures both claim access to an ethno-national Romanian identity which relies on the violent racialisation of Roma as Țigani in EUropean Romania, powered primarily by resistance to the temporal prison of 'post-socialist' society.

We can pay attention to names: where they place us in relation to progress, how we are attached to them, when and where we refuse to answer to them, and who needs to be excluded in order for them to function. We can fight with the knowledge that names bind us, and if there are to be rights, they are the rights to refuse categorisation and to remain queer in time, space, desire and safety.

References

ACCEPT. 2006. Press Statement 5 June 2006. Marşul Diversitaţii: Inca un pas spre toleranţa. Available at: http://Acceptromania.ro/index2.php?option=com_content&task=view&id=52&pop=1 (accessed: 14 May 2008).

ACCEPT, the International Gay and Lesbian Human Rights Commission (IGLHRC) and the European Region of the International Lesbian and Gay Association (ILGA-Europe). 2008 (February). *Romania: The Status of Lesbian, Gay, Bisexual and Trangender Rights*. Available at: http://www.iglhrc.org and through http://www.Accept-romania.ro.

Anon. 1998. 'Homosexualii – Neafectati de Scumpirea Benzinei', *Adevarul* 8 March.

Anon. 2004. 'Mădălin Voicu despre primul festival gay din România "Homosexuali sunt şi oameni săraci, şi politicieni"'. In *Ziarul* 3 May. Available at: http://www.Accept-romania.ro/fest/fest04RO1.htm (accessed: 14 May 2008).

Böröcz, J. and Kovács, M. 2001. *Empire's New Clothes: Unveiling EU-Enlargement*. Central Europe Review e-books.

Borza, I., Grünberg, L. and Văcărescu, T. 2006. *Cartea Neagrăa egalităţi de şanse între femei şi bărbaţi în România*. Bucharest: Editura AnA.

Brenna, M.M. 2009. 'Queer Family Romance: Writing the "New" South Africa in the 1990s'. *GLQ: A Journal of Lesbian and Gay Studies* 15(3): 397–439.

Brezianu, D. 1996. *Cu Mai Puţine Verbe*. Bucharest: Cavallioti.

———. 2000. *Escale*. Bucharest: Cavallioti.

Brown, W. 2006. *Regulating Aversion: Tolerance in the Age of Identity and Empire*. Princeton and Oxford: Princeton University Press.

Butler, J. and Spivak, G.C. 2008. *Who Sings the Nation State? Language, Politics, Belonging*. London: Seagull.

Cesereanu, R. 1993. *Imaginarul violent al românilor*. Bucharest: Humanitas.

Chari, S. and Verdery, K. 2009. 'Thinking between the Posts: Postcolonialism, Postsocialism, and Ethnography after the Cold War'. *Comparative Studies in Society and History* 51(1): 6–34.

Contu, I. 2005. *Those Are All Fags?! Dude, There's So Many of Them!* (online: 4 June). Available at: http://romania.indymedia.org/en/2005/06/851.shtml (accessed: 14 May 2008).

Creteanu, A. and Coman, A. 1998. *Homosexualitatea în presa scrisa din România* [*Homosexuality in the Romanian Written Press*]. Available at: http://accept. ong.ro/presarom.html#presa (accessed: 10 January 2010).

Gheorghe, N. (1991) 'Roma-Gypsy Ethnicity in Eastern Europe'. *Social Research* 58(3): 829–44.

Ghinea, C. 2001. 'Intre noi fie vorba, rromii tot Țiganii sînt'. *Dilema*, 451, 19 October, 3.

Ghodsee, K. 2006. 'Nongovernmental Ogres? How Feminist NGOs Undermine Women in Postsocialist Eastern Europe'. *The International Journal of Not-for-Profit Law* 8(3) May 2006 Available at: http://www.icnl.org/KNOWLEDGE/ ijnl/vol8iss3/art_2.htm (accessed: 11 January 2010).

Grünberg, L. 2008. 'The NGO-ization of Feminism in Romania. The failure of a success'. Available at: http://ana.ong.ro/romana/centrulana/editura/rev700/ lgrunbergeng700.html (accessed: 11 January 2010).

Gunkel, H. and Pitcher, B. 2008. 'Racism in the Closet – Interrogating Postcolonial Sexuality'. *Dark Matter Postcolonial Sexuality* 3 (online 2 May). Available at: http://www.darkmatter101.org/site/2008/05/02/racism-in-the-closet-interrogating-postcolonial-sexuality/ (accessed: 11 January 2010).

Gunkel, H. 2010. *The Cultural Politics of Female Sexuality in South Africa*. New York: Routledge.

Haritaworn, J. 2008. 'Loyal Repetitions of the Nation: Gay Assimilation and the "War on Terror"' (online: 2 May). Available at: http://www.darkmatter101.org/ site/2008/05/02/loyal-repetitions-of-the-nation-gay-assimilation-and-the-war-on-terror/ (accessed: 11 January 2010).

Hoad, N. 2007. *African Intimacies: Race, Homosexuality, and Globalization*. Minneapolis: University of Minnesota Press.

Human Rights First. 2007. *Homophobia 2007 Hate Crime Survey*. Washington DC. (online report). Available at: http://www.humanrightsfirst.org (accessed: 11 January 2010).

Human Rights Watch and the International Gay and Lesbian Human Rights Commission New York. 1998. *Public Scandals: Sexual Orientation and*

Criminal Law in Romania. New York and Washington DC: Human Rights Watch.

Kajinic, S. 2003. *Experiences of Lesbians at the Belgrade Pride 2001 and Zagreb Pride 2002*. Unpublished masters thesis. Central European University, Department of Gender Studies, Budapest. Available at: http://www.labris.org. yu/en/images/SanjaKajinicThesis.pdf (accessed: 14 May 2008).

Kideckel, D.A. 2008. *Getting By in Postsocialist Romania: Labor, the Body and Working Class Culture*. Bloomington: Indiana University Press.

Kligman, G. 1998. *The Politics of Duplicity: Controlling Reproduction in Ceausescu's Romania*. Berkeley: University of California Press.

Miruna and Elena. 2005 'A Belated Report on Gay Pride – 10.06.05'. Available at: http://romania.indymedia.org/en/2005/06/851.shtml (accessed: 14 May 2008).

Munro, Brenna M. 2009. 'Queer Family Romance: Writing the "New" South Africa in the 1990s'. *GLQ: A Journal of Lesbian and Gay Studies* 15(3): 397–439.

Nicolae, V. 2006. 'Fourth Arm of the State' *Index on Censorship 3*. Noua Dreapta. Available at: http://www.nouadreapta.org/actiuni_prezentare.php?idx=110; (accessed: 14 May 2008).

Ockenga, E. 1997. 'Trade Unions in Romania'. *Transfer: European Review of Labour and Research* 3(2): 313–28.

Project on Ethnic Relations (PER). 1997. Report on the Conference 'Images and Issues: Coverage of the Roma in the Mass Media in Romania', 27–28 June, Bucharest.

Popescu, C. 2004. *Cloaca Maxima*. Bucharest: Editura Vremea.

Puar, J.K. 2002. 'Circuits of Queer Mobility: Tourism, Travel and Globalization'. *GLQ: A Journal of Lesbian and Gay Studies* 8(1–2): 101–37.

———. 2007. *Terrorist Assemblages: Homonationalism in Queer Times*. Durham, NC: Duke University Press.

Puar, J.K. and Rai, A.S. 2002. 'Monster, Terrorist, Fag: The War on Terrorism and the Production of Docile Patriots'. *Social Text* 20(3): 117–48.

Reynolds, R. 2002. *From Camp to Queer: Remaking the Australian Homosexual*. Melbourne: Melbourne University Press.

Sedgwick, E.K. 1990. *Epistemology of the Closet*. New York: Harvester Wheatsheaf.

Tismăneanu, V. 2000. *Încet, spre Europă*. Bucharest: Polirom.

United States Department of State Bureau of Democracy, Human Rights and Labor. 2008 *Country Report on Human Rights Practices in Romania 2007* (online March 11). Available at http://www.state.gov/g/drl/rls/hrrpt/2007/100580.htm (accessed: 14 May 2008).

Verdery, K. 1996. *What Was Socialism, and What Comes Next?* Princeton: Princeton University Press.

Ward, J. 2008. *Respectably Queer: Diversity Culture in LGBT Activist Organisations*. Nashville: Vanderbilt University Press.

Weiner, E.S. 2005. 'No (Wo)Man's Land: The Post-Socialist Purgatory of Czech Female Factory Workers'. *Social Problems* 52(4): 572–92.

Whitlock, G. 2007. *Soft Weapons: Autobiography in Transit.* Chicago and London: University of Chicago Press.

Woodcock, S. 2004. 'The Globalization of LGBT Identities: Containment Masquerading as Salvation or Why Lesbians Have less Fun'. In *Gender and the (Post) 'East'/'West' Divide*, eds M. Frunză and T. Văcărescu. Cluj-Napoca: Editura Limes.

———. 2007. 'Romania and EUrope: Roma, Rroma and Țigani as Sites for the Contestation of Ethno-National Identities'. *Patterns of Prejudice* 41(5): 493–515.

———. 2008. 'The *Țigan* Other as Catalyst for the Creation of Modern Romani'. In *Annual Journal of the Centre for Roma Studies*. Bucharest: University of Bucharest.

———. 2009. 'Gay Pride as Violent Containment in Romania: A Brave New EUrope'. *Sextures*. Available at: http://sextures.net/woodcock-gay-pride-romania [accessed: 11 January 2010].

Zizek, S. 2008. *Violence; Six Sideways Reflections.* London: Profile Books.

Zub, A. 2002. *Oglinzi Retrovizoare: Istorie, memorie şi morală în Romania în dialog cu Sorin Antohi.* Iasi: Polirom.

Chapter 5

Travelling Ideas, Travelling Times: On the Temporalities of LGBT and Queer Politics in Poland and the 'West'

Joanna Mizielińska

A Klee painting named 'Angelus Novus' shows an angel looking as though he is about to move away from something he is fixedly contemplating. His eyes are staring, his mouth is open, his wings are spread. This is how one pictures the angel of history. His face is turned towards the past. Where we perceive a chain of events, he sees one single catastrophe which keeps piling wreckage upon wreckage and hurls it in front of his feet. The angel would like to stay, awaken the dead, and make whole what has been smashed. But a storm is blowing from Paradise; it has got caught in his wings with such violence that the angel can no longer close them. This storm irresistibly propels him into the future to which his back is turned, while the pile of debris before him grows skyward. This storm is what we call progress.

(Walter Benjamin, *Theses on the Philosophy of History or On the Concept of History*)

The aim of this chapter is to explore the ways in which 'Western' ideas of LGBT and queer politics have travelled and are deployed in Poland. In doing so, I am particularly interested in the content and functioning of 'time'. I will suggest that Polish LGBT activism cannot be simply categorised as 'identitarian' or 'queer' because it exists in a different geotemporality from the 'West'. I will focus on the Campaign Against Homophobia/Kampania Przeciw Homofobii (CAH/KPH), the largest and best-known Polish LGBT organisation. I will suggest that in their choice of strategies and discourses one can see the queer mixture of ideas that represent various historical stages of Western LGBT activism. From aggressive, in-your-face 'queer' campaigns, through to celebration of coming out and identity politics, to assimilationist 'do-it-slowly-and-unobtrusively' grassroots work, discourses produced by CAH cannot be easily categorised.

I will suggest that one of the reasons is the 'temporal disjunction', a historical void in which CAH works. The 1990s marked the beginning of LGBT activism in Poland, where this transformation saw 'Western' ideas applied without much attempt at understanding their cultural and historical context and functioning. Suddenly, Polish homosexuals (just 'becoming' 'gays' or 'lesbians') accessed differentiated models of LGBT and Q activism developed in the West over more than 40 years, using them for their own purposes. In 1989, when the 'communist time' stopped, 'Western time' began, becoming a 'universal time' for both West and Central and Eastern Europe (CEE). But what is 'continuity' from a Western perspective is a knotted and dehistoricised cultural phenomenon, imposed as much as welcomed, of which Polish LGBT activists and academics are still trying to make sense. Rather than repeating the dominant narrative of CEE 'catching up with Europe' (i.e. a linear narrative of progress), I want to look at the much finer processes of weaving geotemporal realities in Polish LGBT activism.

I will start this chapter with an overview of the contemporary Polish political scene, with examples of sexual politics in Poland. In doing so I want to highlight the limitations of queer politics in Poland. I would also like to show some of the resistance actions performed by LGBT and feminist circles in Poland, and the responses they have received among the political elites. I would argue that queering politics can mean different things locally and that what can be described as an identity approach from the US perspective can have its queer face on the local level.

The Polish Political Situation

It seems that by joining the European Union (EU) Poland has finally chosen its value system, including respect for human rights. However, in 2005 parliamentary and presidential elections were won by the Kaczynski twins, Lech and Jaroslaw, who openly disapproved of the 'public promotion of homosexuality' and banned the annual 'Equality parade' in June 2004. For the first time the parliamentary election campaign in 2005 was built around the issue of the 'gay question' as well as neoliberal vs welfare state. The Kaczynski twins, leaders of Law and Justice, a political party characterised by a mix of nationalism, populism and Catholic conservatism, promised voters to protect equally the welfare state and Polish tradition (in their understanding built on Catholic values, the traditional patriarchal family etc.). In order to fulfil their promises, Law and Justice built a coalition with the extremist League of Polish Families Party and the conservative-populist Self-Defence Party. During the campaign right-wing candidates often appealed to their voters by using homophobic language and warning against the public 'promotion of homosexuality' and presenting themselves as defenders of traditional values. For instance Jaroslaw Kaczynski described homosexuality as an 'abomination' and said that in his opinion homosexuals should not be teachers. His anti-gay rhetoric came as no surprise, as both twins have a long history of openly expressed hatred towards homosexuals (e.g. Lech Kaczynski – later to become president – still as a mayor of Warsaw banned a Gay Pride march in spring 2005, publicly announcing that he respected rights to demonstrate as citizens but not as homosexuals).

Unfortunately, open homophobia sells well in Poland and has brought its supporters political successes. In October 2005 Lech Kaczynski won the presidential elections. In November 2005 the Law and Justice Party, run by Jaroslaw Kaczynski, won the parliamentary elections. Finally, a year later, after dismissing his first PM, Jaroslaw became Prime Minister. He often declared that the promotion of homosexuality could lead to the end of civilisation and therefore must be stopped. After the election, the government started its new regime against women's rights and homosexuals' rights. Its rule can be described as:

- against women's rights (they cancelled and suppressed the post of Plenipotentiary for the Equal Status);
- against birth control: contraceptives were presented as dangerous to life and not refunded by the state ('*becikowe*' – a small amount of money paid to women after giving birth);
- against abortion: the concept of 'a conceived child' replaced the 'foetus' in a public debate; attempts to change the Constitution and totally delegalise abortion also in those instances when it is legal nowadays – namely, when it presents a threat to a woman's life, when it is an outcome of rape, or when a future child is likely to be disabled;
- against homosexual rights: several bans on Gay Pride parades; bans on any educational action that promotes equality and tolerance;
- against any 'immoral' behaviour;
- against sex education.

So after the 2005 parliamentary elections, 'wars over values' were fought on every level: economical, political, educational and cultural. Moreover, nowadays in Poland one can observe a schizophrenic war between two value systems: conservative and liberal/democratic, Catholic and secular.[1] The main victims of this war are sexual minorities and women. One might suspect that 'sexual politics' is the main tool to distract the attention of public opinion from other social and economical problems. What is even worse, Polish politicians nowadays officially voice homophobia or prejudices against homosexual people also at international forums, for example by pretending to be the only 'moral voice' in the 'immoral' EU. In one of his speeches (March 2008) on Polish national TV, President Lech Kaczynski expressed his concerns about the Lisbon Treaty and his lack of support for it. The presentation was built around two issues: Polish national interests ('the fear of Germans' questioning post-war geopolitical agreements) and Polish national traditional morality (the fear of homosexual marriage).[2] In this speech, Polish morality (synonymous with Catholicism) was contrasted with EU 'immorality'.

---

1 Of course one has to take into account that Polish conservatives represented by Kaczynski and others are not the same as the Conservative Party in the UK. As I have already written, it is openly homophobic, sexist and … Catholic.

2 The speech was illustrated with pictures from a gay marriage which, as it appeared afterwards, were not taken in Europe but in Canada. This mistake was widely commented on and the Canadian couple even visited Poland, invited by the Polish private TV channel TVN.

Poland was presented as the moral saviour of the whole of Europe, as the last instance of the Good in the flood of the Evil.

Although in the precipitate elections in October 2007 the major opposition party, Civic Platform, won, Kaczynski's party was second and increased its number of voters compared to 2005. Civic Platform may have a more moderate and (neo)liberal attitude in social and economic spheres, but it remains a 'traditionally conservative' party when it comes to values. For example, its Plenipotentiary for Equal Treatment, Elzbieta Radziszewska, has admitted to being against: the introduction of parity in the Polish Parliament; reimbursement of contraceptives; same-sex partnership; and the anti-hate speech bill drafted by Polish LGBT organisations.[3] She has also failed to establish any relations with those organisations, which explains why many of LGBT and feminist groups called several times to dismiss her.

We can conclude that Polish politicians (no matter the party membership)[4] use/d sexual politics as a meaningful and manipulatory tool to control/focus social fears. 'Sex panic' can be used to rationalise/justify any economic decisions and therefore it serves neoliberal purposes, exemplifying 'an illusion of neoliberalism' (Duggan 2003). In *The Twilight of Equality*, Lisa Duggan has shown the false distinction between economy and values and the failure of the neoliberal project founded on this distinction. I would also claim that 'sex panic' shows the failure of the more primary liberal presumption of divided public and private spheres. For example, in the US case 'sexual politics' was/is used to support the tax-cutting agenda of New York state corporations, which leads to a shrinking of public institutions (Duggan 2003). In Poland, sexual politics is used to justify a new (cultural and economical) policy that reflects a nationalist-conservative ideology of ruling elites – i.e. the Catholic morality – which is called simply 'morality', forcefully subsuming all other ethical systems as non-existent. The best illustration of this approach is given in a cartoon by Andrzej Mleczko (a popular cartoonist and commentator): 'So here is the deal. You give us money and we give you values.' Those values are Catholic, anti-gay and anti-feminist. Queers are often presented as something from the EU (e.g. posters during anti-gay manifestation with slogans such as 'Eurosodomy' or 'Poles don't do Eurosodomy') as a part of European moral relativism.

As Gayle Rubin writes in *Thinking Sex*, 'disputes over sexual behavior often become the vehicles for displacing social anxieties and discharging their attendant

---

3   For instance in an interview on Polish radio she stated that Polish LGBT organisation do not care about same-sex partnership legislation but rather about anti-discriminatory law on the market not taking into account that such a law already exists in the Polish Labour Code. Also instead of – participating in the annual feminist parade on the occasion of the 8 March called Manifa, she chose to take part in meditation in the cloister.

4   It applies also to the Polish left. In spring 2008 a survey of 1569 social democrat (SLD) delegates showed that more than one-third of them thought that homosexuality was against human nature, almost half were against same-sex marriage, 15 per cent were against abortion for social reasons and 45 per cent wanted the return of capital punishment (Majka 2009).

emotional intensity. Consequently, sexuality should be treated with special respect in times of great social stress' (Rubin 1993: 3–4).

Queer(?) Defence?

Taking into account the Polish political situation, what would be the best strategy in Poland to fight this openly expressed homophobia? What kinds of means and methods does the Polish LGBT movement use? What kinds of alliances does it form, and with whom? In this section, I would like to focus on the activism of the Campaign Against Homophobia (CAH). First, I will compare their two social campaigns – 'Let Them See Us' and 'What Are You Staring At, Dyke/Faggot?' – and show the failure of Western 'queer apparatus' when analysing these campaigns. I will try to show that it is impossible to decide on what type of activism is carried out by CAH. Both campaigns could be understood as strengthening identity/minority politics, as well as attempting queer politics, but in different ways from Western/American contexts. Then, I will discuss how this 'temporal disjunction' works when we look at CAH's broader political agenda and different scopes of activism.

I would like to argue that we have to take into account that history is not a linear movement from oppression to liberation, and moreover that it is not universal and does have its local flavours. The history of the LGBT (queer) or feminist movements looks different in every country; and, given the context, many approaches, once used and defined in the US, can have different meanings and produce (or not) different outcomes when transplanted elsewhere.

Project 'Let Them See Us' was started in the autumn of 2002 by Karolina Bregula and CAH. It consisted of an exhibition of 30 portraits of gay and lesbian couples, all of them holding hands in a winter scene, as if they were taking a walk. The pictures, exhibited in art galleries in Warsaw, Cracow, Gdansk and Sosnowiec, were only part of the project, which also involved an outdoor poster campaign as well as an information campaign. The project generated a heated discussion about gay and lesbian rights, especially the right to be in a public space, revealing a great deal of prejudice. Posters were quickly destroyed; after the heat arose, some galleries refused to host the exhibition, after initially agreeing to do so; those that finally did host it faced serious repercussions afterwards (such as their contracts and funding being withdrawn by some local and national agencies).

In March 2007, CAH staged another campaign, putting up 100 posters across Warsaw with the slogan: 'What are you staring at, dyke/faggot?' A month later, they were changed to portraits of young lesbian and gay people with statements such as 'Dyke/faggot! I hear it every day. Hate hurts.' According to CAH:

> initially the aim of this campaign was to cause in viewers the feeling of being attacked, insulted. We wanted in this very symbolic way, to let others feel what is usually felt by persons to whom those words – faggot, dyke – are addressed.

The second stage, aimed to show that lesbians and gays are an integral part of
Polish society. That they have always been here. That we love and respect them,
that they are in our families, among our friends. (Szpak 2007: 9)

This campaign was accompanied by the exhibition called 'Homophobia, that's
what it looks like', at the Austrian Cultural Center in Warsaw (4–15 March
2007). This exhibition consisted of pictures, press cuttings/releases and videos
illustrating instances of homophobia in Poland. According to the exhibition
catalogue, it shows 'how homophobia looks in Poland, how it is expressed and
what kind of consequences it has for gays, lesbians, bisexuals and transgender
people in Poland'.

So, coming back to my initial question: what kind of representational politics
should the Polish LGBT movement strive for? I would like to show that the
answers are not as easy as they seem at first sight. Both campaigns would seem to
take an identitarian approach, as other activities do. For example, LGBT Prides
are never called 'Gay Pride parades' but rather 'marches for tolerance' or 'equality
parades' etc. This could be seen as a closeted strategy of not naming what it is, not
daring to speak its name. But maybe the opposite is true? Maybe by doing this they
try to summon everybody who is in favour of the idea or aim, without having to
define their interest group from the very beginning. Thus it could be an example of
what Judith Butler once called 'coalitional politics' (Butler 1992)? As such, what
is queer and what is not may differ and may depend on local contexts.

'Let Them See Us' was perceived by its opponents as highly provocative. It
recalled emancipatory strategies of the US gay and lesbian identity movement
from the 1960s and 1970s, showing that 'we are everywhere', we are like all other
people, citizens etc. 'What Are you Staring At, Dyke/Faggot?', conversely, seems
to resemble queer politics, with its 'in-your-face' attitudes and attempts to reclaim
insulting names. At the same time it pertains to a rigid binary system with its narrow
focus, making it unapproachable for bi- and trans- people. With both examples we
can see young, middle-class, intellectual (students or academics) men and women,
and this has been widely criticised by queer scholars in Poland. Also I have my
doubts about them; but on the other hand, can those two campaigns be read from
a more queer perspective? Or perhaps the binary 'either/or' description just does
not fit the case?

On the level of representation, we saw a narrow and traditional approach
to gender ('masculine boys and men' and 'feminine women and girls'). But on
the level of description (leaflets) we read that the second campaign was to fight
homophobia, including the problems of bisexual and transgender people. So
'homophobia' here stands for hate of all who transgress the binary gender/sex/
sexuality order. It may be too general and subsuming bi- and trans- under the
homo- dominance, but not necessarily so in Polish reality, where all people who
do not fit into a rigid gender binary system – be they gays, lesbians, bisexuals,
transsexuals, transgenders – are called freaks, dykes, faggots interchangeably.

Using 'homophobia' as an umbrella term for all these prejudices makes sense in such circumstances.

Secondly, it shows that the Polish gay and lesbian movement is aware of discrimination against other than homosexual people. And it is not accidental that the movement often calls itself LGBT, even if B and T act as empty signifiers of a more desired presence. It shows that Polish emancipatory LGBT identity politics can differ from the Western/American 'model' because it developed only after 1989, learning from the mistakes of this model – thus being seemingly more inclusive. Also in terms of the strategies used by CAH they might be 'more queer'.

Queer Asynchrony and Its Consequences

So far, I have tried to demonstrate that CAH activism cannot be easily classified and analysed by using Western theoretical tools that are attuned to different geotemporal circumstances. The concepts of *temporal disjunction* and *asynchrony* (knotting/looping time) that we suggest as a useful way of thinking about this geotemporal difference (see Mizielińska and Kulpa in this volume) is also connected to the question of the split/hybrid LGBT identity. Linear time means linear narration of the movement (from A to B), which produces as a consequence an impression of a coherent identity (in this case, construction of identity within the movement of the 1970s precedes its deconstruction in the early 1990s). In the Polish case, since there is no longitudinal narration, hence the lack of impression of coherence: in a sense a deconstruction coincides with the construction. The same moment marks all.

Zygmunt Bauman, in his analysis of identity, refers to the famous distinction made by Paul Ricoeur, according to which identity consists of two elements: *ipse* (self) and *idem* (same) (Bauman 2007: 15; Ricoeur 1992). The former refers to the need for differentiation (i.e. how unique we are in relation to others). The latter is the continuity of oneself in time, a feeling of remaining the same within time (*idem, la memete*). If we apply this distinction to the Polish LGBT movement we can see that it has problems with its *idem*, its continuity and cohesion within time: its sameness. So its narration about identity cannot become consistent and continuous. Marked by this lack from the very beginning, the Polish LGBT(Q) movement tries to build its identity by taking bits and pieces from all kinds of discourses. Driven by the contemporary demand to construct an identity, the movement's activity becomes a battlefield between – as much as a cross-examination of – those sometimes randomly chosen strategies. This disjunction/crossover/coincidence must necessarily become problematic at certain points, not only for people in CEE, who are trying to 'catch up with' the West, but also for Western communities who see CEE as 'lagging behind' or dragging 'progress' down. I would like to analyse some of the consequences of this 'temporal disjuncture' which, in my opinion, occurs on three levels: (1) identity and naming, (2) stage of development and (3) knowledge production.

Questions of Identity/Naming

In the American historical narratives of the LGBT movement we are dealing with a 'proper' sequence that departs from essentialistm: the homophile 1950s and 1960s, through the gay and lesbian quasi-ethnic model in the 1970s, arriving at the non-identitarian (or less identitarian and more inclusive) queer/LGBT model in the 1990s. We can see this kind of narration in almost all books on LGBT studies (e.g. Jagose 1996; Blasius and Phelan 1997; CLAG 2003).[5]

What happens when we apply this narrative to Poland, where everything happened almost simultaneously?[6] In the 1990s in Poland we dealt with the explosion of discourses that developed and were digested in the West gradually. So instead of a slow adoption of categories, names and ideas, we have had an eruption all at once. Instead of 'time of sequence' we have had 'time of coincidence'.[7]

One example is the self-naming of the movement as 'LGBT' almost from the very beginning. Unlike in the West – where transgender and bisexual groups had a long history of struggle for inclusion within lesbian and gay politics (LG to LGBT) (Meyerowitz 2002; Gamson 1996) – 'bisexuality' and 'transgender' were included alongside lesbian and gay politics beforehand, discursively, without any signals from bisexuals and transsexuals claiming their rights to be included. This 'inclusion before coming-into-being' occurred because of the different temporalities of the West and CEE. Activists in CEE adopted labels already in use in the West, even if they did not denote their new reality.

Let us look at CAH's website as an example, to understand what B and T stand for. First of all there is a huge and significant difference in the self-description in Polish and English. The main difference concerns the question of whom CAH represents and helps. In the English version we have a reference to LGBT people:

> The Campaign Against Homophobia (CAH) is a nationwide public-benefit nongovernmental organization with non-profit status working for the equal rights of lesbian, gay, bisexual and transgender people. ... CAH specializes

---

5   For instance in 'Queer Ideas: The David Kessler's Lectures in Lesbian and Gay Studies' one can read: 'LGBTQ studies has its origins in gay activism that marks its symbolic birth with the Stonewall uprising of 1969' (CLAG 2003: 7).

6   This brings the CEE case closer to post-colonial discourses on sexuality. For instance Liang-Ya Liou, in her article 'Queer Theory and Politics in Taiwan', writes that the concepts of 'gay' 'lesbian' and 'queer' were introduced there in 1990 at the same time. This questions the Western narrative of progress from 'old' gay and lesbian politics to the 'new' LGBT (Liou 2005). One has also to take into account that what is perceived as a Western narrative very often conceals a specifically American perspective. For instance in the Nordic countries the success of the gay and lesbian movement in promoting same-sex partnership legislation pre-dates the import of the concept of queer theory/practice in the region, and is contrasted with the unsuccessful gay and lesbian politics in the US (Wickman 2010).

7   I use the term 'time of coincidence' after Boellstorff (2007).

in organizing large social awareness and educational campaigns aiming at integrating LGBT people into society. These include the poster campaign and photo exhibition 'Let Them See Us' or the annual 'Queer May' festival in Krakow. (CAH 2010)

In the Polish version of the same page, after the first identical introductory paragraph there is a much longer description where 'LGBT' is replaced by 'gays' and 'lesbians' or 'homosexuals'. Sometimes 'bi-' is added:

We are promoting tolerance, fighting with prejudices and stereotypes about bi and homosexuals; forming positive identities of bi and homosexual people. We deal with education, research activity, social integration, activity for women and counteracting gender discrimination ... CAH specializes in organising big social and educational campaigns that present homosexual people in positive light ... We are lobbing towards a respect of gay and lesbian rights on national and international scale ... CAH constantly looks for new ways of increasing tolerance and social inclusion of gays and lesbians. Volunteers and activists of CAH are known from their motivation, engagement, sacrifice, pertinacity and consequence in terms of their work towards inclusion of bi and homosexual people to the society and promotion attitudes free of prejudices. (CAH 2010)

When we look under different bookmarks (e.g. 'Education' or 'Find out what it's like to be LGBT in Poland') we can read only about gays and lesbians. Under 'My rights' a link takes us to a separate website (http://www.mojeprawa.info) that has been set up to inform LGBT people of their legal rights in Poland. But on this site also information relates only to gays and lesbians. Bi- and trans- people, although discursively invoked, remain virtually non-existent, with their specific problems not being acknowledged at all.

This split between naming and the lack of actual inclusion of bisexual and transgender interests/needs into CAH aims/mission raises the question of false representation. This becomes especially apparent when comparing the English and Polish content of the website, where the English one seems to be more attuned to Western readers, and hence more 'B' and 'T' friendly. This could be interpreted as an attempt to 'catch up with the West', explained by financial necessity (i.e. it is easier to get funds on international forums) but also as a way to be open and inclusive 'beforehand' (learning from Western experiences) even if only in the naming. Until recently, there was no transgender or bisexual activity in Poland, and the letters 'T' and 'B' were empty signifiers. This changed quite recently when the group Trans-Fuzja was established in 2007 (2008 as a formal group). Some activities started in cooperation between the two organisations (and some other newly established queer organisations such as Unidentifying Flying Abject – UFA). But one must note that Trans-Fuzja does not (over)use in its naming letters that it does not attempt to represent/include in its activities. The bisexual movement therefore remains unknown.

One of the events that demonstrate a recent growing cooperation between CAH and Trans-Fuzja is the Festival of Rainbow Families (16 February 2009), which aimed to show the diversity of families/relationships that people create in the contemporary world. A large part of the festival was indeed devoted to transgender issues (e.g. workshops on the transgender family, debates on family, transsexuality and law; looking at the Polish legislative system; a screening of the movie *Transparent*). Also, in the CAH bi-monthly magazine, *Replika*, there is an attempt to include transgender and bisexual issues. For instance, alongside homosexual and lesbian coming out stories they published an interview with Anna Grodzka called 'Trans coming out' (no. 21, 2009); and from time to time shorter articles and representations of transgender people appear there. Bisexual issues are far less frequent. For instance, one issue of *Replika* (no. 5, 2006) was advertised as being devoted to bisexuals but contained only one article on this topic. So we can conclude that 'bi' is still an empty signifier. But why is this so?

Such lack of consideration for bi- people by lesbian and gay organisations creates an urgent problem. A recent report by Krzeminski on the situation of Polish gays and lesbians shows huge antipathy, lack of trust and even aversion towards bisexuals (2009: 88). This indicates a need for education and training not only for the Polish homophobic society, but also for lesbian and gay communities. The same report confirms my claims that one cannot measure Polish LGBT by Western standards and time scales. In contrast to the Western LGBT movement the conflict there between lesbians and gays is much weaker. Also there is no gay/straight split or tension between the Polish LGBT and feminist movements (Krzeminski 2009: 88), and the two see each other rather as partners in fighting sexism and homophobia in Poland.

Questions of Stage/Development

In the 'Western' (although mostly American) context the history of 'queer' is rooted in AIDS politics and in opposition to gay liberation of the 'Stonewall' era, which has no equivalent in Poland. However, the American model stands as a universal model of development, where American and Polish activists expect that LGBT movements in CEE countries will follow the same trajectory of development.[8] This raises the question: how does this model foreclose full recognition of separate histories of LGBT movements and of sexuality studies in different countries? Should we follow it and go through the 'necessary preliminaries' of creating a similar form of gay social group identity in order to contest and deconstruct it afterwards? If 'queer' relates to – and presumably rejects – the identitarian politics of the Stonewall era (Jagose 1996), what is left of 'queer' in the CEE context, where

---

8   For example many Polish activists and academics suggest that we are still waiting for 'our Stonewall', or have just had it (i.e. Sypniewskis and Warkocki 2004), or use it as a label (as with the Lambda Warsaw Association naming its small grants fund a 'Stonewall Fund').

no Stonewall ever happened, where it stands as an empty signifier, a meaningless figure, yet still a pervasive and monumental reference?

One of the most important questions is whether it is possible to do 'queer' theory/politics without this historical baggage. Is it possible to do non-identitarian politics (Western model of queer) without first going through the stage of identity politics? And as much as these are open questions without a definite answer, I would like to contextualise them and focus more on the 'cultural translation' of queer in the context of CAH. I have analysed this above, in relation to CAH's two campaigns, and showed how context-specific locations can influence the notion of 'essentialist' and 'queer'. Below, I will concentrate on the two most recent projects: 'Coming out' actions (2008 and 2009) and CAH Queer Studies (from 2008).

The 'coming out' project seems to be part of a larger educational purpose and as such it follows on from the 'I am gay, I am lesbian' educational CAH campaign that was carried out in 2003. It is mostly presented on the webpage http://www.homoseksualizm.org.pl[9] run by the CAH Youth Group and in the series of 'coming out' interviews in *Replika* magazine. On the webpage of CAH Youth, one of its aims is stated as being to encourage and facilitate coming out. The group organised 'The Day of Coming Out' in 2009, a year after the 'We are coming out' action, with significant support from other lesbian and gay organisations and from the *Gazeta Wyborcza* newspaper (which published letters and interviews about coming out in Poland in June 2008 before the annual Equality Parade in Warsaw). Both the printed series of interviews and the stories published on the webpage constructed a specific and constraining 'coming out narration'[10] that excluded a significant number of people. This was also noted by some of the 'ordinary people' in their responses (Gazeta Wyborcza 2008), and not only by academics. 'Coming out' as a strategy promoted by CAH is also seen in every issue of *Replika*, which contains 'coming out' interviews with well-known gays and lesbians.

In any case, as a result we have a strong notion of essentialised sexual identity, around which the group identity is being constructed. In addition, an 'LGBT genealogy' is constructed in *Replika*'s pages: e.g, Krzysztof Tomasik outing Polish medieval King Boleslaw II Smiały (Tomasik 2006: 20). Tomasik is also the author of a recently published book, *Homobiografie* (2009), in which he writes about Polish writers who, in his opinion, were 'hidden homosexuals'. Although he has proven elsewhere to be aware of the constructedness of homosexuality as a category, his insensitivity is bold. Also the fact that the category of bisexuality is largely neglected or even ridiculed (as in the case of Gombrowicz or

---

9   The webpage in itself is a very interesting exemplification of an inclusive/exclusive mixture of ideas. It contains highly essentialist ideas about what is like to be a lesbian (e.g. 'Why it is worth being a lesbian' or '10 things that every lesbian should stop doing') next to texts on intersexuality or transsexuality. Also since October 2009 it has cooperated with Trans-Fuzja and co-organises events such as the already mentioned Rainbow Family Festival.

10   Closet, pain and dissatisfaction of a 'hidden lie', coming out, some obstacles in the process but ultimate reward at the end, joy and happiness of 'open life'.

Iwaszkiewicz), and treated as a way to hide one's supposedly 'true' homosexual identity is noticeable.

In this way, CAH maintains and strengthens the essentialist notion of identity and also becomes a gatekeeper of its very strict definition. In doing so, CAH ignores the more disruptive queer approach that undermines the homo/hetero dichotomy, becoming a 'guardian of gayness' as in 'coming out interviews'. Those who 'refused' it for many reasons were punished and accused of being in the closet; for example, Jacek Dehnel, a prominent Polish writer who rejected the offer from *Replika* although publicly mentioning his boyfriend on a much broader forum in *Gazeta Wyborcza*. But it seems that for the editors of *Replika* those who said it in a different way, in different media, did not say it at all. Their punishment was the publication of 'an interview that has never happened', sarcastically called 'I won't tell I am gay' (7/2007).

Perceived this way, 'coming out' and the revelation of one's homosexual identity becomes an exemplification of the outside/inside figure described by Diana Fuss. Instead of problematising the notion of homosexuality and heterosexuality as both products of the same knowledge/power system and acknowledging their mutual co-dependence, CAH concentrates on developing essentially understood identity. But in doing so, it strengthens the whole homo/hetero dichotomy and the privileged position of heterosexuality (Fuss 1991; Phelan 1994; Foucault 1995). This ignores and omits all those who transgress the mutually exclusive homo/ hetero borders. It is no surprise, therefore, that the question of bisexuality is left out as it disintegrates/blurs those clear notions.

At the same time, while publishing *Replika* and promoting coming out, CAH organised the first Polish 'Queer Studies' course, consisting of 'traditional' lesbian and gay studies but also 'queer theory'. However, it is hard to judge the content from the description. For instance, it is hard to say whether the courses entitled 'Social situation of bi- and homosexuals in Poland' (Marta Ambramowicz) or 'International law and LGBT' (Krzysztof Smiszek) really address the problems of bisexuality or are just another type of misuse of naming. The whole programme seems to be very inclusive. One can also notice the presence of courses run by Polish scholars who for years have been trying to introduce queer theory into the Polish context, such as Jacek Kochanowski ('Introduction to queer social theory') or Tomasz Basiuk ('AIDS representation in Polish and American cultures'). Worth noticing is the presence of courses on gender stereotypes run by well-known Polish feminists. This again confirms the close cooperation between LGBT and feminist circles.

Interesting also is the example of *Replika* magazine. On the one hand, it explains queer theory in academic terms with the voices of Polish queer writers (Basiuk, Kochanowski). On the other hand, it contradicts itself with 'anonymous' voices (editorial?) who neglect and ignore the academic explanation. The concern is about 'queer' being 'new closet', hiding one's sexual identity[11] (which is 'against' *Replika*'s strong promotion, if not imposition, of 'coming out').

Is an answer about sexual orientation such as 'I don't like to define myself' a queer one or the voice from the closet? How to differentiate between them? Does behind this unwillingness to define oneself stand a true impossibility of univocally sexual self-definition or fear of homophobia and self-denial of one's homo- or bisexuality? This is my problem with queer theory (*Replika* no. 17/2009).

This shows a gap between knowledge of what queer theory is about, and the assumption that it can (not) be applied to Polish practices or translated into certain radical political activities. Especially problematic for me is how in the above example queer theory has been equalised (and simplified) with the position of being in the closet. Of course one can also blame Polish queer theorists for not trying hard enough to introduce queer and then explain the radicalism of queer theory projects, which resulted in the lack of translation of political queer practices (Mizielińska 2007).

The accusation of queer (theory) as being another modern closet seems to be more and more popular among Polish gay and lesbian activists. For example, Anna Laszuk, editor-in-chief of the recently reactivated *Furia* magazine, published an article provocatively entitled 'A Modern Closet or About Queer in Polish' (Laszuk 2009).[12] Her call for political efficiency stands in opposition to the lack of recognition for, or even ignorance of, the problem of exclusion and hierarchisation within the LGBT community. According to her, undermining the notion of a strict and coherent gender and sexual identity queer theory weakens the Polish LGBT movement:

> So instead of undermining [an] already weak LGBT movement from within in the argument over gender and sexuality categories, maybe we should express diversity within the movement? Win a space, instead of moving back to snobbish marginality. Community of gays, lesbians, bisexual, transsexuals and transgenders suffers less if only one is excluded; and more because of its small size, fear and apathy of all those who are not politically engaged. (Laszuk 2009, 74)

---

11   Worth noticing here is the lack of differentiation between queer theory/practice and its use of the term queer that has an interesting genealogy of its own as an umbrella term and the misuse and commercialisation of the term queer that is observed worldwide – where queer is shorthand to refer to gays and lesbians. Moreover, in the Polish context queer has a far less radical connotation and is very often used because it serves as a safe word, whereas 'gay' or 'lesbian' do not. I have written extensively on this in my book and articles. See Mizielińska 2007, 2010.

12   It seems ironic that in the new version and first number of the magazine – which I used to co-edit with Olga Stefaniuk 1997–2000 and which published the first articles on queer theory in Polish (a whole issue devoted to queer theory and practice with a translation of Butler's and Fuss's canonical texts) – appears an article that shows such a misunderstanding.

Her words, however, contrast meaningfully with those by Aleksandra Sowa, who in the same issue claims that discrimination of bisexuals by homosexuals is an important internal problem of the Polish LGBT movement and postulates either serious inclusion of bisexuality or omitting the letter 'B' from the official naming:

> If we agree for inclusion of the bisexual minority into the abbreviation that shows the direction of our activity, if we talk about creating a space for discussion about discrimination of sexual minorities, we should fulfil. Not because of the sense of obligation but because of the real conviction of the fact that breaking stereotypes and myths that we create is necessary for discussing the problems of non-heterosexual people and not their idealised pictures. In any case, we should omit B not to be hypocritical. But we should take into account that so castrated LGBT won't be the same. (Sowa 2009: 62)

So we can see a split attitude within the same organisations, or sometimes the same people or magazines. In practice, however, most Polish activists think that 'coming out' and identity politics built around the naturalised concept of one's sexual identity (biological/given) are more accurate and successful political strategies. 'In-your-face politics' and the anti-identity approach that queer theory offers seem not only less appealing but also largely misunderstood as reproducing the closet. The example of CAH activism illustrates a much broader tendency and reflects the previously mentioned mixture of ideas taken from queer theory (or hidden under this term) or/and from traditional gay and lesbian studies. What is worrying is the fact that one can see a growing split between theory and practice. That is, queer theory is perceived by some only as a useful theoretical approach and some of its concepts enter the mainstream (i.e. heteronormativity), but more often as academic snobbery and/or an excuse not to be involved in politics (see Laszuk 2009). So the radicalism of queer practice is largely misunderstood or neglected.[13]

In general, in LGBT practice, the identitarian approach dominates and the construction of group identity is centred on a clearly defined core. As such, identity politics is perceived as a necessary step to gain equal rights. But one must also ask whether it is the same identity politics as in the Western/American past? If we refer to Judith Butler's idea of performative repetitions (she had in mind gender norms but I think it could be broadened to any repetitive acts), the possibility of change/ subversion is always already contained there. Even if we repeat certain steps in Poland we might do it differently (Butler 1990). 'Time never dies. The circle is not round' (Manchevski 1994). What is repeated within the Polish LGBT movement uncovers the falsity of the origin and shows the particularity of one model, which becomes not *the one* but just one of many. It helps to see the US/Western model as an accidental one, which does not mark the general and universal pattern. It questions the very origin of the 'Real'. The Polish case clearly demonstrates that in their daily struggles and self-representations LGBT people have used and

---

13   The same problem is noticed by Wickman in the Nordic context (Wickman 2010).

connected (perhaps even played with) different types of rhetorical tools (referring to EU standards, rights-based 'Rainbow flag' discourse and queer theory/politics) that complicate our way of thinking about 'queer global progress narrative' and 'CEE belatedness'.

Questions of Knowledge Production and Transmission: Whose Voice Counts?

The hegemonic temporality of the West is connected to the hegemony of knowledge production by queer theorists. One can see it in many publications where the Western time and space paradigm is taken for granted and perceived as general – for example, in Annamarie Jagose's *Introduction to Queer Theory* (1996), Wiliam B. Turner's *A Genealogy of Queer Theory* (2000) or Nikkie Sullivan's *A Critical Introduction to Queer Theory* (2003). These and other publications hardly touch on other cultures apart from Anglo-American; and if they do, these 'others' are usually token examples. Occasionally, a collection of essays from randomly chosen countries (usually post-colonial) under the heading of a 'global' or 'transnational' perspective appears (e.g. Hawley 2001; Cruz-Malave and Manalansan 2002). One such book reflecting North American hegemonic scholarship is *The Global Emergence of Gay and Lesbian Politics: National Imprints of a Worldwide Movement* (Adam, Duyvendar and Krouwal 1999), where all articles have approximately 20 pages, except for the USA, which has 61 pages. At the end, the editors compare all countries, but do not reflect upon the model of their comparison. In fact, the book was about the 'universal' American movement, which has been seen as a model for other national variations which are perceived to be at different stages of development.

Another example is found in Donald Hall's *Queer Theories*, where the author notices the limited geographical scope of the book. Yet still, in a very short passage called 'Queery', although he lists some 'other' examples, Hall finishes as follows: 'While such works are (unfortunately, but inevitably) peripheral to the present study because of its focus on British and American literature and applications of critical theory, they are provocative and commendable. *Read them when you have time*' (Hall 2003: 50, my italics). These examples show the American hegemony of time and space, and set its teleological development as 'universal' and 'ultimate'. Others are perceived as the derivation of such a model, without recognising their heterogeneity. This raises questions about how artificially constructed is the field of LGBT and queer studies around the world, and by which parameters is the development of those studies/movements measured.

What is surprising for me is that it happens also in texts discussing queer time and space. While problematising heterotemporality, Western scholars very often (re)produce a Western homonormative timeline. They take for granted what has happened/is happening in their geotemporality (and it does not even have to be national; it can be regional, state or even city based) and theorise about it as if it were universal. Lee Edelman's already 'canonised' book, *No Future: Queer Theory and the Death Drive* (2004), serves as an example.[14]

In a roundtable discussion on queer temporalities, Carolyn Dinshaw tried to envision the project where 'different nonlinear temporalities might meaningfully be brought together figuring out how to make heterogeneity analytically powerful' (Dinshaw 2007: 186). She writes that 'one way of making the concept of temporal heterogeneity analytically salient and insisting on the present's irreducible multiplicity is to inquire into the felt experience of asynchrony ... Such feelings can be exploited for social and political reasons' (Dinshaw 2007: 191). Perceived from this perspective, Poland/CEE could be an exemplification of such asynchrony and anachronism, and as such 'viewed as a queer phenomenon' (Freeman 2007: 163). It symbolises an expended 'now' in which past, present and future do not follow one after another in an already Western-defined sequence, but coincide and coexist. It/they question/s the teleology of progress and the construction of history as a linear development. This recalls the figure of Walter Benjamin's Angel from *Theses on the Philosophy of History* (1969: 262). The Angel is 'blown backwards' and sees time not as a sequence of events (past, present, future) but in the full light of a sudden epiphany. Catastrophe is what we often call progress.

Also Judith Butler in her recent book *Frames of War*, while criticising the use of the hegemonic concepts of progress, refers to the writings of Walter Benjamin's graphic rethinking of time. In doing so, she wants to stress that 'there can be no consideration of sexual politics without a critical consideration of the time of the now ... Thinking through the problem of temporality and politics in this way may open up a different approach to cultural difference, one that eludes the claim of pluralism and intersectionality alike' (Butler 2009: 103). She wants not only to make readers aware of the temporal and spatial presuppositions of some progressive narratives, but also of how they restrict other possibilities of realising sexual politics. Therefore, Butler describes the time of sexual politics as a 'fractious constellation' (2009: 104). The figure of 'fractious constellation' of time, where progress is just one of many strands (perhaps also in crisis), seems to be a much more open and inclusive operationalisation, especially when compared to hegemonic narrative of 'progress'. 'Fractious constellation' resembles the figure of 'time of coincidence' which I use to broaden the scope of sexual temporalities in different cultural locations (see Mizielińska and Kulpa in this volume).

While writing this chapter and trying to confront Western queer theory with the CEE locality, I have realised how difficult it is to avoid preconceptions about LGBT development around the world. 'We' all name American tools, concepts, linear narration of temporality as 'ours'. But are they truly ours? What do they obscure and what do they silence in different histories of sexuality? I have constantly struggled with relaying Polish data to produce knowledge, as well as addressing the constant need/attempt to collect enough Western/American theory to support my argument and make it more 'reliable'. It is because I have internalised the idea

---

14   See Mizielińska and Kulpa in this volume for further critique of this book.

that it is expected of me to reproduce *the* theory, not to produce one; although it was exactly what I wanted to avoid. This experience is excellently described by Renata Salecl's *The Spoils of Freedom: Psychoanalysis and Feminism after the Fall of Socialism*:[15]

> What does a feminist intellectual from Eastern Europe have to say about the issues addressed by contemporary critical theory? Could such an intellectual speak from a purely theoretical position, or must his or her position be marked by the course of events that happened in his or her own country? ... Whenever I was invited to speak at a Western university I was always expected to speak about what was going on in Eastern Europe. Even the most abstract theoretical paper I delivered provoking questions such as 'How are things for women in Eastern Europe?' In a way, there is a special kind of prejudice at work in this attitude of Western intellectuals. If, for example, Western feminists speak about feminism, they can discuss such abstract issues as 'women in film noir', 'the notion of the phallus in feminist theory', etc.; but someone coming from Eastern Europe must speak about the situation of women in her own country. (Salecl 1994: 1–2)

So I would like to perceive this text also as part of a much broader project that calls not only for de-centralisation or de-Westernalisation/Americanisation of queer theory – and recognition of the heterogeneity of CEE (and also the complexity of both Western and Eastern) sexualities – but also for the courage to do queer locally, which means to build a theory which is more suitable to our practice.

Conclusion

As I have tried to show, it is difficult to classify/define Polish LGBT politics using Western/American measurements of time and space. This approach seems to be concerned with identity issues, but also tries/pretends to be inclusive and open to all willing to fight against heteronormativity. So, perhaps we should think about this identity politics from a different angle. Tuija Pulkinnen, Finnish philosopher and queer theorist, asked an important question about my essay on queer theory in Poland during its presentation in 2004: Is identity politics possible outside the essentialist framework of 'sameness'? She claimed that collective identities in politics are needed; therefore she would rather call for their different conceptualisations. I think it corresponds with Judith Halberstam's warning in *In a Queer Time & Place* against the blanket dismissal of identity politics by

---

15   I have also described this problem in my text 'Is Queer Theory Always Already American' pointing out that many Eastern but also less-Western (i.e. Finnish in the described case) scholars experienced an attitude that they should reproduce the theory, not build it, and in doing it they should prove the rightness of American thinking (Mizielińska 2010).

intellectuals on the left. She suggests that various communities use different methods to make room for themselves in a crowded world (Halberstam 2005: 20). Halberstam's point is to subvert this false logic of 'either/or' and move beyond the rigid binary division. She quotes Steve Pile: 'the subjects of resistance are neither fixed nor fluid, but both and more. And this 'more' involves a sense that resistance is resistance to both fixity and to fluidity' (Pile quoted in Halberstam 2005: 21). Also Judith Butler, in *Undoing Gender*, warns us against the false logic of the dichotomy when she writes about international human rights. Her point is that we must find a way between the universal and the particular; between reductive relativism, which does not allow us to make any universal claim, and the dangerous generalisation: 'We must follow a double path in politics: we must use this language to assert an entitlement to conditions of life in ways that affirm the constitutive role of sexuality and gender in political life and we must also subject our very categories to critical scrutiny' (Butler 2004: 37).

Finally, I want to come back to my point that history is not linear – in itself not a novel one (see e.g. Jenkins 1997). Emancipation/s go/es its/their own way/s in various countries. We cannot translate stages of Western/American development on to other contexts without risking mistakes of not noticing local specialities (thus making the American model hegemonic). In Poland this linear narrative does not work because of lacking equivalents. In a way, in Poland everything happened at once, which also testifies in our favour. Forcing linear narrative is futile because it does not account for specific Polish history.[16] And because it prolongs Americo-centrism by elevating American history to the status of a universal pattern, it posits anything that happens in non-US contexts as its local, less ideal equivalent. This has been criticised heavily also in queer studies, but more broadly from a post-colonial perspective (e.g. Cruz-Malave and Manalansan 2002). I think we also need stronger 'European' critiques and problematisations, which this text aimed at encouraging.

References

Adam, Barry D., Jan Willem Duyvendar and Andre Krouwal, eds. 1999. *The Global Emergence of Gay and Lesbian Politics: National Imprints of a Worldwide Movement*. Philadelphia: Temple University Press.

Bauman, Zygmunt. 2007. *Tozsamosc: Rozmowy z Benedetto Vecchim*. Gdansk: GWP.

Benjamin, Walter. 1969. *Theses on the Philosophy of History or on the Concept of History: Illuminations*. New York: Schocken Books.

---

16   The same can be true of a feminist movement in Poland and the false attempts by some Polish feminists to look at it by translating the concept of feminist waves (first, second and third) to describe Polish specificity.

Blasius, Mark, and Shane Phelan, eds. 1997. *We Are Everywhere: A Historical Sourcebook of Gay and Lesbian Politics*. New York: Routledge.

Boellstorff, Tom. 2007. 'When Marriage Falls: Queer Coincidences in Straight Time'. *GLQ* 13:2–3: 227–48.

Butler, Judith. 1990. *Gender Trouble: Feminism and the Subversion of Identity*. London and New York: Routledge.

———. 1992. 'Contingent Foundations: Feminism and the Question of "Postmodernism"'. In *Feminists Theorize the Political*, eds Judith Butler and Joan W. Scott. London and New York: Routledge, 3–22.

———. 2003. *Bodies That Matter*, London and New York: Routledge.

———. 2004. *Undoing Gender*. London and New York: Routledge.

———. 2009. *Frames of War: When is Life Grievable?* London and New York: Verso.

(CAH) Campaign Against Homphobia. 2010. http://www.kph.org.pl (accessed: 20 January 2010).

(CLAG) Center for Lesbian and Gay Studies, CUNY. 2003. 'Queer Ideas. The David R. Kessler Lectures in Lesbian and Gay Studies'. New York: The Feminist Press at the City University of New York.

Cruz-Malave, Arnaldo and Martin F. Manalansan IV, eds. 2002. *Queer Globalization: Citizenship and the Life After Colonialism*. New York: New York University Press.

Dinshaw, Carolyn. 2007. 'Theorizing Queer Temporalities: A Roundtable Discussion'. *GLQ* 13:2–3: 177–96.

Duggan, Lisa. 2003. *The Twilight of Equality*. Boston: Beacon Press

Edelman, Lee. 2004. *No Future: Queer Theory and the Death Drive*. Durham, NC and London: Duke University Press.

Foucault, Michel. 1995. *Historia Seksualnosci*. Warsaw: Czytelnik.

Freeman, Elizabeth. 2007. 'Introduction'. *GLQ* 13:2–3: 159–76.

Fuss, Diana. 1991. *Inside/Out: Lesbian Theories, Gay Theories*. New York and London: Routledge.

Gamson, Joshua. 1996. 'Must Identity Movement Self-Destruct? A Queer Dilemma'. In *Queer Theory/Sociology*, ed. Steven Seidman. Oxford: Blackwell, 395–420.

Gazeta Wyborcza. June 2008.

Halberstam, Judith. 2005. *In a Queer Time & Place: Transgender Bodies, Subcultural Lives*. New York and London: New York University Press.

Hall, Donald. 2003. *Queer Theories*. New York: Palgrave Macmillan.

Hawley, John, ed. 2001. *Postcolonial, Queer: Theoretical Intersections*. Albany: State University of New York Press.

Jagose, Annamaria. 1996. *Queer Theory: An Introduction*. New York: New York University Press.

Jenkins, Keith, ed. 1997. *The Postmodern History Reader*. London: Routledge.

Krzeminski, Ireneusz, ed. 2009. *Naznaczeni: Mniejszosci seksualne w Polsce*. Warsaw: Instytut Socjologii UW.

Laszuk, Anna. 2009. 'Nowoczesny closet, czyli queer po polsku'. *Furia* 1:64–76.

Liou, Liang-Ya. 2005. 'Queer Theory and Politics in Taiwan: The Cultural Translation and (Re)Production of Queerness in and Beyond Taiwan Lesbian/ Gay/Queer Activism'. *NTU Studies in Language and Literature* 14: 123–54.

Long, Scott. 1999. 'Gay and Lesbian Movements in Eastern Europe: Romania, Hungary, and the Czech Republic'. In *The Global Emergence of Gay and Lesbian Politics: National Imprints of a Worldwide Movement*, eds Barry D. Adam, Jan Willem Duyvendar and Andre Krouwel, Philadelphia: Temple University Press, 242–66.

Majka, Rafal. 2009. 'Lewica bez etyki?' Feminoteka. http://www.feminoteka.pl (accessed: 12 March 2009).

Manchevski, Milcho. 1994. *Before the Rain* (film).

Meyerowitz, Joanne J. 2002. *How Sex Changed: A History of Transsexuality in the United States*. Cambridge, MA: Harvard University Press.

Mizielińska, Joanna. 2010. *Is Queer Always Already American? Basque and European Perspective on Cultural and Media Studies*, (ed.) Maria Pilar Rodriguez. Reno: Centre for Basque Studies and University of Nevada.

———. 2007. *Plec/cialo/seksualnosc. Od feminizmu do teorii queer*. Cracow: Universitas.

Muñoz, Estaban Jose. 2007. 'Cruising the Toilet: LeRoi Jones/Amiri Baraka, Radical Black Traditions, and Queer Futurity'. *GLQ* 13: 2–3, 353–67.

Muñoz, Estaban Jose. 2009. *Cruising Utopias: The Then and There of Queer Futurity*. New York: New York University Press.

Patton, Cindy. 1993. 'Tremble, Hetero Swine!' In *Fear of a Queer Planet: Queer Politics and Social Theory*, ed. Michael Warner. Minneapolis: University of Minnesota Press.

Phelan, Shane. 1994. *Getting Specific: Postmodern Lesbian Politics*. Minneapolis: University of Minnesota Press.

Ricoeur, Paul. 1992. *Tozsamosc osobowa. Filozofia osoby*. Cracow 1992: 33–44.

Rubin, S. Gayle. 1993. 'Thinking Sex: Notes for a Radical Theory of the Politics of Sexuality'. In *American Feminist Thought at Century's End*, ed. Linda S. Kauffman. Oxford: Blackwell, 3–64.

Salecl, Renata. 1994. *The Spoils of Freedom: Psychoanalysis and Feminism after the Fall of Socialism*. London and New York: Routledge.

Sowa, Aleksandra. 2009. 'O bi miedzy innymi'. *Furia* no. 1: 54–63.

Szpak, Agnieszka. 2007. 'Pedal, Lesba – nienawisc boli/Faggot, dyke – hate hurts'. *Replika* no. 7: 9.

Sullivan, Nickie. 2003. *A Critical Introduction to Queer Theory*. New York: New York University Press.

Tomasik, Krzysztof. 2006. 'Geje i lesbijki sprzed lat'. *Replika* no. 5: 20–21.

———. 2009. *Homobiografie*. Warsaw: Krytyka Polityczna.

Sypniewskis, Zbyszek and Blazej Warkocki. 2004. *Homofobia po polsku*. Warsaw: Wydawnictwo Sic!

Turner, B. Wiliam. 2000. 'A Genealogy of Queer Theory'. Philadelphia: Temple University Press.

Wickman, Jan. 2010. 'Queer Activism: What That Might Be?' *Trikster* no. 4. http://trikster.net/4/index2.html (accessed: 7 February 2010).

Chapter 6

Researching Transnational Activism around LGBTQ Politics in Central and Eastern Europe: Activist Solidarities and Spatial Imaginings

Jon Binnie and Christian Klesse

Introduction

In this chapter we examine the transnational dimensions of LGBTQ politics and activism in Poland. We draw on material from an empirical research project we have conducted on contemporary transnational activism and solidarities around gender and sexual politics in Poland, the data collection for which ran from April 2008 to June 2009. Our research focused on the links between activists from abroad and Polish groups and associations organising LGBTQ-oriented cultural and political events. For this purpose we participated in a variety of events (mainly cultural festivals and political demonstrations) and interviewed activists in Poland, Germany, the Netherlands, Belgium and the United Kingdom.

We address the question of whether the term 'solidarity' is suitable to conceive of elements of this activism and cooperation. We suggest that although solidarity discourses have been used by some of our research participants, this has not been generally the case. Moreover, solidarity discourses are complex, manifold and highly contextualised. We advance the argument that an understanding of transnational politics in Poland – and other Central and Eastern European (CEE) countries – is seriously limited by the operation of an East/West dichotomy. Binary thinking structures many features of current discourses on sexual politics in Central and Eastern Europe, including the dimension of temporality (manifested in the tropes of 'progress', 'democratisation', 'modernisation' and 'liberation'). Western European LGBTQ movements tend to be treated as the model case of an advanced political culture around gender and sexual equality, which has significant consequences for the conceptualisation of solidarity discourses in the field of transnational politics. Under the influence of an East/West binary, the notion of solidarity can sometimes be problematically understood to mean Western European activists acting 'in support' of struggles in Central and Eastern Europe. Such discourse then reinforces Western European cultural hegemony in sexual politics.

Many of our respondents in Poland did not use the language of solidarity or even questioned its relevance for the context of their activism. Others did refer to instances of practices of solidarity, but applied it to other and often quite specific forms of collaboration. In this chapter we draw on Krakow and Poznan based activists' narratives to examine the local and transnational dimensions of solidarity discourses. References to the transnational may not be the most salient feature in many of these understandings of solidarity. Yet, as we will argue throughout this chapter, the local itself tends to be constituted in transnational terms. This insight is obscured through evolutionist thinking along an East/West dichotomy, reinstalling the logic of the *national* in the trans*national*.

This chapter will proceed as follows: In the next section we will trace the main contexts for the project, and discuss how we undertook the research. We will then go on to reflect some of our main concepts and categories. We will channel this discussion towards the third section, a theoretical consideration of the question of solidarity, which is a key perspective in this chapter. The fourth section will analyse discourses on solidarity as they have been used by some research participants. In the conclusion we suggest that solidarity discourses both support and are supported by specific geopolitical imaginaries such as the notion of an East/West binary.

The Study

In 2007 we decided to work together on a joint research project focusing on the transnational dimensions of the struggles around lesbian, gay, bisexual and queer sexualities and transgender lives. Christian had just joined Manchester Metropolitan University, where Jon had been working for a longer period of time. We were looking for a joint project in which we could work on shared research interests. Jon had already conducted interviews with some international human rights campaigners who worked in LGB(T) politics in Central and Eastern Europe as part of his long-standing research interest in transnational sexuality studies (Binnie, 1997, 2004; Bell and Binnie, 2000). Christian's interest in sexual politics in Poland intensified through his experience of the debates at the conference 'Europe without Homophobia: Queer-in(g) Communities' at Wroclaw University in May 2004, one of the annual queer studies conferences which were held in Poland between 2000 and 2004 (Sikora, Basiuk and Ferens, 2008; Klesse, 2006).

At the time when we were discussing joint research opportunities there was a heightened public awareness in the UK and other Western European countries of the violent oppression of LGBTQ activism in Poland. This was due to the controversy around political demonstrations with an LGBTQ focus in the cities of Warsaw, Krakow and Poznan in the years 2004 and 2005, which led to the legal prohibition of some marches and violent attacks by far right groups on others (for details, see Törnquist-Plewa and Malmgren, 2007; Ferens, 2006; Gruszczynska, 2009; Kowalczyk, 2006; Warkocki, 2006; see also Mizielińska, this volume). These events were widely reported in the British media and occurred at a time of considerable anxiety in the UK around EU enlargement in 2004 and the growth of Polish migration to the UK. Furthermore, reports in the British media discussing the migration of Polish lesbians and gay men to the UK (Graham 2007) in response to the situation in Poland made us want to understand more about these processes and the relative importance of sexuality and economics in transnational migration. We observed the greater interest in Central and Eastern Europe in both the pink and the mainstream British media (see for instance Gilliver 2009; Ronson 2009; Watt 2006), and we were interested in exploring the impact that events in Poland had on the politics of groups and organisations campaigning around LGBTQ issues in the UK. We witnessed an increase in transnational links and exchanges focused on LGBTQ issues in Poland. For example, a delegation of activists from an organising group of the Culture for Tolerance Festival in Krakow talked about their work and the situation in Poland at the QueerUpNorth and the Get Bent festivals in Manchester in 2007. Also in Germany the growth of interest in Polish LGBTQ activism was noticeable. Like many of the activists from Western Europe we later interviewed in our project, we were drawn to conduct research in response to the political crisis around an escalating homophobic discourse in Polish politics since 2004. One of our research questions was whether these forms of cooperation can be understood in terms of 'solidarity'. If this is the case, in what discourses are these solidarities articulated? At the same time, we were wary of the evolutionist narratives that were used in the UK media to characterise the state of sexual politics in Central and Eastern Europe as being backward and lagging behind the West. In the context where the discourses on homophobia in Poland seemed overdetermined by the cultural, political and economic power relations in Europe (Kulpa 2009), we sought to understand the cultural frames organising solidarity discourses in transnational sexual politics and the political economy within which they were enacted.

In total we interviewed 35 activists in Poland, Germany, the Netherlands, Belgium and the United Kingdom. These included a wide range of activists from diverse backgrounds affiliated to different types of organisations: from professional LGB(T) rights organisations to queer anarchist groups; from those working in trade unions to those who were not affiliated to any formal organisation. We also participated in equality marches and cultural festivals in Warsaw and Poznan in 2008; the Krakow Culture for Tolerance Festival in 2008 and 2009; the Krakow Queer in May event in 2009, as well as the Krakow March for Tolerance in 2008 and 2009. In addition we took part in the 2007 Get Bent Festival in 2007 and the 2008 Queer Up North event (both in Manchester), as well as the 2009 Pink Saturday Event in The Hague. We also took part in international networking events of the Dutch Centre for Culture and Leisure (COC) and local organisations in The Hague and Arnhem in 2009. In addition we conducted archive research on Polish LGBTQ politics in the International Gay and Lesbian Information Centre and Archive (IHLIA) in Amsterdam. We have not yet systematically analysed the entirety of the interview transcripts, documents and field notes. In this chapter we present some preliminary thoughts and findings.

Terms, Concepts and Definitions

In the following section we briefly explain our understanding of some of the key concepts of categories which are repeatedly referred to in this chapter, namely the terms 'activism', 'transnational', 'LGBTQ' and 'queer'. We will then deal in closer detail with the concept of 'solidarity' in section 4. All these terms are problematic to the extent that they are based on assumptions and generalisations which cannot be categorically applied to the complex multinational, multi-issue and multistrategy political terrain we have been concerned with in this research project.

We use the term *activism* as shorthand to describe, or label, the actions of those people who contributed towards the realisation of the marches, festivals and other artistic and/or political events we studied. This may include assuming roles within the larger process of organisation of and participation in these events and actions. We apply the term further to people who consider themselves part of LGBTQ organisations, groups or initiatives (in Poland and other countries) or who cooperated with or supported the work of LGBTQ organisations, groups or initiatives in Poland – for example by creating or maintaining networks, exchanging information, sharing resources, raising funds etc. The term *activism* carries meanings relating to agency (Beger 2004), and it has been a prominent concept in research on various social movements, including social movements around gender and sexual diversity (Darnovsky, Epstein and Flacks 1995; Rahman 2000; Monro 2005).

However, not all the people we interviewed necessarily identified with this term, saw themselves as activists or saw their actions as being political. Some participants talked about their actions in terms such as 'friendship', saying that they took part in equality marches as an act of friendship in support of their friends. Others saw their actions as a form of labour in preference to activism, as activism suggested a level of radicalism they did not identify with, or wished to be associated with. We see activism as an inherently diverse category, which continuously reshapes our definitions of the political. We acknowledge that even in its deployment as an 'open category' it remains a problematic label for the actions of some research participants.

We use the term '*transnational activism*' to refer to all kinds of activism that cross or transcend the boundaries of nation-states or articulate modes of citizenship that cannot be contained in a model of 'national citizenship'. Our perspective on transnational activism aims at the globalised dimension of sexual and gender politics (both on the levels of interaction and intertextuality) and the multilayered character of active citizenship (cf. Yuval-Davis 1997; Werbner and Yuval-Davis 1999). This provides the rationality for our methodological choice to interview not only activists who reside in Poland, but also activists from other countries. The advantages of the *transnational* over *global* are that it acknowledges the resilience of the nation-state as a significant mediator of power in the regulation of the interconnections between the cultural, the political and the economic

(Ong 1999; Binnie 2004: 34–5). The fact that significant power remains attached to the nation-state or to multistate agencies such as the European Union (EU) is exemplified in the enabling or inhibiting effect of migration regulations and citizenship or residency laws for various forms of transnational activism. Yet there are also drawbacks of the term *transnational activism*. It reinforces the symbolic significance of the national in the conceptualisation of politics (cf. Malkki 1994). This may be at odds with some activists' intentions to consciously defy appeals to the nation-state in their activities. A further problem derives from an equation of the transnational with an international or 'cross-border' orientation of politics. This may obscure the fact that already local political initiatives are constituted through the transnational. That is the case with the networks we studied in North-Rhine Westphalia, where some of the key local activists originated from Poland; or in Krakow, where migrants from Germany and the USA were active in LGBTQ organisations. The *international* as a paradigm of the transnational becomes even more problematic if it is mapped along an East/West division represented through flows between Poland and Western European countries. If transnational activism is cast as 'solidarity work', all the cultural and political connotations of the East/West dichotomy get mobilised. From Western perspectives, the 'politics of solidarity' start to appear then as forms of 'support' for LGBTQ struggles in Poland. Our research demonstrates how reductionist such perspectives can be. Rather than a simple focus on transnational links between West and East, we came across a much more complex pattern of transnational flows. For instance we noted transnational exchanges within Central and Eastern Europe, between activists between Poland and the Czech Republic, Lithuania, Belarus and Ukraine. A number of Polish activists were highly mobile in transnational European space, and had spent a number of periods living, studying and working in Ireland, the UK and Belgium for instance. A number of the activists we interviewed, who lived in Krakow, had migrated there from abroad. Moreover, some activists based in Germany were themselves of Polish origin or background.

Our research is concerned with the transnational dimensions around lesbian, gay male, bisexual, transgender and queer politics, shortened to LGBTQ. We will refrain from a general or categorical definition of the various forms of activism we studied as LGBTQ. There is a range of problems with this practice of naming. First, it lends itself to essentialist readings. If we define activism in these terms, we risk feeding the assumption that it is lesbian, gay, bisexual, trans or queer people only who are engaging in this kind of activism. This renders invisible, for example, the participation of non-trans heterosexuals as a strong component of marches. If identity ascriptions are consciously avoided, the LGBTQ abbreviation still remains problematic since it suggests that there is an agenda that is common to the members of its various constituencies. It reinforces the notion of homogeneous communities at the heart of social movement activism. Moreover, it insinuates a common agenda between these constituencies. It thus symbolises easy alliances, which with regard to the B and the T are often not even aspired by political organisations that dedicate themselves primarily to a lesbian and gay male rights struggle (cf. Beger 2004; Erel et al. 2008). Despite these reservations, we have decided for pragmatic reasons to use variants of the acronym in this chapter. We will to do this in a contextualised and qualified way. This means we will not refer to an organisation or local event as Q or T or B if we do not see such a reference as being warranted.

We do not think it is appropriate to use *queer* as an umbrella term for all these various struggles either. This would conflict with our own understanding of queer and the manifold interpretations of it, which we have encountered in our research across various terrains of politics. Debates in the Anglo-American academy tend to focus on the problematic way queer is sometimes used as an umbrella term of a variety of non-heteronormative identity categories, as opposed to a resistance to the classification of acts and practices into fixed identity categories (Beger 2004). However, we need to recognise that there are significant cross-national differences in the meanings attached to queer (Duyvendak 1996; Beger 2004). Queer has certainly a strong resonance among quite a lot of people engaged in politics around LGBTQ issues in Poland. Yet different interpretations and usages of the term *queer* seem to prevail. Different understandings and deployments of queer may even commingle in the discourse of distinctive political actors, as Joanna Mizielińska's (2009) reading of Kampania Przeciw Homofobii/Campaign Against Homophobia (KPH/CAH) discourses clearly illustrates (see also her chapter in this collection). The fact that queer is not universally applied by activists in Poland, and the co-presence of various and competing interpretations of queer, provides sufficient reasons not to use the term in any generic manner. The same is the case for any other of the countries we researched in. In the remainder of the chapter we wish to focus on one key aspect of our project – namely the concept of solidarity, how it has been theorised in relation to sexual politics in Poland and how the concept was understood, articulated and deployed by the informants in our project.

Solidarity and Transnational Gender and Sexual Politics

Our pilot web-based research of international LGBT activism around events in Poland since 2004 showed the common use of the concept of *solidarity*. A particularly interesting case is the use of 'gay solidarnosc' by the main German lesbian and gay social and political organisation, the LSVD, to describe their activism regarding LGB(T) politics in Poland and other Central European countries. It symbolically affiliates these actions to Solidarnosc (Solidarity), the most influential anti-communist workers' movement in Poland throughout the 1980s. By using 'gay solidarnosc' the LSVD inscribes itself in historical memory, suggesting linguistic and historical familiarity and a shared interest and unity in struggle.

At the same time, in the critical literature on transnational sexual politics, the notion of global LGBT solidarity has been widely challenged and criticised for its ethnocentricity – insensitivity to cultural difference in the same way that the concept of global sisterhood has been challenged by postcolonial feminist scholars and activists (see for instance Mohanty 2003). The will by Western LGBT activists to act in solidarity with LGBT people elsewhere has been criticised for the imposition of Western values often reflecting a neo-colonial mindset (Haritaworn 2008; Haritaworn et al. 2008; Puar 2008). The notion of transnational solidarity is thus often seen as suspect.

We were therefore interested in examining empirically the transnational practices of Western European LGBT activist interventions in Poland. How were they seen by Polish LGBT activists? Postcolonial criticism has drawn attention to the ethnocentricity of Western LGBTQ politics, and the neo-colonial power relations that, for instance, characterise connections between activists in the UK and Zimbabwe (Phillips 1997; Stychin 2004). Postcolonial theory and criticism are now being deployed to understand and conceptualise the experiences of post-transition Central and Eastern Europe (see for instance Kuus 2004; Light and Young 2009), so we were concerned to understand how a postcolonial theoretical persepctive might help us in understanding the transnational politics of sexuality in Poland. By researching the experiences of activists who are differently located within the same transnational activist networks, we aimed to get a sense of what is 'good practice' in doing transnational activism, which could contribute to more effective, culturally sensitive cooperation. How do discourses on solidarity figure in transnational gender and sexual politics? Who is using what kind of solidarity discourses and to what ends? In the following we will delve into the tradition of solidarity theory in order to discern a suitable perspective for our project.

Solidarity in Social and Political Theory

Reflecting on academic discussions of solidarity, Jean Harvey notes (2007: 22): 'there seems to be no agreed upon meaning of the term "solidarity," nor even a clear consensus as to the kind of item it refers to. Is it an action, a motive, an attitude, a piece of political activism, or something else?' However one dominant framing of solidarity is that solidarity is assumed to designate mutual obligations to aid each other. Yet these positive obligations to act, according to Carol Gould, usually pertain to members of the community to which one belongs oneself (Gould 2007: 150). In its history, the term 'solidarity' thus has been defined mostly in terms of an 'intragroup solidarity'. The idea of intragroup solidarity is most nuanced in Émile Durkheim's notion of solidarity as the precondition for social cohesion, as the basic ties, which ground a sense of connectedness and make social forms functional (ibid.).

Durkheim (1964) distinguished between 'mechanical' and 'organic' solidarity. He reserved the first term for the relations in traditional and less differentiated societies. 'Organic solidarity' was supposed to capture the interdependent relations in larger (modern) social formations, which were marked by a significant division of labour. The Durkheimian model of organic solidarity – or 'social solidarity' in the words of Sally J. Scholz (2007) – could be used to map social relations on different levels, ranging from the 'domestic', through small face-to-face networks, to the regional or the national (Brunkhorst 2007; Gould 2007; Gould and Scholz 2007). It fosters the fellow-feeling within a certain group context. This notion of intragroup solidarity has often been called upon to promote policies and ethics, which may help sustain the cohesion of the nation-state. Social solidarity of this kind has been central to the process of nation building (Gellner 1983; Anthias and Yuval-Davis 1992). This is the point, where it left an imprint on civic forms of solidarity, which defined the relationship between the welfare state and its citizens. As we will argue later in more detail, racist and heteronormative practice may be well in tune with such kinds of solidarity. Due to the prominence of an intragroup orientation in modern (European) solidarity discourses, it is necessary to revise basic tenets of its discourse in order to conceive of transnational or global solidarities. Carol Gould (2007) proceeds in this direction by suggesting the concept of 'transnational network' solidarities.

Transnational Political and Networked Solidarities

Transnational activism may be theorised through a model of 'network solidarity', since network solidarity is understood to be based on plural solidarities (Gould 2007: 150). The term 'network' solidarity does not contain any preperceived assumptions on group membership or identification, and thus is distinct from older identity-based solidarity conceptualisations (ibid.: 159). People of diverse social positioning may partake in network solidarity groups or forms of activism, allowing for the enactment of various and overlapping forms of solidarity. Similar theories of solidarity have for a long time been promoted by anti-racist and anti-colonial feminist activists and scholars. Jacqui Alexander and Chandra Talpade Mohanty, for example, argue that global critical solidarities between women are only possible if they are based on a politics of conscious alliance building which takes account of the differential affects that current ideologies and politics in the neo-imperial capitalist world order have on women of different positioning and locations (Alexander and Mohanty 1997, in Bhavnani 1994).

Similar ideas are expressed in Sally J. Scholz's definition of 'political solidarity'. We think the notion of political solidarity has a strong relevance for our research, since it refers to forms of solidarity derived from shared commitment to a political project. It lends itself as a tool to think of cooperation and collective action in the context of social movements, since 'activism' is a central element of its practice. 'Activism is the public side of political solidarity', argues Scholz (2007: 45). 'Political solidarity' aims to affect social change. It is born out of a mutual commitment to a joint struggle to challenge injustice or oppression (cf. Mohanty 2003). It is thus possible to speak of political solidarity if individuals are prepared to form networks to pursue a political goal by various means of activism. The notion of 'shared interest' is relative and limited to the ambition to challenge certain modes of oppression or to pursue a path of liberation: 'it is the mutual commitment ... that forms the unity of solidarity, not shared feelings, experiences, identities or social locations' (Scholz 2007: 40). Political solidarity is thus represented as a form of coalition politics, which may include dissenting voices and disagreements (including ones regarding the definition of the political goals) (ibid.: 38).

We think that a generalised assumption of the 'mutuality' of commitment in coalitional struggles renders this certainly attractive vision of solidarity slightly over-euphemistic, subsuming it to an ultimately liberal understanding of the *political*.[1] The assumption of mutuality obscures to a certain extent the awareness of the various material differences and cultural hegemonies across which solidarity work inevitably needs to be constructed. To what extent do differences in experience and position (in terms of gender, class, race/ethnicity, citizenship, economic power, privileged ideological support etc.) obstruct balanced mutualities? The assumption of a mutuality of commitment comes along with the connotation that the various commitments at stake are essentially alike and similar in kind. This may go hand in hand with the idea that the motivation for the commitment is the same, i.e. the struggle for a 'good cause'. We do not mean to argue that this cannot be the case. Yet the reasons to become engaged in solidarity work may be less 'pure' in many instances than the idea of mutuality seems to suggest. In the terms of transnational politics, they may include organisational and geopolitical considerations and interests, which may intermesh with a dedication to the 'good causes' of human rights and equality. We therefore think that the concept of difference has to be placed at an even deeper level, close to the core of the theoretical understanding of solidarity discourses and practices. Moreover, it needs to be a concept of difference, which is attuned to the material power relations that structure the field of transnational politics.

Sameness and Difference

The emphasis on 'difference' as such is nothing new in the theory of solidarity. Our discussion so far may have revealed that representations of sameness or difference are in fact central to many conceptualisations of solidarity. This is most obvious in the case of 'intragroup solidarities', such as the ones which have given rise to social cohesion arguments, or the normative ideas which govern the 'civil solidarity' enacted through certain welfare state measures: welfare states often limit their provisions to people with documented residency, if not full legal citizenship status. Solidarity thus is curtailed according to a boundary process, which marks

---

1   We are grateful for the feedback we got on our presentation of a paper on these themes in 'Violence, Solidarity, Affect: A Workshop on Transnational Genders and Sexualities' at LSE, London on 8 May 2009. In particular we are indebted to the response by Jenny Petzen and our discussions with Sarah Lamble, who encouraged us to develop our analysis along these lines.

certain people as meeting the criteria necessary for being considered within acts of civic solidarity (cf. Yuval-Davis 1997; Werbner and Yuval-Davis 1999). Critics of hegemonic welfare state practices have further revealed that 'civil solidarity' often operates on the grounds of heteronormative assumption. If the heterosexual nuclear family is idealised as the basic unit of society and promoted and fostered through social and economic policies, queer and other alternate relationships (or individuals) inevitably get sidelined (Cooper 1993; Stychin 2004). Since LGBTQ people are excluded from many welfare state provisions, it can be said that they hold an ambiguous citizenship status in many European societies (cf. Evans 1993; Richardson 2000; Bell and Binnie 2000).

If solidarity is conceived as acts of support on behalf of members of one towards another group, the boundary processes inherent to group definition inevitably impact on the way solidarity is practised (cf. Young 1990; Squires 1999). Network solidarities or political solidarities, as we have defined them above, do not apply such rigid group definition. The idea of network solidarities acknowledges that people may be members of all kinds of different groups and that they may enter different kinds of solidarity relationships. Yet inasmuch as activism or aid is motivated by a sentiment of 'solidarity with …', boundary processes and group representations based on assumptions of sameness and difference may still be at play here too. For example, Chandra Talpade Mohanty has criticised the stereotypical representations of 'Third World' women at the heart of hegemonic (Western) feminist solidarity politics in the name of 'global sisterhood'. 'Third World women' all too often were represented as 'universal dependents' and victims of violence and exploitation, and appeared as mere receivers of well-meaning support from their white ('First World') sisters (Mohanty 1988: 1992). In a similar vein, Jin Haritaworn (2008) suggests that the current concern about the issues pertaining to LGBT Muslims in mainstream lesbian and gay organisation in European countries such as the UK and Germany is driven by a politics which denies queer Muslim agency and stylises white LGBT activists as experts on 'Muslim homophobia'. In the political climate set by the 'war against terror', this may help to pave the way of mainstream lesbian and gay organisation into the centre of society (see Puar 2008). Transnational network solidarities, too, may be enacted in a tension emerging from conflicts around dominant modes of 'othering'.

In this section we have seen that solidarity has been framed in a heteronormative way within social and political theory. Theories of solidarity often coalesce around notions of *sameness* and *difference*. For instance the nation is theorised as solidarity between those who share a common identity and allegiance to the nation-state. However we need to recognise the distinctive way in which solidarity has been conceptualised in different national contexts. We have argued that the notion of 'queer solidarity' may itself be highly problematic in erasing differences between sexual dissidents on the basis of race, class and gender and other forms of difference. Having identified the different national trajectories and understandings of solidarity in both politics and theory, we now wish to discuss how the activists in our project understood solidarity.

Given the way sexuality has been theorised in relation to solidarity, we sought to understand how activists participating in transnational networks conceived their actions in relation to notions of *sameness* and *difference*. We were therefore interested in what solidarity meant to activists who were differently located (politically, socially, economically and geographically). What were the practices of solidarity – how certain actions were seen as 'solidaristic'? In this chapter we will concentrate on the thoughts on solidarity of some of the research participants from Poland. It further helps us to recognise the multiple ways that solidarity has been understood within national polities across Europe.

Solidarity Discourses among Activists in Poland

The notion of 'solidarnosc' has a particular set of meanings in Poland that sets it apart from other understandings of solidarity in social and political theory – though we also recognise the diverse constructions, legacies and meanings of solidarity in social democracy and Christian democracy in different national contexts in Europe (Stjerno 2004). We are more concerned about the way in which contemporary claims for inclusion within Polish civil society try to invoke, or draw upon, the memory of the Solidarnosc movement to promote their political claims. In this context, we are heavily indebted to Anna Gruszczynska's work on the political uses of solidarity in the political claims around the Poznan March for Equality in 2005. In her discussion of the Poznan march in 2005, Gruszcyznska (2009: 48) argues that the socially conservative Law and Justice Party claimed the memory of Solidarity in order to promote their political agenda in opposition to that of the left, rooted in the communist past. She argues that: 'Solidarity functions in the Polish national imaginary very much in the form of hegemonic "frozen memory"; one of the recurring images of being that of the ZOMO squads breaking up illegal demonstrations' (ibid.: 49).

Gruszczynska further describes 'the emotional spaces of solidarity' associated with the Poznan march in November 2005 in terms of the rallies that were held across Poland in solidarity with the Poznan marchers. Participants in the Poznan march could invoke the memory of the Solidarity movement's protests against an unjust communist state to legitimise their own spatialised claims for sexual citizenship constituted through walking through urban space to raise the issue of the state's treatment of its gay and lesbian citizens. 'The Poznan activists were able to inscribe the Solidarity 'memory package' as relevant to issues of sexual politics' (ibid.: 49). There was therefore a conscious attempt to invoke the memory of Solidarnosc in order to create legitimacy for a project of LGBT equality and citizenship. She goes on to argue that:

by defying the ban of the Poznan mayor, the Poznan March of Equality organizers could be seen as representing the core values of Solidarity, as opposed to newly elected government. Through the spatial and emotional context of the event, the Poznan March organizers could actively challenge what they argued was re-appropriation of Solidarity legacy by the right-wing in power. (Gruszcyznska 2009: 49)

A specific feature of solidarity practice in current sexual politics in Poland can also be identified in the prominence of an approach of intergroup solidarities. From our point of view this becomes most obvious in the organisation of the Poznan March for Equality. The march in Poznan is usually organised on the UN International Day of Human Rights. According to our interviews with the organisers of the 2008 march, feminists, and anarchist civil rights activists have been influential in the loose networks which are revitalised every year to make the march possible. Over the years, the organising committee has sought to build coalitions with different oppressed groups: women, disabled people, the aged, fat people and, of course, lesbians, gay men, bisexuals and transgender people. The emphasis on solidarity across the boundaries of oppression is most pronounced in the march in Poznan. It is expressed in the title of the march: *Equality March*. For instance, Gruszczynska (2009: 50) notes that: 'the coalitional aspect of the Poznan Marches in 2006 and 2007 was apparent already in the preparatory phase, where the activists took great care to include representatives of local anarchist, ecologist and disability rights groups among the organizing team.' Yet there are similar currents in other localities of Polish activism. Discussions about coalition politics (for example with the Jewish community) has been on the agenda of the debates among activists who organise the March for Tolerance in Krakow too. It could be argued that the choice of political slogans such as 'tolerance' and 'equality' has also served to deflect public attention from the sole issue of homosexuality.[2] Recourse to equality and tolerance may also be a conscious strategy to tap into political opportunities opened up by the European Union (EU), its specific anti-discrimination politics and discourses, spread during a 'Europeanisation' of political discourses in the course of EU accession. However, all these considerations do not explain the cross-group solidarity element in contemporary sexual politics in Poland. In our conversations we have seen a commitment to a conscious effort to build bridges and coalitions, rather than an instrumentalist approach to political strategies.

According to Gruszczynska (2009), references to Solidarnosc activate the 'frozen memory' of solidarity during oppression under the communist government. It has a strong appeal in many social movement milieus. Yet the legacy both of the Solidarnosc movement and of the contemporary connotations of solidarity

---

2   According to Robert Kulpa (personal communication), the attempts to deflect from a pure focus on (homo- or bi-) and to build strong coalitions across sexual identities played a role in the creation of the name 'Equality Parade' for the events that took place in Warsaw after 2001.

discourses is contested. Informants in our project saw the value in contesting the dominant meanings of solidarity in Polish society and seeking to challenge the way it had been appropriated by Law and Justice politicians. This was a dominant theme in our interviews. For instance Samuel sees solidarity as a term that has been appropriated by the nationalist conservative right to articulate their conservative political vision that excludes many – not just lesbians and gay men:

> The plan is just to show that the way the word is being used excludes a lot of people, except for heterosexual, conservative men and women. It's much more about stealing the meaning, the essential meaning and to show that this platform, which was supposed to be a starting point to develop society, was so exclusive. (Samuel, Krakow)

Samuel links the discussion of solidarity with another concept – that of tolerance. He sees an equivalence between the conservative appropriation of the concept of solidarity and the appropriation of the concept of tolerance for LGBTQ politics:

> So in this case it's not only about solidarity and being ... sharing their experience, supporting them. It's a little bit more about fighting with words and stealing the meaning, the essential meaning. Somehow we managed to steal the word tolerance. (Samuel, Krakow)

References to solidarity in struggles against homophobia and transphobia thus have specific meaning on the level of resignification. It is about reclaiming words and histories for a particular political stance. According to Samuel, tolerance has become strongly associated with homosexuality within popular discourse, which he sees as a success of the movement he has been part of. This focus on the politics of representation and contesting terms points towards the power of 'solidarity' within Polish political discourse.

One significant and interesting way in which solidarity was conceived among our respondents was that of solidarity as intergroup coalition. The conceptualisation of the protest as a coalition-driven multi-issue directly involves the value of solidarity. Aska had linked the concepts equality, tolerance and solidarity in one sentence earlier in the interview. When we asked her about the significance of solidarity for the larger activist movement around the Poznan protests, she replied:

Christian:	Do you think that the work you're doing, you know, organising this demonstration and this week, do you think that solidarity is ... a value which is important in that?
Aska:	Yeah.
Christian:	Do you think it has something to do with solidarity?
Aska:	Yeah. I think, yeah it has a lot to do with solidarity. It stems from this idea that all the discriminated groups are, you know, some kind of minority and the mechanisms of discrimination are the same,

> so, you know, every group alone could be, you know, fighting discrimination, but if we join in this solidarity, okay solidarity between those groups, you can go do something more.

Solidarity is described as a strategic orientation to build a stronger movement. There are different forms of discrimination. They can be challenged; yet if each group struggles on its own the effectivity of its struggle will ultimately be limited. Aska's view further rests on the assumptions that discriminations work along similar mechanisms. Even if she does not elaborate on this issue, we can draw from this point that the advantage of a politics of solidarity is not simply a question of strength based on numbers. People who are faced with certain forms of discrimination can learn from each other's experiences and utilise these experiences in their own or independent struggles. Political struggles are then a matter of mutual learning and collaboration.

This notion of solidarity as based on coalition between different groups that are marginalised by the conservative political mainstream is articulated by other activists. For instance Pawel talks of a 'new Polish solidarity', which revolves around the coalitions of feminists, lesbians, gay men, bisexuals, left-wing groups (including anti-globalisation actors and anarchists), democratic actors from within previous periods of anti-communist movement struggles, artists and curators, progressive academics, and sometimes workers too. This new solidarity is a networked solidarity, based on the readiness to engage in forms of collective action or to address local forms of support work for other groups. In particular the marches become rallying points for the articulation of this new kind of solidarity:

> They [i.e. the marches] gathered people from many left wing groups ... You will have, in the Polish parade, many straight men ... you will have, like, left-wing straight men, or anarchists, participating in these activities. They have this gathering of left-wing, intellectual activists ... young people mostly, but not only, or people who are against [the] Church, against Catholicism in Poland. ... But the critics of the parade and people who attack the parade, they see only the gay ingredient, and they attack the parade because of the gay ingredient.
>
> So I think this is the solidarity, the new solidarity, which gathered in Poland around the far right and this could happen only because of the parade's repression; only because the far right became so powerful in Poland in the beginning of the twenty-first century with powers like the League of Polish Families or Law and Justice, or even the current ruling party, which is a right wing party, Civic Platform ... central right wing, but still right wing, that there is such a disappointment among the youth and the left people in this country ... that you have this new solidarity where the gays, the feminists, the left-wing intellectuals and activists ... and even the workers sometimes work together against the far right politics in Poland.

Pawel sees a new kind of solidarity emerging, which is born out of a general dissatisfaction with the cultural conservatism and the political authoritarianism which drives the far right's government politics. It gives birth to a social movement (or a coalition of social movements) which goes far beyond the issue of homosexuality, even if solidarity with LGB(T) people is a theme around which these various groups and actors fight together. The understandings of solidarity articulated by Pawel and Aska demonstrate elements of both intergroup and intragroup discourses on solidarity in the sense that the members of these coalitions of different activist groups share a common conservative, authoritarian enemy while they recognise the variety of distinctive political actors and projects that make up these coalitions.

We find it noteworthy that the primary frame of reference encompasses the collaboration between various groups within Polish society. Pawel refers to the most striking solidarity he has experienced over recent years of LGBTQ struggle as the 'new Polish solidarity'. This does not mean the accounts of our informants did not contain references to 'transnational solidarities'. The transnational dimension may add a further element. The emphasis on 'transnational solidarities' would vary according to the context of the event or the context under consideration. The march in Poznan, for example, has seen relatively few participants from abroad over the years and has been organised without any financial support from abroad; whereas other events, such as the Krakow Culture for Tolerance Festival and the associated march, have been attended and supported in manifold ways by various groups and institutions in other countries. David Featherstone (2008: 44) has argued that 'Solidarities are not produced on a smooth surface between discretely bounded struggles, but rather are part of ongoing connections, relations and articulations between places. Further, they are interventions in the social and material relations between places.' In our project we sought to understand the nature of these connections between places and how they were imagined by our respondents. In this concluding section we wish to draw the discussion of transnational activist solidarities together by focusing on their spatial politics. We found major differences in character between the marches and associated cultural festivals in Krakow, Warsaw and Poznan. Each city is differently embedded within transnational networks. In a similar way, each respondent deployed different imaginaries of solidarity, which linked different groups and places with each other. For Western European activists, the transnational dimension of solidarity was the primary frame, whereas for activists in Poland it was secondary. For many of them, Western Europe was not necessarily the dominant frame of reference.

When we asked Samuel and Ania about their ideas on the relevance of transnational solidarity in the current moment of struggle, Samuel's reply made it quite clear that their political strategy is primarily designed to respond to 'local' discourses:

Christian: Yes, the question for us would be … How is it possible to conceive
               of something like queer, or lesbian, gay, bisexual solidarity? Is

Samuel:
>there something [like that] and what are the emotions underpinning it? [Or] ... would you suggest [that] ... it's not an appropriate concept ... to carry to the field of sexual politics in Poland at all. You know, maybe we should just discard it ... let's stop ... thinking there's solidarity we need to find.
>
>I'm sorry to disappoint you, but to be honest our perspective is quite narrow here. We don't think that much on the global scale. I think we should start, but it's still like we really created measures to deal with the local issues and that's why sometimes one might find us a little bit narrow minded. (Samuel, Krakow)

Samuel then goes on to talk about the international orientation of the arts festival, but his point about priorities and orientations is quite clear. For Samuel, LGBTQ politics in Poland first of all need to find a response to the specific construction of Polish national identity. All transnational strategies need to be mediated via the requirements defined by this basic conditionality.

Many respondents replied to our question about the relevance of solidarity to their activism by mapping a social and spatial imaginary which evolved primarily around local or regional solidarities. Yet the local and the regional cannot be collapsed into the 'national'. This becomes evident in Lukasz's response:

Christian:
>Do you think that the concept of solidarity or the idea of solidarity is something which is important to the work you're doing or the kind of struggles about queer art and queer politics?

Lukasz:
>Of course. I mean ... I wouldn't use the word solidarity, but I would use the word recognition. We need to recognise each other as working and being active and doing things in the same context, and do things maybe individually as well, but be sure that there are other people as well and that we can work with each other and create something bigger ... You know those young guys from art academy, they're obviously queer and obviously interested in art, but I believe they might be afraid of doing something openly queer because the academy is so conservative, but maybe through bringing them to the exhibition and they meet each other ... they will be able to do something more radical and that's what I want. I'm searching for Polish artists who are willing to do this. So, I hope it's working. (Lukasz, Krakow)

Lukasz prefers the term 'recognition' over the term 'solidarity'. The scale of action linked to recognition (which is distinct from but similar to solidarity in Lukasz's eyes) is clearly a local one. The mutual recognition of radical queer artists is the basis for unity and for creating a Polish queer art movement. Yet Lukasz's vision of a creative network of queer artists who through their work may contribute to fighting back dominant homophobic attitudes and policies goes far beyond the frame defined by the 'national'. As it becomes evident at various points in Lukasz's description of his map for a creative movement born out of mutual recognition, it is particular artists in Central and Eastern Europe he likes to call upon:

> [S]o I'm really conscious about doing things that they are specifically Central or Eastern European. ... A few people are involved in that ... but, you know, more and more people start to do it and I'm trying to map them and bring them here as well, because again I want to create that kind of circle. I want all of us to get recognised and see how powerful we can be. ... And because it's Eastern Europe, so all that homophobia and intolerance is also effective to fight with and we can do it by bringing all those people together and be stronger. ... If you want to hit something with a fist, you know, we have to have all fingers and we're trying to have that fist strong, and obviously we need to create a circle, a network, regional wise because this region is highly homophobic; it doesn't recognise queer artists as serious artists, so it needs to be lifted up there, the whole concept of artists here working together or having an opportunity to exhibit and influence the audience. (Lukasz, Krakow)

Multiple Solidarities

Another interesting observation is that many respondents saw solidarity as something that is not one-dimensional. This means that even if activists referred to what could be called 'transnational' acts of solidarity, it was not necessarily the transnational dimension in that encounter and interaction that people found most noteworthy. At the start of the project we had envisaged that activists would conceive of solidarity as being constituted primarily in cross-cultural or national differences. However, our respondents pointed towards other forms of difference that were at least as significant as national, or intercultural, difference that we had not envisaged, or could not have anticipated from the outset of our project. These were namely differences along the lines of age and sexual orientation. For example Bettina, one of the organisers of the 2008 Krakow Festival for Tolerance, suggested that the difficulties of transnational cooperation are aggravated by gender, intergenerational and cultural differences:

> Christian: Would you say the cooperation turned difficult because of primarily personal, emotional or political issues ... or a mixture of it?
>
> Bettina: I think it's more about personal ... but I think it was just misunderstandings because of culture and because of generation, because the activists who came, they were all, like fifty years old. They were all like twice the age of the average Polish activist's age ... and they were also sometimes, like ... because our activists are almost all women ... and it was a little, sometimes, strange. It

> was like the fifty-year-old German gays come and tell the young, Polish lesbian feminist women what to do. ... Germans have this tendency, may be, to discuss everything and to make it clear and Polish people don't have, maybe, this much this culture ... and then the generational thing, that they have the experience of twenty, thirty years' activism.

Bettina argued that the interplay of various factors and positions resulted in a situation in which some (female) Polish activists read the behaviour of some (male) German activists as patronising and domineering. Cultural differences in styles of communication, andro-centrism and gender-normative behaviours, age differences and differences in experience are the perspectives through which Bettina interprets certain 'transnational' dynamics. Geopolitical hegemony gets reinforced through uneven geotemporalities (here with regard to the histories of social movement activism) and forms of gender power. While Bettina talks of generational difference as a source of problems in this quote, she sees them as an inspiration – a specific articulation of (positive) solidarity in other parts of the interview (Binnie and Klesse 2009). Apart from intergenerational solidarity, Bettina also stresses a moment of solidarity across sexual identities:

> And I think there is also within the march a big solidarity because most people marching with us are heterosexual, like 50 per cent, so it's like a real a big issue because the majority of lesbians and gay [men] from Krakow don't go to the march ... so therefore other heterosexual people are coming because they are in favour of tolerance and equal rights. This is really positive I think but on the other hand it is also a little problem in that ... the march is even hetero dominated..in that there are very few gay and lesbian couples visible ... and there are even heterosexual couples visible – like holding hands and may be kissing ... so this is also a little strange because it would be also nice to have a visibility of gay and lesbian people in Krakow which is the only day where we are visible in the whole year ... but ... it's just great that they are coming because ... there are very very many gay people who don't come because of being afraid of being seen and so it's good that we have these groups like Social Democratic and Green Party, anarchists and feminists who support us ... it's great we have these groups who support us. (Bettina, Krakow)

Bettina, like many others, emphasises that the support of heterosexual participants was vital to the early marches. At the same time, the above quote reveals grains of ambiguity with regards to heterosexual and LGBTQ visibilities. Solidarities across sexual orientation, too, are enacted across uneven terrain. Many activists from Poland described an understanding of solidarity as a complex and multilayered process of intersecting inter- and intragroup solidarities. The transnational is one element among them, and often not the most prominent. This calls into question hegemonic understandings of solidarity in gender and sexual politics in Poland, as operating along an East/West binary, and centres on cross-national flows and links which structure popular, media and activist discourses on sexuality and sexual politics in Europe.

Conclusion

In this chapter we have examined the way in which the concept of solidarity has been used by the research participants within our study on transnational activism around contemporary LGBTQ politics in Poland. We have seen that the key terms in our study – 'transnational', 'queer', 'activism', 'solidarity' – have multiple and contested meanings, and that we have sought to understand how our informants have understood and used them. We have argued that notions of sameness and difference have been central in social and political theories of solidarity. Concentrating on interviews with respondents in Poznan and Krakow, we found that many of them did not use the term 'solidarity' directly to articulate their sense of connection to others involved in common projects to challenge heteronormativity in Polish society. Because of the hegemonic meaning of Solidarnosc within contemporary Polish politics and its appropriation by socially conservative Law and Justice politicians, we noted that some respondents saw the need to contest the dominant meanings associated with terms such as 'solidarity' and 'tolerance'. One of the most significant ways in which solidarity was envisaged among our respondents was the notion of solidarity as intergroup coalition. This is particularly true of the activists in Poznan, where there was evidence of a conscious attempt to establish and mobilise connections between different but related groups of activists focusing on diverse political projects with roots in feminism, anarchism, anti-capitalism, age awareness and fat activism.[3] In terms of the transnational dimension of activism (which was the primary focus of our project) we saw that our understanding of the transnational basis of solidarity needs to be set into the context of other and overlapping forms of solidarity which we had not envisaged at the outset of our project, such as intergenerational solidarities. We also recognise that it is imperative that the transnational mobility of the respondents in our project is not overstated, and that more research needs to be conducted on the transnational dimensions of Christian right and far right activism within Poland.

---

3   The 2008 Poznan Equality and Tolerance event and Equality March included a specific commitment to age awareness and fat activism, as evidenced by the declaration on the organisation's website that: 'This year we want to put up a problem of women over 50 and talk about discrimination of overweight women' (Organizational Committee of the Equality and Tolerance Days in Poznan 2008).

References

Alexander, Jacqui M. and Mohanty, Chandra Talpade. 1997. 'Introduction: Genealogies, Legacies, Movements'. In *Feminist Genealogies, Colonial Legacies, Democratic Futures*, eds J.M. Alexander and C.T. Mohanty. New York, Routledge, xiii–xlii.

Anthias, Floya and Yuval-Davis, Nira. 1992. *Racialized Boundaries: Race, Nation, Gender, Colour and Class*. London: Routledge.

Beger, Nico. 2004. *Tensions in the Struggle for Sexual Minority Rights in Europe*. Manchester: Manchester University Press.

Bell, David and Binnie, Jon. 2000. *The Sexual Citizen: Queer Politics and Beyond*. Cambridge: Polity Press.

Bhavnani, Kum-Kum. 1994. 'Tracing the Contours: Feminist Research and Feminist Objectivity'. In *The Dynamics of 'Race' and Gender: Some Feminist Interventions*, eds H. Afshar and M. Maynard. Bristol: Taylor and Francis, 26–40.

Binnie, Jon. 1997. 'Invisible Europeans: Sexual Citizenship in the New Europe', *Environment and Planning A*, 29: 237–48.

———. 2004. *The Globalization of Sexuality*. London: Sage.

Binnie, Jon and Klesse, Christian. 2009. 'The Politics of Age and Inter-Generational Relations in Transnational Lesbian, Gay Bisexual and Transgender Activist Networks', unpublished paper, presented at RGS-IBG Annual Conference, 26–28 August 2009, University of Manchester.

Brunkhorst, Hauke. 2007. 'Globalizing Solidarity: The Destiny of Democratic Solidarity in the Times of Global Capitalism, Global Religion, and Global Public', *Journal of Social Philosophy*, 38(1): 93–111.

Cooper, Davina. 1993. 'An Engaged State: Sexuality, Governance and the Potential for Change'. In *Activating Theory: Lesbian, Gay, Bisexual Politics*, eds J. Bristow and A.R. Wilson. London: Lawrence & Wishart.

Darnovsky, Marcy, Epstein, Barbara and Flacks, Richard. 1995. 'Introduction'. In *Cultural Politics and Social Movements*, eds M. Darnovsky, B. Epstein and R. Flacks. Philadelphia: Temple University Press, 190–218.

Durkheim, Émile. 1964. *The Division of Labor in Society*. New York: Free Press.

Duyvendak, Jan Willem. 1996. 'The Depoliticization of the Dutch Gay Identity, or Why Dutch Gays Aren't Queer'. In *Queer Theory/Sociology*, ed. Steven Seidman. Oxford: Blackwell, 421–38.

Erel, Umut, Haritaworn, Jin, Gutiérrez Rodríguez, Encarnacíon and Klesse, Christian. 2008. 'On the Depoliticisation of Intersectionality-Talk: Conceptualising Multiple Oppressions in Critical Sexuality Studies'. In *Out of Place: Interrogating Silences in Queerness/Raciality*, eds, A. Kuntsman and E. Miyake. York: Raw Nerve Books, 190–218.

Evans, David T. 1993. *Sexual Citizenship: The Material Construction of Sexualities*. London: Routledge

Featherstone, David. 2008. *Resistance, Space and Political Identities: The Making of Counter-Global Networks*. Chichester: Wiley-Blackwell.

Ferens, Dominika. 2006. 'The Equality March – Introduction', *Interalia*, 1: 1–4.

Gellner, E. 1983. *Nations and Nationalism*. Oxford: Basil Blackwell.

Gilliver, Andrew. 2009. 'Poland's First Married Couple Start Action Group', *PinkPaper.com*, http://news.pinkpaper.com/NewsStory.aspx?id=1163 (accessed: 18 December 2009).

Gould, Carol C. 2007. 'Transnational Solidarities', *Journal of Social Philosophy*, 38(1): 148–64.

Gould, Carol C. and Scholz, Sally J. 2007. 'Introduction', *Journal of Social Philosophy*, 8(1): 3–6.

Graham, Colin. 2007. 'Gay Poles Head for the UK to Escape State Crackdown', *The Observer*, Sunday 1 July, p. 52.

Gruszczynska, Anna. 2008. 'Radicalising Public Space: Looking at Lesbian and Gay Public Activism in Poland', paper presented at the Queering Central and Eastern Europe: National Features of Sexual Identities conference, UCL SSEES, April.

———. 2009. '"I Was Mad About It All, About the Ban": Emotional Spaces of Solidarity in the Poznan March of Equality', *Emotion, Space and Society*, 2: 44–51.

Haritaworn, Jin. 2008. 'Loyal Repetitions of the Nation: Gay Assimilation and the "War on Terror"', *darkmatter*, no. 3, http://www.darkmatter101.org/site/author/jin/ (accessed: 20 December 2009).

Haritaworn, Jin, Tauqir, Tamsila and Redem, Esra. 2008. 'Gay Imperialism: Gender and Sexuality Discourse in the "War on Terror"'. In *Out of Place: Interrogating Silences in Queerness/Raciality*, eds A. Kuntsman and E. Miyake. York: Raw Nerve Books, 71–96.

Harvey, Jean. 2007. 'Moral Solidarity and Empathetic Understanding: The Oral Value and Scope of the Relationship', *Journal of Social Philosophy*, 38(1): 22–37.

Klesse, Christian. 2006. 'Beyond Visibility, Rights, and Citizenship – Critical Notes on Sexual Politics in the European Union', *Interalia*, no. 1, http://www.interalia.org.pl/numery.php?nid=1&aid=8 (accessed: 20 August 2007).

Komter, Aafke. 2005. *Social Solidarity and the Gift. Cambridge*: Cambridge University Press.

Kowalczyk, Izabela. 2006. 'The Equality March: Media Response to the Poznan Equality March', *Interalia* 1: 1–19.

Kulpa, Robert. 2009. 'Discussion Paper for the Workshop: Debating Anglo-Polish Perspectives on Sexuality Studies', *Interalia*, no. 4, http://www.interalia.org.pl/pl/artykuly/autorzy/robert_kulpa.htm (accessed: 20 December 2009).

Kuus, Merje. 2004. 'Europe's Eastern Expansion and the Reinscription of Otherness in East-Central Europe', *Progress in Human Geography*, 28: 472–89.

De Lange, Sarah and Guerra, Simona. 2009. 'The League of Polish Families between East and West, Past and Present', *Communist and Post-Communist Studies*, 42: 527–49.

Leszkowicz, Pawel and Kitlinski, Tomek. 2009. 'Extremes Meet: Anglo-Polish perspective on Sexual Politics', The Manchester Seminar, *Interalia*, 1: 9.

Light, Duncan and Young, Craig. 2009. 'European Union Enlargement, Post-Accession Migration and Imaginative Geographies of the "New Europe": Media Discourses in Romania and the United Kingdom', *Journal of Cultural Geography*, 26(3): 283–305.

Malkki, Liisa. 1994. 'Citizens of Humanity: Internationalism and the Imagined Community of Nations', *Diaspora: A Journal of Transnational Studies*, 3(1): 41–68.

Mizielińska, Joanna. 2009. 'Ideas for a Workshop Transnational Perspectives on Queer Theory in the UK and Poland – Challenging Anglo-American Perspectives in Queer Theory', The Manchester Seminar, *Interalia*, 1: 5.

Mohanty, Chandra Talpade. 1988. 'Under Western Eyes: Feminist Scholarship and Colonial Discourses', *Feminist Review*, 30 (autumn): 61–88.

———. 1992. 'Feminist Encounters: Locating the Politic of Experience'. In *Destabilizing Theory: Contemporary Feminist Debates*, eds M. Barrett and A. Phillips. Cambridge: Polity Press, 74–93.

———. 2003. *Feminism without Borders: Decolonizing Theory, Practicing Solidarity*. Durham, NC: Duke University Press.

Monro, Surya. 2005. *Gender Politics: Citizenship, Activism and Sexual Diversity*. London: Pluto.

Organizational Committee of the Equality and Tolerance Days in Poznan. 2008. 'Equality and Tolerance Days in Poznan, Poland (10–16 November 2008)', http://www.dnirownosci.most.org.pl. (accessed: 10 March 2010).

Pankowski, Rafal. 2009. *The Populist Radical Right in Poland*. London: Routledge.

Phillips, Oliver. 1997. 'Zimbabwean Law and the Production of a White Man's Disease', *Social and Legal Studies*, 6: 471–91.

Puar, Jasbir. 2008. 'Homonationalism and Biopolitics'. In *Out of Place: Interrogating Silences in Queerness/Raciality*, eds A. Kuntsman and E. Miyake. York: Raw Nerve Books, 13–70.

Rahman, Momin. 2000. *Sexuality and Democracy, Identities, Strategies in Lesbian and Gay Politics*. Edinburgh: Edinburgh University Press.

Richardson, Diana. 2000. *Rethinking Sexuality*. London: Sage.

Ronson, Henrietta. 2009. 'Rightwing Politician Angry at Elephant's Gay Tendencies', *Pink News*, http://www.pinknews.co.uk/news/articles/2005-12131.html (accessed: 18 December 2009).

Scholz, Sally J. 2007. 'Political Solidarity and Violent Resistance', *Journal of Social Philosophy*, 38(1): 38–52.

Sikora, Tomasz, Basiuk, Tomasz and Ferens, Dominika. 2008. 'Introduction'. In *Local and International Perspectives in Queer Studies*, eds D. Ferens, T.

Basiuka and T. Sikora. Newcastle upon Tyne: Cambridge Scholars' Publishing, 1–7.

Squires, Judith. 1999. *Gender in Political Theory*. Cambridge: Polity Press.

Stjerno, Steinar. 2004. *Solidarity in Europe*. Cambridge: Cambridge University Press.

Stychin, Carl. 2004. 'Same-Sex Sexualities and the Globalization of Human Rights Discourse', *McGill Law Journal*, 49: 951–68.

Törnquist-Plewa, Barbara and Malmgren, Agnes. 2007. *Homophobia and Nationalism in Poland: The Reactions to the March against Homophobia in Cracow 2004*, no. 23, Trondheim Studies on Eastern European Cultures and Societies. Trondheim: Norwegian University of Science and Technology.

Warkocki, Błazej. 2006. 'The Equality March, Poznan 2005', *Interalia*, 1: 1–5.

Watt, Nicholas. 2006. 'Prejudice Forms a New Line between East and West', *The Guardian*, Monday 8 May, p. 25.

Werbner, Pnina and Yuval-Davis, Nira. 1999. 'Introduction: Women and the New Discourse of Citizenship'. In *Women, Citizenship and Difference*, eds N. Yuval-Davis and P. Werbner. London: Zed Books, 1–38.

Young, Iris Marion. 1990. *Justice and the Politics of Difference*. Princeton: Princeton University Press.

Yuval-Davis, Nira. 1997. *Gender and Nation*. London: Sage.

Chapter 7

Rendering Gender in Lesbian Families: A Czech Case

Kateřina Nedbálková

Introduction

Gay and lesbian families have been discussed in the context of the lesbian and gay community and the academy extensively since the 1970s (Green 1978; Golombok, Spencer and Rutter 1983; Tasker and Golombok 1997; Patterson 1994; Stacey and Biblarz 2001, 2010; Stein 1997; Warner 1999). This topic has been researched so widely that we can actually detect a canon to which studies of North American or Western European provenance adhere (Green 1978; Patterson 1994). In other words, researchers often attempt to refute concerns and stereotypes surrounding homosexuality or homosexual parenthood. This chapter attempts to surpass efforts to prove that lesbian/gay (l/g) families are good or bad. My concern in this study is to explore the extent to which the concept of the same-sex family transforms the institution of the family as a gendered institution in the Czech context. I will consider whether and to what extent gender is produced and reproduced in the context of homosexual partnership. This question will be unfolded based on qualitative research and also in relation to the Western literature published on the topic of homoparentality. In the chapter I proceed from 1) outlining the topic of homosexuality, gender and family in the Czech Republic; 2) introducing the conceptual background of the study and its methodology; through to 3) analysing the research material and concluding with the comparison to the Western findings.

(Homo)sexuality and Homoparentality in the Czech Republic

Long-term research has shown that in comparison with other Central and Eastern European (CEE) countries, the Czech Republic is relatively more tolerant to same-sex marriages and child adoption.[1] Public perceptions of homosexuality have been associated here with medicine and sexology. In 2006, the Czech Republic

---

1 *Češi jsou vůči sňatkům a registrovanému partnerství homosexuálů vstřícnější než Poláci, Maďaři a Slováci* (2005). Public Opinion Research Centre of the Institute of Sociology of the Academy of Sciences of the Czech Republic (CVVM) press release.

was the second of all post-communist countries to legalise registered partnership for same-sex couples. As part of the European Year of Equal Opportunities for All (2007), a Working Group for Sexual Minority Issues was established in the government, aimed at improving the LGBT minority status in the Czech Republic. The members of this team are both activists from non-governmental, non-profit organisations focused on the LGBT minority and academic experts.

Although there is no geographically concentrated gay and lesbian community in particular neighbourhoods or cities, and the first Gay Pride march took place only in 2008, Prague tends to be described in LGBT guidebooks as the gay metropolis of the former Eastern Europe.[2] The public space of the gay and lesbian community is represented by bars, cafés, restaurants, sex clubs and saunas situated especially in larger cities such as Prague, Brno and Olomouc. The private space of the subculture is then represented by informal groups of friends who meet in private households and who do not opt for commercial gay and lesbian clubs. A more formally organised part of the community is represented by non-profit LGBT organisations; there are several dozen of them in the Czech Republic. These organisations endeavoured to put into law a Registered Partnership Act (accomplished in 2006) and organise discussion and support groups, film festivals or lectures, and sports or other leisure events. Furthermore, the central platform for the formation of an LGBT community is the TV programme *Queer* (formerly *Legato*), which has been broadcast regularly by one state TV channel since 2004. In 2007 the first lesbian publishing house, *Le Press*, was established. The transsexual community is concentrated predominantly in Prague around Transfórum, a single civic association representing transpeople's interests (Nedbálková and Polášková 2009).[3]

The existence of gay and lesbian families is not taken into consideration on either legal grounds or in public awareness. The topic stays academically under-researched and it is usually the students of psychology or sociology who are most interested in writing about it. Adoption is available to individuals and to couples in the Czech Republic. Homosexual couples (if registered) are excluded from adopting. Also artificial insemination by unknown donor at a clinic is available only to women who prove to have a male partner. Despite the reported tolerance of homosexuality, the atheism of the Czech population and empirical data that point to the decline of traditional family, the notion of family in the Czech Republic is rather traditional. For example, discourse on child development is dominated by psychologists who strongly favour women staying at home with children almost till they reach school age (Matějček 2008).

Retrieved on 11 November 2006 from http://www.cvvm.cas.cz/upl/zpravy/100533s_ov51128.pdf.

2   See e.g. http://www.prague4gay.com/noframes/infogayguide1.htm; http://praha-gaybars.com/page/about; or http://come2prague.com (accessed: 24 April 2010).

3   For publications on homosexuality, g/l community and lesbian families, see Nedbálková 2005, 2007; Polášková 2007; Sokolová 2001; Lišková 2008).

Conceptual Background and Methodology

In this chapter I am concerned with one of the fundamental social institutions (the family) in a relatively 'new' context of homosexuality. At the analytical level I have adopted an interpretative approach, still not very popular in Czech sociology of the family. The interpretative approach enables the exploration of the social reality of the 'family', 'family life' and 'life in a family'. It helps to see them as a continuous flow of 'everyday activities through which people live their lives and which form the basis of exploring what families really do rather than what form these families have' (Almack 2005: 250). 'The *family* is thus the result of material and symbolic practices. It involves assistance, visits, gifts' exchange, kindnesses, favours, and the work of memory: unity through photographs, wedding and engagement rings. The safekeeping of cohesion often falls on women' (Bourdieu 1998: 98). These practices involve inaugural acts (naming, weddings) and are further ingrained and strengthened in a series of other practices.[4] This situated action, saturated with meaning, can be understood as a practice that does not represent the individual actor's 'free choice', but is always structured by social systems and categories of meaning. Hence the family is the outcome of the concrete activities of particular individuals, and at the same time a founding principle of social reality (Bourdieu 1998).

I find this concept appealing for it allows seeing the day-to-day negotiated character and hard work of 'doing' families, as well as explaining why on the surface the family operates as a universal, natural, unimpugnable basis of society. Family and intimate partnership are both institutions that are deeply gendered in the traditional conceptions, and therefore they are utterly (hetero)normative. Martin characterised heteronormativity as 'the mundane, everyday ways that heterosexuality is privileged and taken for granted as normal and natural. Heteronormativity includes the institutions, practices, and norms that support heterosexuality (especially a particular form of heterosexuality – monogamous and reproductive) and subjugate other forms of sexuality, especially homosexuality' (Martin 2009: 190).

It is not surprising that research on gay and lesbian partnerships and families confronts the heteronormativity and seeks to answer the question of gender differences in l/g and heterosexual families. Western researchers were so far mostly interested either in the character of the adult partnership (division of labour, motivation for having children) or in the children (their gender identity, sexual orientation, well-being, social adaptation, stigmatisation). Some studies (Kurdek 1988; Sullivan 2004) characterise gay and lesbian partnerships as egalitarian, lying outside the asymmetrical division of labour, with the breadwinner on one side and the homemaker on the other. Very few studies questioned this egalitarian

---

4   Carrington (1999) distinguished the following spheres of practical activities in the family: feeding work, emotional work, interaction work, presentation of the family status and kinwork.

model and argue for division of labour based on the partner's participation at the labour market (Carrington 1999).

In the following section I focus on the negotiation of gender in the lesbian relationship in the Czech Republic. The chapter is empirically based on ethnographic research on 14 lesbian families with children either planned in the context of a homosexual partnership (nine families) or with children from a previous heterosexual marriage (five families). During the years 2004–2008 I conducted semi-structured interviews with these families.[5] Five families were interviewed repeatedly, and with seven partners I sustained email conversations. The families were chosen via a snowball method, and approximately one-third of the women knew me from my previous involvement in the lesbian and gay community. All the interviews were recorded and transcribed. I also took field notes after each interview, which also served as empirical data. The vast majority of the women lived in the two largest cities in the Czech Republic and they also shared a similar middle or upper middle-class background.[6]

The Partner (Dis)comfort of Gender

The following situation, although not drawn directly from my own research, eloquently opens up the topic of doing gender in the family and, respectively, in the same-sex family. In an episode of the reality show *Wife Swap* (aired 4 April 2009, TV Nova, IV-5) female partners in a lesbian and a heterosexual couple swapped places. In the course of the week with her new family, Gita, a lesbian, repeatedly criticised her temporary heterosexual partner for not acting as a man at home. 'He is half female and half male. He nods to everything, he agrees with everything, whatever you tell him to do, he does it. He is not enough of a man.' She repeatedly challenged him not to help so much at home, to leave homecare and childcare to her. In the final section, while assessing the experience of the past days, both couples end up in tears (of sentiment and empathy) and the man says 'in terms of my dominance, I'll have to work on that', to which his wife responds 'I keep telling you that.' The reality show confronts two different families and everyday lives: the more the men and women are taken aback, surprised, shocked or angered by the given situations, the better. In this respect the homosexual couple promised a juicy bite exactly because it seemingly turned upside down all that the family was based on. The lesbian in this case represents very strong views on the masculine role in the family that would contradict the widespread notion of the egalitarianism of lesbian couples. She strives to be seen and portrayed as a 'proper' and essential

---

5   Between 2004 and 2005 I interviewed families with my colleague from the psychology department. Because later (and especially in the phase of interpreting and writing) we worked separately, I use the singular form while referring to the research.

6   This was not intentional and it coresponds with the situation of other researchrs who have difficulties finding respondents out of this group (Stacey and Biblarz 2010).

part of such propriety in this context – family (and moreover family presentation on commercial TV) means also properly gendered. Being a 'proper woman' here encompasses being feminine, which in relation to the family means taking care of the household, children and husband.

As I have already suggested, a significant amount of information on the egalitarian division of labour in same-sex families formed part of the knowledge with which I approached my research. In fact I treated this topic as a specific area in the interview and its structure was planned in advance. It became clear only after a few interviews that direct questions about the division of roles were not suitable. If the topic of the division of roles appeared in a question formulated by us, the answers that followed included expressions like 'It is completely egalitarian; we all do everything; the roles are not really divided between us; we take turns' (Matylda). When we think about it, such answers represent a logical reaction, as the so-called 'traditional' division of roles is no longer a gold standard even in the case of heterosexual couples (Šmídová 2009). At the same time, and mainly in the manifest content, we can expect the rhetoric of egalitarianism particularly in the case of younger and more educated couples. Hence these answers are predictable already due to the composition of the sample, as it is dominated by women with secondary and higher education, living in larger cities. Rather than answers to direct questions, it was the unprompted interactions and exchanges between partners in the course of the interviews that proved more fruitful, as they often concerned the un/equal division of roles. In the course of the interviews, or when analysing transcripts, it was similarly fascinating to detect how women contradicted themselves in the course of a few hours of talking; their individual statements and utterances are thus always context bound.

Although I have suggested that, manifestly, women often referred to an equal division of childcare and homecare, it does not imply that women would understand such an egalitarian division as universally positive. In the interviews women mentioned situations in which egalitarianism can be understood as a disadvantage. The contradictory signification of the same phenomenon becomes clear in the following two quotes:

> We have a certain advantage as no one can tell us, you are the man, you should do this and that. If we need to divide tasks, we have to do the rock/paper/scissors. (Agáta)

> I sometimes feel that I no longer like being that, that emancipated and feminist lesbian without roles. Sometimes I'd like to say: now, you do this because, you know, how she can say it, the woman can say it. And why should I do it? Because you are a man, as if. (Štěpánka)

While the first interviewee understands the traditional division of roles in the family as an oppressive stereotype, for the second one a reliance on the stereotype provides (at least hypothetically) a respite in the territory of the known, the expected, the understandable – a means to unproblematic comfort or support. In the interview Štěpánka identified the reliance on the traditional division of roles mainly with the role of the breadwinner. While she thinks that in the case of a heterosexual family it is possible and predictable to rely fully on the father's role as breadwinner responsible for the family's financial well-being, in the end she resists this asymmetry in the case of a lesbian couple and expresses the view that she 'would not feel like a kept woman in any case'.

As I suggested, views on the division of roles in the context of same-sex couples are closely linked to the heterosexual gender structure of society. Štěpánka can imagine the model of breadwinner/homemaker only in a heterosexual family, while she believes that in the case of a same-sex couple one cannot rely on it with equal ease. Similarly, the difference between homosexual and heterosexual coupling is outlined in the following quote, with Míša and Ivana recalling their previous heterosexual relationships:

> Míša: When I was with Zdeněk, he was somehow my support and I was his support, and with Ivana it is the same but it is somehow a different support. It is as if he used to be greater support for me than I for him. Although with Zdeněk it was, he is a very kind boy and I was very dominant in that relationship.
>
> Ivana: Well, he would look after the car, you know, I do not. Or let's say driving, well, I rather dislike driving with Míša, I'm glad when she drives all the way. Sometimes she happens to be tired so I take the turn to drive but there it was somehow natural.

When Michaela (Míša) lacks words to describe her feelings, Ivana readily comes up with the example of driving the car, which she picked as a situation when, according to her, the man takes the initiative completely. Despite the fact that in retrospect Michaela understands her dominance in the relationship with Zdeněk, she habitually perceives support in a heterosexual relationship as asymmetrically gendered, with the man seen as a greater support than the woman. Driving the car is an example selected also by Inge when she says: 'I am not a masculine type, not at all. In no way. And I think that for example Mirka likes cars, that yes, she likes to drive. I do not like to drive.' In this case driving represents a prototype of a masculinity-coded activity.

The same way as Michaela does not question Zdeněk's greater support in the first quote, in the following quote Eva gradually realises that men are a priori more suited to certain activities than women:

> I tend to be the kind of a person who strikes with a hammer somewhere. I can do a load of things, like I'm not afraid of taking the hammer and taking a nail. Well, in case something more fundamental is concerned I rather tell my father; in the end a man always does it better, but drilling or hanging something, I do not only mean pictures but also more complicated stuff, I do that myself. I can

certainly even make something out of wood. Well, that's my kind of attitude, I'm not afraid; I am quite good with my hands. (Eva)

Eva interprets her skills not as a result of conscientious efforts or of necessity that stems from the fact that in a lesbian couple a man (in the role of a person who is expected to conduct house repairs and have manual skills) is missing; but rather she understands them in the context of the kind of a person she is. Jarka makes a similar point in the following fragment:

I do the masculine stuff, so-called, and Klára does the sort of feminine chores, don't know, she does the washing, the cooking, the cleaning, looks after the children but the reason tends to be that it so happened. Partly because she cannot do the other stuff, she is not the kind of person, but then equally, neither is the father-in-law or the uncle or our young master [son from a previous marriage], he really is not good with his hands, he actually likes cooking. (Jarka)

In the above quote we find noteworthy and contradictory statements – one that Klára cannot do something, hence does other things in the family; and at the same time they insist that roles are divided as happened. Neither Eva nor Jarka operates with 'kind of person' as a gendered category. That is, they do not talk about the man and woman as a 'kind of person' who would naturally do this or that; rather it is understood as one's disposition, one's character. While idealised heterosexual relationship represents (e.g. in the account given by Ivana and Michaela) relationship that structures behaviour so that it were (is) perceived as gender-related and gendered, in a same-sex relationship we do not find an a priori reliance on the sexually differentiated division of labour. Even though the division of labour is to some extent negotiated also in heterosexual couples, there is still a strong taken for granted aspect of it that stems from the presumably natural origin of masculinity and femininity. The homosexual couple, on the other hand, might appeal to be freed from this dichotomy. This, however, should not lead us to a clear conclusion that these relationships are not marked by gender.

One of the decisive criteria in this respect appears to be biological motherhood. Dita and Pavla (biological mothers) talk about this difference in the following way:

Simply, the one who gives birth to the children has the legal responsibility. The difference is monstrous, really. (Dita)

One thing is the same and it will not change, when a child cries, when it comes to the crunch, then it is the mother who always must. While the other partner is the one who can, if willing. But you actually must. (Pavla)

In this case the asymmetry is not only understood through legal regulations, but is also manifested in everyday activities connected with childcare. Despite the stress on the key role of the biological mother, a number of women stressed at the same time the help provided by themselves and their female partners.

> We are constantly close to each other and the helpful hand is always present, the traditional model lets you down in this respect. (Kamila)

> I do not like planning, I do not like duties, I do not like basic things like going shopping, having to go somewhere, I don't know, the council etc. So Lucie does all of this, I just get home from work, Patrička is almost asleep or she actually sleeps, and that is somehow like I do not do anything at all in the family. I am here just to play with Patrička occasionally, in my free time and that's all. (Karla)

Karla defines her role in the family either in a negative terms, referring to what she does not do, or in relation to the child, when she describes it as playing in her free time. Her description is not a proud declaration of a breadwinner as we could expect in the breadwinner/homemaker configuration, on the contrary, she understands her conduct as inefficient, leading to a sense of guilt. Although it is likely that in their families Kamila and Karla contribute to the everyday running of things to a similar degree, they signify their engagement very differently. While Kamila claims that she and her partner are always nearby and willing to help, Karla insists that she hardly does anything for the family. Nonetheless, both views are strongly gendered as feminine. At least at the manifest level Kamila is at her partner's disposal to help (partly because her job allows her to work from home); at the same time, as a woman, she is able to value her partner's housework as hard labour. Sullivan's (2004) findings are similar in this respect: a woman who worked more within the family (in employment) praised the housework that her partner did as demanding and tiring. Housework does not represent an unnoticed, matter-of-course issue; rather it is the outcome of everyday routine and often tiresome efforts.

Although in the earlier quote Kamila states that she and her partner are always near each other, she addresses the issue further in the interview:

> I give Dita space so that she is in a closer relationship with children. I also care for them, I am not an aunt that lives with them, we are simply two mothers. But I give Dita space when the children need someone, in this the role is clearly divided. In terms of running the household, from looking after the garden, the car, mopping the floor and cooking, in these there is complete equality. (Kamila)

The quote again refers to, on the one hand, the duties of the biological mother and, on the other, the possible willingness of the partner to substitute for her. Kamila talks about 'giving space', which might be seen as delegating competences. When negotiating or activating the participation of the social mother, a decisive role is played by her engagement in the public sphere, her participation in the labour market. In the Czech context biological mothers are usually not provided with a space for childcare as, symbolically and materially, they are invested with it from the beginning. The partner who stays at home not only provides childcare but also conducts household maintenance. It is usually considered 'natural' and fair. The 'working' partner is exempt from these duties on the ground of lacking home presence while securing financial income (Carrington 1999; Sullivan 2004).

The same way as women in the role of breadwinners value the care provided by their partners, women who stay at home value the work that their partners do outside the family. In the following quote Dita stresses the professional abilities and performance of her partner, who, in return, downplays her contribution:

Dita: Well, it's that I'm at home and Kamila works; this is because, Kamila does not say this, but this is because she is more competent, it's that simple.

Kamila: Maybe, it depends in what and how.

Not only do family members appreciate the care, work or effort of their partners in order to keep (save) the family's face but researchers also might become a part of this appreciation. When reading the transcript of the interview with Tereza and Karla, which I did not attend, I noticed how my colleague who conducted the interview repeatedly stressed that earning money is also important, as if trying to rehabilitate the small value that Karla (as documented above) ascribed to her own conduct. This situation is a telling example of teamwork in Goffman's (1997) sense, when actors help and support each other in the conduct of their roles and actions. In this case a normal, i.e. good and well-functioning, family is presented in the course of the interview. Karla's partner does not blame her for not taking part in housework; on the contrary, she blames herself for the situation and she rushes to help, saying: 'Me and the fact that I didn't allow her to do anything, it is my fault and I have myself to blame and it works the way it always did.' However, it is not only the partners who aim for a shared objective and a good result. When the interviewer realises that the family's attempts at a good presentation are falling apart in some places, particularly due to Karla's continued underestimation of her role, she makes an effort to help the family not to fail in presenting its performance as it would put the family in an unpleasant position (because of the loss of face that would be uncomfortable also for the researcher).

Gender for Children and Gender in Children

Apart from doing gender in a relationship, the interviewees also perceived the gender structure of society as relevant in relation to children. Hence they anticipated the occurrence of a frequent objection to same-sex families, that of not providing 'normal' and 'favourable' (i.e. heterosexual) socialising. In the following quote

Dáša explicitly addresses this issue, stressing that socially cherished gender complementarity is not only mediated at home:

> Since her birth Petruška had those two women, she knows that there are men and there are women. She knows that men and women marry, she sees grandma and grandpa, she sees that Radek [brother] has a girlfriend. We have guinea pigs so she sees that this is a male and a female. She herself certainly has no problems with not identifying with a man, a woman … . Definitely, if you conducted specialised research, I believe you would find that her psychological and sexual development is completely all right. (Dáša)

Such completely conscious exposure of families to the wider kin, friendship and social bonds and structures was typical of accounts that I also heard in other families. This is in line with Patterson's (2000) findings, who argues that lesbian mothers were (in comparison with divorced heterosexual mothers) more concerned for their daughters to have opportunities to interact with adult men. In general, lesbian couples were adamant that their families should not to appear closed and isolated. Parents stressed the importance of active involvement with the grandparent generation as well as with other adult relatives and friends.

In the following quote Pavla considers the nature and causes of gender differences:

> Well, I have *Aspekt* [feminist cultural magazine] here, 'We are not born women, we become them' and I read everything, read it in detail, right now before giving birth I thought I'd read *Aspekt* about it, I really did change my opinion. Actually with Tomáš some stuff is just given as male. We didn't force it on him. He also has a play kitchen, you saw him cooking there. Well, but how, don't you think. And who showed him that he should smack play dough with a hammer? He was a year and a half, he did not speak yet but he was already humming. He took a car in the sand pit and started riding with it immediately. I know that even a girl can do that but who taught him, for example, to hold a lid like a steering wheel and run around the flat and shout: 'Crash, crash'? Who taught him? (Pavla)

Zuzka and Pavla define themselves critically in relation to the traditional gendered model of the family. They appreciate feminism, as they understand it from literature available in the Czech Republic, mostly mediated by the Slovak feminist magazine *Aspekt*. The example of this family supports findings summarised by Stacey and Biblarz (2001), who argue that in the case of daughters, mothers did not adhere so anxiously to gender stereotypical games and toys. The above quote also confirms the findings of a different study, i.e. that mothers' preferences had only a small influence on their children's preferences, as they chose toys and activities that tended to be gender stereotypical (Tasker and Golombok 2002). In contrast with the previous family, in Kamila and Dita's family both mothers preferred toys and clothes that are gender traditional, and they happily shared the story about their three-year-old daughter putting on high-heel shoes, which may be understood as adopting a desirable image of femininity.

The last quote is a good example of how the upbringing of children by lesbian couples involved a mixture and confrontation of normative gender expectations with an often explicitly expressed effort at overcoming these:

> Tomáš [four-year-old son] is simply a technical type. He has a child electric screwdriver and he held the screw like this, fitted it like this and I watched him and thought to myself: 'My goodness, he holds it better than me. That stupid little screw.' Well, it does not involve anything, does it, but suddenly I had the feeling that he has a grip. (Pavla)

Pavla characterises her son's treatment of the screwdriver as his having 'a grip'; and similarly Eva in an earlier quote proposes that she leave the 'more fundamental [technical] stuff' to her father. Both women confirm the superiority of men/boys in this field, although Pavla does so with a certain amount of surprise and 'motherly prejudice'. At the same time, similar to the case of the three-year-old daughter putting on high-heel shoes, the mother comments on this performance with apparent joy – related exactly to the fact that the child demonstrates an 'appropriate' gender role.

Reflexive Relationships

Only when the research was completed did I realise a somewhat surprising fact: the topic of sex did not come up in the course of the interviews with almost any of the families. To the contrary, it was a frequent topic in interviews with heterosexual women (carried out for another project). The single reference to sex was made by Irma:

> She was very strict and consistent in preventing him [son] from seeing us in an intimate relationship that is in action. You get home, kiss your partner in front of the child, on the contrary, explicitly in front of the child – the sign that we love each other, all of us – love each other, that all is well, on the contrary, the child can see, the child likes to see that all's fine. This is *extremely* important and that is also why I know now in retrospect that there wasn't a slightest problem. (Irma)

The context in which sex appears seems typical, in a sense that it refers to the knowing constitution of the family as a harmonious and loving unit. However, in Irma's narration, in a lesbian relationship the expression of emotional fondness in front of the child needs special monitoring. Lesbian sex represents a problem; therefore she applies strict heteronormative criteria of 'normality' and 'deviancy' in her relationship. In the quotation presented above Irma presents the stereotype of a lesbian relationship that might be seen as presumably double loaded with femininity, and therefore based on mutual support, care, empathy and affection.[7]

In the mentioned episode of *Wife Swap*, the couples sitting at the table at the final meeting were really different at first sight. However, they actually shared much in common: an idea that 'real men' are dominant and that 'real women' should work together with men to render women more submissive. If femininity is usually understood as communicative and empathetic, then our female respondents, often completely consciously, met this image.

(Self-)reflexivity was a frequent characteristic in my cases – particularly in relation to the gender order through which women disciplined themselves (often more consciously and strictly than I would have expected before conducting the research). This could also be observed in the discussed episode of *Wife Swap*. The egalitarian model of lesbian relationships found in Western literature (Kurdek 1988; Sullivan 2004) would imply that one of the partners from the lesbian couple would appreciate the 'modern man' in her household. Conversely, we see Gita trying to 'fix' the man into the 'appropriate' (i.e. traditional) gender role. In doing so, Gita conforms to (and confirms) the dominant position of heteronormative gender roles. This also implies that Western scholarship on non-normative kinship needs to be critically reassesed in and against the Czech context, as the implications of both are different.

West and East

The adopted interpretative approach to the study of 'homo-families' offers an opportunity to highlight those aspects of partnerships and parenthood that would be problematic in the context of heterosexual families, disguised in 'taken-for-granted' 'normality' and 'transparency'. Research on the everyday lives of homoparental families suggests that gender and sexual orientation become a structural component of interactions, a principle that organises their social space.

---

7   We can find similar desexualising tendencies in the l/g movement as, for example, during the first queer Pride (2008) in the Czech Republic: s/m participants were over the internet discouraged from participating in the march in order to present the gay and lesbian community in a less alternative and opposing manner.

Another explanation of the absence of sex in interviews with lesbians occurred to me in conversation with my colleague. She pointed to the fact that not only do heterosexual women seem to talk more about sex, but they are also more likely to verbalise their dissatisfaction with sex. She suggested that if heterosexual relationships are more gendered and women are the ones who are responsible for domestic duties and childcare, they are also likely to be the ones who are at times more or less displeased with this asymmetry in relationships. Unsatisfactory sex is then an indicator of frustration and miscommunication in the partnerships. If lesbian relationships are more egalitarian (as some research proves) it might mean more satisfaction also in sexual life and less need for bringing up the issue in conversation.

This contradicts the Western research that is narrowed to the comparative study of lesbian families against the traditional models of 'family' (Chan et al. 1998). Although such an approach dominates the public debate in the Czech Republic, in sociological terms it is highly problematic for the uncritical use of analytical categories. Research frequently explores sexual orientation as a defining element in how one grasps and performs the parental role. With reference to selected authors (Hicks 2005; Butler 2002) I argue for an approach that takes into account the circumstances, contexts and purposes for which sexual orientation is mobilised as a defining characteristic for exercising the parental role or, in contrast, the contexts in which sexuality is deprived of its significance or is silenced.

In my study I explored same-sex marriage and parenthood as topics that involve public, civic and political discussions. Although it may seem that gays and lesbians will welcome the right to marriage (or partnership) as a clearly positive development, there is also an ambivalent aspect to this consecration (Warner 1999; Butler 2002). No matter how much we may agree with conferring the right to marriage on gay and lesbian couples or disagree with homophobic arguments that appear in public debates about same-sex unions, we cannot be blind to the fact that the granting of gay marriages also brings about a new set of hierarchies, inequalities and disciplinations. This is because the granting of marriage declassifies all those types of relationships and intimacy that do not involve couples and monogamy to a category of lower quality; these do not represent very good life strategies and paths (Butler 2002). In this respect then we can consider the founding of a lesbian family consisting of two mothers and a child (or children) a completely conformist act. On the other hand the women often had to invent and work up non-standard strategies in order to conceive a child under conditions that legally do not support homoparentality. Also their daily practices of parenthood in a situation where one partner is not biologically linked to the child challenge the notion of biological and social in a family.

The difference of the lesbian family often stems not so much from the identity defined by sexual orientation but rather from the dominance of heterosexuality in the society which renders other forms of partnership deviant or insufficient. Heteronormativity does not only exercise its influence from the outside as a coercive and disciplining force; its power also lies mainly in internalisation and somatisation. As a result, women in lesbian families may at times perceive themselves as members of 'not good enough' families. This difference or 'inadequacy' that is experienced symbolically and materially, abstractly and also very concretely, had its antithesis in the (at times) conscious effort to withstand the test, which often actually meant fitting within two categories that provide consolation and identification – femininity and family. In relation to both, women relied on distancing themselves from the gay and lesbian community which then does not seem to work as a source of identification patterns and values – at least in a sense that tends to be described in the Western academic writings (Stein 1997; Weston 1991).

My findings also contradict the research that argues that traditional parental roles do not apply in the case of lesbian families, that traditional gender roles are absent and that, in replacing these, women invent new forms of parenthood and partnership (Kurdek 1988). No matter how attractive such arguments may appear at a theoretical level, they seem to expect the disappearance, elimination or invalidation of gender roles and traditions once we move away from the context of the heterosexual family – an expectation that is rather naive. Gender as an element of social structure is embedded in our everydayness through a series of more or less significant interactions, abstract and everyday apparatuses of knowledge and practice (Harding 1986; Bourdieu 2000). Consequently, lesbian families do not necessarily endorse 'equality' of monogendered familial organisation; similarly heterosexual families do not necessarily involve the traditional division of roles.

Whether the ideal of the 'normal' family is explicitly uttered or not, we can say that it is at least implicitly always present in discussions about alternative families (Stacey and Biblarz 2001). Lesbian families, when confronted with the 'ideal' dominating Czech culture, seem to inevitably apply heteronormative gendered scenarios when performing their parenthood and partnership roles. These are, however, not only conformist, but also have transformative potential by the simple fact that they are enacted within the (by definition) non-normative lesbian partnership. The women in this research did not tend to be proud pioneers of changes in the organisation of family, partnership or intimacy. To the contrary, lesbian families share with the majority of Czech society conventional normative ideas of the family as an entity based on a solid couple with children under one roof. Nonetheless, the configuration and division of motherhood (as biological and social), dominant in my research sample, represents an unspoken repudiation of the traditional model of the family.

Neither Subversive nor Traditional

The study shows that Czech lesbian families are neither traditional nor subversive. Their depiction as such is always the outcome of opinionated interpretations embedded in a concrete position that can always be identified and allocated an ideology. To understand homoparental families as conformist or deconstructivist entails what Bourdieu terms the anthropomorphic concept of the family. According to him, the family appears to be a transparent person endowed with a common life and spirit and a particular worldview (Bourdieu 1998: 95). In relation to this anthropomorphic image of a family, one may recall Eric Fassin's words:

> Homoparental families share with other families solely (and this is by far sufficient) 'the appearance of the family': a mouth similar to this one, eyes like another's, a chin like that one and a nose like this one. They can fall apart and re-unite just like heteroparental families. They can centre on one parent like monoparental families. They can be based on multiple filiations and

shared parenthood like families with adopted children. In exactly the same way as heteroparental families that utilize the means of assisted reproduction or adoption, they as well sometimes question and sometimes do not question the principle of biological origin. In short, homoparental families show partial similarities, they have entered the 'family of families', yet it is not necessary and not even possible to search for a new common denominator for families (and that not even for homoparental families themselves) as demonstrated in the many ways in which they are formed. (Fassin 2003: 32)

Moreover, with the help of Goffman (1967), upholding the metaphor of face, we can see it as a positive value and recognition that people demand in concrete situations using verbal and non-verbal practices of action. Thus lesbian families attempt to maintain the face of a good family, based on a solid and monogamous partnership and childcare. The effort to 'keep face' – also a meaningful concept in heterosexual families – acquires, however, a special status in same-sex families, especially in relation to popularly held convictions about homosexual people as 'promiscuous', somehow 'without families' and without the will to have them.

Thus, in their everyday efforts lesbian families in the Czech Republic strive for a balance between the stigmatising stereotype of a lesbian and the image of the autonomous 'good family'. In this case a 'good family' also means an 'invisible family' – a family that does not attract attention and is not marked as 'different'. As said above, the women in my research did not tend to embody activist attitudes for lesbian and gay rights. If this type of political activism in the Czech Republic is often associated with the stress put on *coming out* in public, then lesbian families from my study do the opposite. They rather perform '*coming into*' 'normality and expectancy' associated with traditional and heteronormative models of family.

Bibliography

Almack, K. 2005. 'What's In a Name? The Significance of the Choice of Surnames Given to Children Born Within Lesbian-Parent Families'. *Sexualities*, 8(2): 239–54.

Bourdieu, P. 1998. *Teorie jednání* [*Practical Reason: On the Theory of Action*]. Prague: Karolinum.

Bourdieu, P. 2000. *Nadvláda mužů* [*Masculine Domination*]. Prague: Karolinum.

Butler, J. 1991. 'Imitation and Gender Insubordination'. In *Inside/Out: Lesbian Theories, Gay Theories*, eds D. Fuss et al. New York: Routledge.

———. 2002. 'Is Kinship Always Already Heterosexual?' *A Journal of Feminist Cultural Studies*, 13(1): 14–44.

Carrington, C. 1999. *No Place Like Home*. Chicago: University of Chicago Press.

Fassin, É. 2003. 'Užívání vědy a věda o užíváních: K tématu homoparentálních rodin'. *Biograf*, 9(30): 19–35.

Chan, R.W., Brooks, R.C., Raboy, B. and Patterson, C.J. 1998. 'Division of Labor Among Lesbian and Heterosexual Parents: Associations with Children's Adjustment'. *Journal of Family Psychology*, 3: 348–56.

Goffman, E. 1997. 'Frame Analysis of Gender'. In *The Goffman Reader*, eds C. Lemert et al. Malden: Blackwell.

Golombok, S., Spencer, A. and Rutter, M. 1983. 'Children in Lesbian and Single-Parent Households: Psychosexual and Psychiatric Appraisal'. *Journal of Child Psychology and Psychiatry*, 24: 551–72.

Green, R. 1978. 'Sexual Identity of 37 Children Raised by Homosexual or Transsexual Patents'. *American Journal of Psychiatry*, 135: 692–7.

Harding, S. 1986. *The Science Question in Feminism*. Ithaca: Cornell University Press.

Hicks, S. 2005. 'Is Gay Parenting Bad for Kids? Responding to the "very idea of difference" in research on lesbian and gay parents'. *Sexualities*, 8(2): 153–68.

Kurdek, L.A. 1988. 'Perceived Social Support in Gays and Lesbians in Cohabitating Relationships'. *Journal of Personality and Social Psychology*, 54: 504–9.

Lišková, K. 2008. 'Spříznění bez volby: Pornografie v sexuologickém, kriminologickém a feministickém diskursu'. *Sociální studia*, 5(1): 77–97.

Martin, Karin. 2009. 'Normalizing Heterosexuality: Mothers' assumptions, talk, and strategies with young children'. *American Sociological Review*, 74: 190–207.

Matějček, Z. 2008. *Co děti nejvíce potřebují*. Prague: Portál.

Nedbálková, K. 2005. 'Lesbické rodiny: Mezi stereotypem a autenticitou'. *Biograf*, 38: 38). Available at: http://www.biograf.org/clanky/clanek.php?clanek=v3802.

———. 2007. 'The Changing Space of Gay and Lesbian Community in the Czech Republic'. In *Beyond the Pink Curtain: Everyday Life of LGBT in Eastern Europe*, eds R. Kuhar et al. Ljubljana: Peace Institute (Politike Symposion series).

Nedbálková, K. and Polášková, E. 2009. 'The Czech Republic'. In *The Greenwood Encyclopedia of LGBT Issues Worldwide*, eds C. Stewart et al. Westport, CT: Greenwood Press.

Patterson, C.J. 1992. 'Lesbian and Gay Families'. *Current Directions in Psychological Science*, 3: 62–4.

———. 1994. 'Children of the Lesbian Baby Boom: Behavioral Adjustment, Self-Concepts, and Sex Role Identity'. In *Lesbian and Gay Psychology: Theory, research, and clinical applications*, eds B. Greene and G.M. Herek. Thousand Oaks, CA: Sage Publications.

———. 2000. 'Family Relationships of Lesbians and Gay Men'. *Journal of Marriage and the Family*, 62: 1052–69.

Polášková, E. 2007. 'The Czech Lesbian Family Study: Investigating Family Practices'. In *Beyond the Pink Curtain: Everyday Life of LGBT People in Eastern Europe*, eds R. Kuhar et al. Ljubljana: Peace Institute (Politike Symposion series).

Šmídová, I. 2009. 'Changing Czech Masculinities? Beyond Environment and Children Friendly Men. In *Intimate Citizenships: Gender, Subjectivity, Politics*, ed. Elzbieta Oleksy. New York and London: Routledge.

Sokolová, V. 2001. 'Representations of Homosexuality and the Separation of Gender and Sexuality in the Czech Republic Before and After 1989'. In *Political Systems and Definitions of Gender Roles*, eds A.K. Isaacs et al. Pisa: Edizione Plus.

Stacey, J. 1997. *In the Name of the Family: Rethinking Family Values in the Postmodern Age*. Boston, MA: Beacon Press.

Stacey, J. and Biblarz, T. 2001. '(How) Does the Sexual Orientation of Parents Matter?' *American Sociological Review* 66(2): 159–83.

———. 2010. 'How Does the Gender of Parents Matter?' *Journal of Marriage and Family*, 72(1): 3–22.

Stein, A. 1997. *Sex and Sensibility: Stories of a Lesbian Generation*. Berkeley: University of California Press.

Sullivan, M. 2004. *The Family of Women: Lesbian Mothers, Their children and the Undoing of Gender*. Berkeley: University of California Press.

Tasker, F. and Golombok, S. 1997. 'Toward Living in a Lesbian Family: A Longitudinal Study of Children Raised by Post-Divorce Lesbian Mothers'. *Journal of Divorce & Remarriage*, 23: 183–202.

———. 2002. *Growing Up in a Lesbian Family: Effects On Child Development*. New York and London: The Guilford Press.

Warner, M. 1999. *The Trouble with Normal: Sex, Politics, and the Ethics of Queer Life*. Boston, MA: Harvard University Press.

Weston, K. 1991. *Families We Choose: Lesbians, Gays, Kinship*. New York: Columbia University Press.

Chapter 8

The Heteronormative Panopticon and the Transparent Closet of the Public Space in Slovenia

Roman Kuhar

'We only wanted to express our viewpoint. It disturbs me to see [gays] express their sexual orientation in public and in front of children. A child needs a father and a mother, not a father and a father.'[1] This is a court statement of one of three young men, aged 18 to 22, who were arrested in early July 2009 for a physical attack on gays and lesbians in a gay-friendly bar, Café Open, in Ljubljana. They had thrown a lit torch into the bar during a gay literary reading, and physically attacked Mitja Blažič, a gay activist, who happened to be in front of the bar at the moment of the attack. They burned his neck with the torch and injured his head, most probably with a stone. Although he received three stitches in his head, the physical pain he suffered could not be compared to the psychological consequences. He reported to the court that he was no longer comfortable walking the streets alone, especially at night, that he did not feel at ease if somebody was walking behind him, and that he was haunted by disturbing dreams. 'People also stop me in the street [his image was featured in every major media in the country] and insult me,' he claimed.[2]

The gay literary reading in Café Open was one of the events accompanying the 2009 Pride parade in Ljubljana. The immediate reaction to the attack from politicians and the general public was condemnation, extensive and supportive media coverage and the decision of the Minister of the Interior, Katarina Kresal, to march in the parade. Thus the ninth Pride parade in Slovenia met with a much wider (and more positive) response than its organisers could have hoped for. However, this does not change the disturbing fact that first Pride parades, organised in Ljubljana since 2001, did not encounter any contra-protests and no physically attacked and injured participants; while in the past few years the organisers of Pride annually report violent incidents. It seems as if such homophobic violence has become a constitutive element of Pride parades, which – unlike the ones in the West, where they have become more commercial, playful and even depoliticised – still hold the shape (and the content) of political protest.

---

1   Furlan, Mojca Rus. 2009. Napadalci so se gejevskemu aktivistu Mitji Blažiču na sodišču opravičili. *Dnevnik*, 25 November 2009.

2   Ibid.

Although, as Kuhar and Takács (2007) point out, social and cultural homophobia remains a 'unifying experience' of LGBT people in the West and East and therefore we need to look beyond the Pink Curtain,[3] beyond such political and geographical divisions it is also true that Pride parades in Eastern Europe – in cities where they are allowed to be organised – are defined by the fear of potential homophobic violence. Furthermore, despite the fact that the Slovenian gay and lesbian movement has the longest tradition in Eastern Europe[4] – and this might partly explain why the Pride parades are not met with violent organised protests during them (as is the case in Croatia and elsewhere in Eastern Europe) – the effect of the city's heteronormative geography on the everyday life of the LGBT community remains undiminished.[5]

This chapter is based on the empirical research results of several studies which looked into the everyday life of gays and lesbians in Slovenia.[6] Although the most comprehensive study to date on the everyday life of gays and lesbians in Slovenia (Švab and Kuhar 2005) found that the 'geography of homophobic acts' is gendered

---

3   *Beyond the Pink Curtain* is the title of a collection of 21 texts discussing the everyday life situation of LGBT people in Eastern Europe. The title of the book was later used in Matthew Charles's documentary on the lives of gays and lesbians in Eastern Europe (2009): see Kuhar and Takács (2007).

4   Homosexuality was decriminalised in Slovenia in 1976, eight years before the establishment of an organised gay and lesbian movement. The first gay organisation was established in 1984 and encountered no problems from the socialist government of the time.

5   In Slovenia the term 'LGBT' is used as an inclusive and politically correct term (mostly in the LGBT community). However, it does not mean that the politics, based on these identities, equally addresses all four of them. The 'L' and 'G' (or even better 'G' and 'L') are the dominant identities. There are some efforts from non-governmental organisations and a popular transsexual person to address the specific 'T' issues (but so far with no feedback from the government agencies); while the specific position of the 'B' is not addressed politically, but rather socially and culturally (for example through texts, focusing on bisexual identity, in the LGBT magazine *Narobe*). The relation with 'queer' politics is an awkward one. Mainstream society is not familiar with queer (as elsewhere there is no translation for 'queer' in the Slovenian language), while some people in the LGBT community consider themselves queer. The term is quite often used as a criticism of the male/female binary, but at the same time as a 'fixed identity' (rather than a 'non-identity'). While instances of queer politics can be traced in several political actions and protests, the prevailing approach to LGBT issues remains that of identity politics. In the contemporary debate over the proposal of the new Family Code, which puts heterosexual and homosexual partnerships on an equal legal footing, including the right to adoption, there is no distinct queer voice which would oppose 'gay marriages' present in the debate.

6   These research studies include: 'Family and Social Contexts of Everyday Life of Gays and Lesbians in Slovenia' (Švab and Kuhar 2005, N=443); 'Everyday Life of Young LGBT Persons in Slovenia' (Kuhar et al. 2008, N=221); 'Consequences of Discrimination on Social and Political Inclusion of Youth in Slovenia' (Švab et al. 2008); and 'Activate: Research, Monitoring, and Recording of Cases of Discrimination and Rights Violations against LGBT People in Slovenia' (Kuhar and Magić 2008, N=149).

– lesbians are more often the victims of violence in private life than gays – gays and lesbians generally reported the highest share of violent incidents taking place in the public space, perpetrated by strangers in the streets and in bars. This chapter therefore explores how gays and lesbians organise their everyday lives in the public space, defined by heteronormative images.

I will first sketch some conclusions from the (feminist) debate on citizenship, the separation of public and private spheres and its consequences. These effects will be illustrated with empirical data and then discussed further in the context of Foucault's interpretation of the panopticon and Arendt's thematisation of the social and political dimensions of the public sphere ((Foucault 1984; Arendt 1996). In conclusion the chapter suggests that the concept of the 'transparent closet' (Švab and Kuhar 2005; Kuhar 2007), originally used in discussions on 'coming out' in family contexts (the private sphere), could also be applied to the public sphere. The transparent closet draws attention to the relational nature of coming out as an act. While it is often understood that coming out is a process, a chain of never-ending acts (one needs to come out over and over again in new situations), the single act of coming out is rarely understood as relational; it is understood that once one comes out, one is out. However, in order for the coming out to be 'successful' it needs to be acknowledged and acted upon by the other side – the person one comes out to. The transparent closet, therefore, refers to situations where one comes out of the closet, and is then pushed back into it. It is now clear that there is a person in the closet (the closet becomes transparent), but the person/society refuses to acknowledge the new piece of information. It seems that similar mechanisms, informed by heteronormativity and sexual shame (Warner 1999), function in both spheres, public and private, with similar effects.

Public/Private Sphere and Sexuality

The understanding of citizenship rights as being related only to the public sphere overlooks the complex, interwoven nature of public and private spheres. In such understanding, which is clearly shared by the perpetrator of the violent act in front of the Café Open, one's sexuality and sexual orientation is seen as a private matter which should not be publicly displayed. As a private matter, it is understood, it cannot be a matter of state intervention.

Such reductionism results in gays and lesbians being second-class citizens. The state, for example, remains uninterested in the verbal, emotional and physical violence gays and lesbians face in the private sphere due to their sexual orientation. As Young (1991) suggests, such reductionism is in accordance with the legitimisation of the privileged view of the world, which is represented as universal. The reductionism – or, as Richardson (1998: 89) calls it, the heterosexist division between the private and public sphere – again and again establishes and preserves the heteronormativity of the public sphere in such a way that it becomes 'naturalised'. Here, heteronormativity is understood through Hennessy's interpretation of heterosexuality as an 'institution that organises more than just the sexual: it is socially pervasive, underlying myriad taken-for-granted norms that shape what can be seen, said and valued' (Hennessy 1995: 146). It means that in the context of the heteronormative geography of the space, where everything is permeated by factual or imagined heterosexuality, signs of homosexuality (which equal disturbance) are immediately noted and, as the empirical research presented in this chapter shows, accompanied by attempts at its removal. The dichotomy of private/public in the political and spatial sense, as Duncan suggests, is in fact 'frequently employed to construct, control, discipline, confine, exclude and suppress gender and sexual differences preserving traditional patriarchal and heterosexist power structures' (Duncan 1996: 128).

Such employment of the private/public division does not mean that the solution lies in the abolition of such a division, but rather in its deconstruction. In such a way the hidden controlling and disciplining effects of the division can be made visible and consequently changed. While Young (1991) correctly outlines the importance of privacy in a sense that privacy can empower us, the optic of this interpretation needs to be turned to the opposite direction as well. Not only should one be able to exclude others from one's privacy, but one should also be able to talk about and display one's privacy in public. Isin and Wood (1999: 85) explain that the access of one's privacy to the public sphere is not linked with the performance of sexual acts in the public sphere. It is rather linked with the right to participate in the public sphere as sexual beings. Interestingly enough, while gays and lesbians are primarily defined through their sexuality, or even reduced to 'sexual bodies', they are at the same time often denied the right to be sexual beings in the public sphere (Kuhar, 2005).

The understanding of same-sex orientation as a matter of privacy which does not, or should not, have an effect on a person's public life implies a demand that gays and lesbians (and other non-heterosexuals) undress the '*clothes of same-sex orientation*' each time they enter the public space. The process of undressing, which includes the removal of not only the physical signs of homosexuality, but also the movement and gestures of the body recognised as 'gay', is a form of discipline. Furthermore, the heteronormative logic of the public space consequently demands that gays and lesbians should *dress up their bodies* in 'civilian clothes' – those of heterosexuality. In other words: their presence in the public space should not be disturbing to the heteronormative matrix of everyday life. The heteronormative assumption is inscribed in the distinction between the private and public sphere and functions as a form of social control over sexualities which are constructed as 'deviant'.

Through the process of the 'privatisation' of homosexuality, heterosexual norms, as Duncan (1996) points out, are being naturalised. It means that heterosexuality is also explained as being a matter of privacy and not being 'exercised' in the public space. However, the manifestations of heterosexuality in the public space could not be more obvious: heterosexuality is exercised in young nuclear families taking a walk in the park; in a boy and a girl holding hands while walking down the street; in the big advertisements which address us in shopping malls; on the cover of a toothpaste carton where a happy heterosexual couple expose their white teeth; it can be traced in the assumption with which the assistant at the florist's addresses a man (assuming that he is buying flowers for his girlfriend). The same assumption is at work in bureaucracy, most explicitly in forms asking us about our marital status; heterosexual assumption is inscribed in job ads in which a newly opened bar offers employment only to young waitresses (despite the fact that such differentiation is prohibited by law); it is inscribed in the majority of songs echoing through speakers in the streets, in shopping malls, in bars. One can see a heterosexual assumption wherever one turns. However, as it pervades every aspect of social life, not only those dealing with sexuality, it can easily become invisible, naturalised and unquestionable. It actually becomes visible only when this assumption is incongruent with our own 'intimate assumption'.

Despite the correctives in the form of tolerance, heterosexuality remains a structural part of social institutions and relations, and of the public sphere as such. In fact, as suggested by Morgan (2000), the 'tolerant correctives' actually help in reproducing heteronormativity. The heterosexual majority is namely asked to tolerate the homosexual minority, which automatically places homosexuality in a subordinated position and reproduces the binary opposition of heterosexuality as the norm and homosexuality as 'the other':

> The very notion of 'tolerance' implies subordination: you don't 'tolerate' something which is good (you celebrate it), you only 'tolerate' things you would rather didn't exist. Tolerance is thus a practice of oppression. In the area of sexuality, at the very moment 'tolerance' is deployed to justify the recognition of rights, it sends the message that hetero is good and non-hetero is bad. 'Tolerance' is thus also a technology for extending the panoptic gaze. It opens up new terrains of subjectivity for the state to colonize (those being tolerated) whilst maintaining the disciplinary effects of heterosexuality (because those being tolerated are *merely* that). (Morgan 2000: 220)

It is impossible to address the public and private spheres as anything but interwowen and interrelated. Public decisions and politics indisputably structure not only the public but also the private sphere. As Walby (1994: 80) points out, we cannot talk about any social spheres which would be completely protected from state intervention, as the state itself most often sets the limits of (non)intervention. The construction of the private/public divide is therefore a political action in itself.

Gays and Lesbians in the Public Sphere – Some Empirical Data

Empirical studies on the everyday life of gays and lesbians in Slovenia show how the private/public divide affects their everyday life experiences. The most comprehensive study to date in Slovenia (Švab and Kuhar 2005) showed that

53 per cent of lesbians and gays surveyed had reported at least one incident of violence due to their sexual orientation. Most of them experienced verbal violence (91 per cent), a quarter of respondents reported physical violence (24 per cent), followed by those reporting sexual violence (6 per cent). As already mentioned, the experiences of violence are gendered (more men than women experience physical violence and, vice versa, more women than men experience verbal violence) and are also site specific. The geography of homophobic incidents shows that over 60 per cent of attacks occurred in public spaces and were committed by strangers. Furthermore, 68 per cent of those experiencing violence due to their sexual orientation, reported several such incidents (Švab and Kuhar 2005: 117–23).

Small-scale research on homophobic violence lists the most commonly occurring forms of such violence. The most frequent are name-calling and the use of offensive nicknames, ignoring, threatening or excluding. Respondents from this research reported people in the public space being disturbed by signs of homosexuality, such as holding hands. Some of them had been told that holding hands with a partner of the same sex was improper behaviour or had been called names such as 'poofs' or 'dykes'; or, as reported by one respondent, people threw stones at him and his boyfriend as they were holding hands. Yet another respondent reported an incident with a street musician who refused to continue playing his instrument when he realised that a lesbian was listening to him (Kuhar and Magić 2008: 14–21).

Over 92 per cent of respondents from the research on homophobic violence never reported homophobic incidents. 36 per cent of them believed that the violence they had encountered was not 'serious enough' to be reported or, as 27 per cent of respondents claimed, by reporting homophobic violence they would not achieve anything. It seems that victims often rationalise such incidents and minimise their importance or they anticipate negative experiences with the police. However, those who reported homophobic violence did not describe police proceedings as a negative experience: 60 per cent of them described police officers as being neutral and 40 per cent as being supportive (Kuhar and Magić 2008: 22–4).

What is the story behind all these numbers? How does the heterosexualisation of the public space, established either by physical violence or subtle regulative mechanisms (such as verbal comments, staring, gazing, whistling), affect non-heterosexuals? Valentine (1996: 148) suggests that the regulative mechanisms spread the discomfort and send out the message to 'non-heterosexuals' that they do not belong to society at large. These mechanisms establish self-control in non-heterosexual people and consequently enable the preservation of the heteronormative geography of the public space.

On the basis of interviews conducted with the respondents in focus groups[7] (Švab and Kuhar 2005), we can say that most of them adjusted to the heterosexualised

---

7   The research on the everyday life of gays and lesbians in Slovenia consisted of two parts: a quantitative part (443 face-to-face questionnaires) and a qualitative part (seven focus groups that included 36 people).

public space through a certain degree of mimicry. Mimicry is therefore a mechanism of self-control and self-protection, imposed by the heteronormativity of the public space. As a mechanism of self-control it can be propelled also by internalised homophobia. While mimicry in the homophobic public space functions as self-protection, it also consequently enables keeping of the heterosexuality of the street intact. The results showed that in private milieus, for example among friends, the gays and lesbians who participated in the research express their sexuality through visible signs (for example expressing kindness to their same-sex partners). These signs are then removed once they enter the public space: there their same-sex partnership is transformed into 'just friendship'. This false public image is transgressed only in some exceptional moments, when they believe that the threat of violence has momentarily abated. It seems that spontaneous expressions of intimacy in the public space are much less characteristic of gays and lesbians than they are of heterosexuals. The spontaneous gestures are disabled by a constant awareness of the heteronormativity underpinning the public space:

> One feels the pressure. You take a look around yourself and if there is no one, then you do it [you express your homosexuality]. Or you do it if the environment is such that it allows it. If there are no primitive people around you, then you do it. However I don't walk hand in hand with my boyfriend around Ljubljana, definitely not. ... It seems as if all this is already in your DNA, that we live in a heterosexual society with certain rules and that you must not provoke it. (Igor, 27)[8]

As gays and lesbians have to choose carefully moments of when and how to express intimacy in the public space, the spontaneous nature of such gestures is suppressed. In such a way, as some respondents claimed, the gesture loses its point as it is pervaded with fear:

> At the beginning there is a wish, which is then always accompanied by fear, which blocks you. Everything is blocked. ... You ruminate upon holding hands so much that it eventually loses the initial purpose of a spontaneous love gesture. At the end, everything is quite absurd. Even if I hold his hand, it seems as if I was holding a piece of wood. I don't know ... we are simply not relaxed. We hold hands and walk down the street like two paraplegics, and we just wait for someone to say something. (Borut, 30)

While some respondents in the focus groups expressed their discomfort (and the threat of violence) they had experienced when trying to break down the heteronormativity of the public space – knowing that by silencing themselves they helped to reproduce the heterosexualisation of the public space – some respondents resignedly believed that it is simply 'the way of the world' and that one should

---

8 All names have been changed. The number next to the name represents the age of the respondent.

respect the norms of society. Although the invisibility of gays and lesbians in the public space was considered as something negative by the respondents in the focus groups, some of them believed that is it not in their power to resist it. The focus group participants expressed a rather high level of conformity when it comes to public expressions of same-sex intimacy. Švab and Kuhar called this situation 'the unbearable comfort of privacy': on one hand the fact that the limit of tolerance towards homosexuality is set between the private and the public (homosexuality can be tolerated only if it is pushed into privacy) is unbearable, but on the other hand confronting the heteronormativity of the public space might be straining. Therefore enjoying the 'comfort' of privacy can be rewarding: 'If we are cloaked in privacy, we do not need to face discrimination, stand up for our rights and expose ourselves. In this sense, privacy can equal 'comfort'. An illusionary comfort' (Švab and Kuhar 2005: 22).

Although such responses from the focus group participants can be interpreted as protection from possible homophobic reactions to signs of homosexual intimacy in the public space, they might also be, as already suggested, an expression of internalised homophobia and of social control. In such a way socially acceptable identities are created and rewarded and, consequently, other identities are pushed (physically and/or symbolically) towards the margins of society. Expressions of homosexuality are thus limited to selected moments, when one believes they are not in the view of the heteronormative panopticon:

> Sometimes I want to hold his hand, but he pushes it back. I can understand he is afraid, but I am afraid as well. I wouldn't hold hands in Fužine [part of Ljubljana where mostly immigrants reside], that would be too much. But if there is a chance, like at night, why not? (Andrej, 25)

> You can get one strange gaze in the street and you will change your mind. (Amalija, 26)

In his study on the closet in America, Steven Seidman (2002) suggests that young generations tend to organise their everyday life beyond the closet, while for older generations the closet represented an inescapable part of their lives. The studies on the everyday life of gays and lesbians in Slovenia only partly confirm such a conclusion.[9] While living beyond the closet might be characteristic of the new generation, they still – according to our research – do not or cannot organise it beyond the closet in every aspect of social life. The closet loses its power in the narrow social circles of close friends and in family contexts, but remains an obstacle in the public sphere: in the streets (the majority of gays and lesbians surveyed hide their sexual orientation in the streets); in the workplace (over 50 per cent of respondents hide their homosexuality at work); in schools (the official curriculum for primary schools excludes homosexuality and same-sex families as a

---

9   Seidman, of course, does not claim that his conclusions hold true for Eastern Europe.

topic to be discussed in public schools) and so on. It seems that the privatisation of homosexuality in Slovenian society is successfully implemented: homosexuality is acceptable as long as it is not visible and remains in the closet.

Heteronormative Panopticon

The empirical results discussed above show how self-control is established in the public sphere, serving the social norms of society. These norms can be interpreted in the context of Foucault's thematisation of the panopticon. The 'all-seeing' space of the prison – where the continuous surveillance from a central location is being conducted, and where no prisoner can ever know whether they are being watched or not – is in fact an experience of gays and lesbians in the public space. Foucault (1984) explains that the panopticon sets up the awareness of being permanently visible – even in those instances when the surveillance is momentarily ceased. In such a way being aware of the existence of the panopticon surveillance establishes automatic control, which is being exercised by the prisoners themselves. Similarly, the awareness of continuously being watched in the public space, the awareness of being 'imprisoned' in the heteronormative panopticon of the public space, results in self-control or the use of mimicry. Foucault explains that 'there is no need for arms, physical violence, material constraints. Just a gaze. An inspecting gaze, a gaze which each individual under its weight will end by interiorising to the point that he is his own overseer, each individual thus exercising this surveillance over and against himself' (Foucault 1980: 155). This puts immense psychological and emotional pressure on gays and lesbians who, in order to avoid potential violence, are forced to conceal their own homosexuality. The heteronormative panopticon is actually one of the most dangerous forms of violence, as it establishes numerous subtle, invisible and latent mechanisms of control. However, following Foucault (1984), disciplinary techniques (as hidden power) need 'compulsory visibility' of subjects in order to function. While traditionally power, embodied in the sovereign, was visible and the object of the power was invisible, modern societies exercise controlling systems of power and knowledge through visibility. Foucault suggests that modern societies are characterised by the 'carceral continuum', where supervision is exercised on every level of one's existence. As power is ubiquitous, supervision – also as the application of the norms of acceptable behaviour – is now exercised by everyone over everyone else. Visibility is therefore, as Foucault writes, a trap. This brings us to the question of how control over gays and lesbians can be exercised in the city if they are basically invisible in the public space? Furthermore, are the endeavours of the gay and lesbian movement to make gays and lesbians 'more visible' not a way into the Foucauldian trap, where visibility will only enable more control?

    In order to answer these questions, a distinction between the different modes of visibility needs to be introduced. What Foucault understands by visibility is not necessarily 'physical visibility', but rather the discursive production of visible subjects. The visibility of gays and lesbians is therefore ensured through the existing discourse on homosexuality. It is the knowledge of the existence of the other (the homosexual) that enables control. Control over gays and lesbians in the street is closely connected with the understanding of homosexuality as a problem, as shame, as something degenerate and unacceptable. Following Foucault (2000), such visibility of homosexuality is linked with the discursive production of the homosexual as a subject at the end of the nineteenth century, when psychiatric discourse constructed 'the homosexual' as a mentally ill pervert. The continuous reproduction of such discourse (despite detours in the discourse towards tolerance in the late twentieth century) maintains the control/discipline over the perverted body. Gordon writes that 'if a discursive practice ceases to be articulated by constant repetition, it loses its power and may eventually disappear. Thus, the practice maintains its power only insofar as it is visible' (Gordon 2002: 132). In the context of the public space, the visibility of homosexual signs is actually enabled by the omnipresence of heterosexual signs in the public space. The omnipresence of heterosexual signs creates the ostensible invisibility of such signs (as they are everywhere we no longer notice them); while signs of homosexuality, if they emerge, for example in the street, automatically present a disturbance to the system. 'The omnipresence of heterosexual signs in fact magnifies homosexual signs, which are then immediately accompanied by the potential threats of homophobic violence' (Kuhar and Švab 2008: 270). The visibility which enables discipline is maintained by the congruent effect of the heteronormative discourse and the discourse on homosexuals as the others.

The second mode of visibility – the 'physical visibility' (also cultural, political and social visibility) – for which the gay and lesbian movement is striving, might be understood as a 'trap' which enables control. However, as Gordon explains, drawing on Foucault's discussions on power and surveillance, visibility is also a necessary component of resistance: 'Any form of resistance is also dependent on visibility, on the ability of people to see and hear defiant acts. Without visibility, all confrontations are meaningless' (Gordon 2002: 137). In such a way Pride parades, which establish gay and lesbian visibility *par excellence*, are a necessary condition for resistance. Resistance is namely possible, as Foucault writes, everywhere power is being exercised – such as in the heteronormative public space.

Normalisation as a Condition to Escape the Panopticon

Having the heteronormative geography of public space in mind, I would now like to turn to Arendt's differentiation between the social and the political. Arendt (1996) defines the 'social' as an intermediate sphere between the private and the public. The social dimension represents the abolition of the political sphere, which is, in Aristotelian terms, the space of equality; it is a space of plural speech. While the political sphere seems to shrink due to the rise of the social dimension, the sphere of plurality is also abolished. The 'social' is namely defined by only one voice – that of social norms which are believed to be shared among all of us and are allegedly in the best interest of all of us. In this sense, according to Arendt, *action* (as a political act) is now replaced by *behaviour*. Behaviour is determined by numerous rules aimed at controlling individuals, making them 'socially acceptable'. Individuals become social, rather than political beings; one's deliberation is thus replaced by social norms, and conformity is the door through which an individual enters the social dimension (and not the political dimension) of the public sphere. In other words (and using the same metaphor): in the context of homosexuality, coming out of the closet is the entrance through the door into the political sphere. Such an act is namely a political act (not behaviour), as it publicly challenges social norms. Arendt's understanding of the 'social' is actually 'heteronormativity' in the language of queer theorists as it denotes *behaviour* in accordance with hetero-norms. If I simplify it even further, I could say that 'coming out' is a form of Arendt's action, while the 'closet' represents behaviour congruent with heteronormativity. It seems that coming out in the public sphere therefore corresponds to the 'political' or, in Foucauldian terms, to 'resistance'.

However, this is not necessarily the case. It seems that coming out in the public sphere, at least in some (Western) milieus, is becoming more and more social rather than political. Contemporary Western societies have slowly been incorporating homosexuality into their social norms, in a sense that a homosexual couple in the street does not necessarily evoke indignation. Such a shift (which might not be the reality in all Western societies) can be classified as 'tolerance', which is, as Kuzmanić (1994) points out, primarily a *social* not a *political* phenomenon. 'Tolerance' is namely a sign that the 'political' does not exist or that political equality does not function properly. For that reason the above-mentioned shift does not mean the loosening of heteronormativity. It is only broadened as far as including some dimensions of homosexuality. Heteronormativity is therefore a flexible practice/discourse, but only as much as keeping the social power relations intact. The flexibility of heteronormativity as practice is enabled by tolerance, which can be accommodated into heteronormative practice (and discourse) as it actually reinforces the power relations between the subject who tolerates and the object which is being tolerated. Bauman (1997) explains that such a power relation is circular: one group tolerates another in order to keep control in their hands; but at the same time the tolerating subject (the group which subordinates another group) depends on the tolerated object in order to legitimate its own power.

Homosexuals in the heterosexualised street are like Simmel's (1950) strangers: persons who are near and far at the same time. Bauman (1997) suggests that strangers are actually those who appear between the clearly defined in-group and out-group. Strangers therefore transgress the clearly defined boundaries between the two groups, and this is exactly what happens when gays and lesbians come out in the heterosexualised street; they transgress the clearly defined boundaries between the centralised heterosexual majority and the marginalised homosexual minority – or, as Bauman writes, strangers transgress the clear boundary between friends and enemies:

> [U]nlike other, 'straightforward' enemies, he is not kept at a secure distance, nor
> on the other side of the battle line. Worse still, he claims a right to be an object of
> *responsibility* – the well-known attribute of the *friend*. If we press upon him the
> friend/enemy opposition, he would come out simultaneously under- and over-
> determined. (Bauman 1991: 59)

According to Bauman (1997), there are two ways modern societies deal with
strangers: either they swallow them (the process of assimilation through which
strangers become like us) or they vomit them (the process of exclusion through
which strangers are kept outside society, for example in ghettos). It seems that
Western European societies (and less so Eastern European societies), by applying
tolerance towards gays and lesbians, tend to 'swallow them' (their specific identities,
cultures etc.) more and more. Although this seems a positive step forward (for
example legal protection and recognition), here lies also the core of the problem.
Contemporary Western societies have namely included homosexuality on condition
of its normalisation. Such normalisation is a 'heterosexual' normalisation,
increasingly pervading the popular media. Normalised homosexuality is such that,
as Seidman writes, it 'implies a political logic of tolerance and minority rights
that does not challenge heterosexual dominance' (Seidman 2002: 133). In other
words: normalised homosexuality is a form of 'social' behaviour (in the Arendtian
sense) as the 'normalisation' is actually a way to abolish its political potential to
surpass the hetero/homo binary opposition, which now enables power relations
and conceptualises tolerance as acceptance (cf. Warner 1999; Seidman 2002;
Duggan 2002).[10]

Let me borrow yet another Arendt concept – that of Parvenus and Pariahs
(2003) – better to illustrate the difference between coming out as 'social behaviour'
and coming out as a 'political act'. Arendt introduces the categories of Parvenus
and Pariahs in her discussion on Rahel Varengahen, a Jew, who tried to do all in
her power to establish a respectful position for herself in an anti-Semitic society.
In order to do that she had denied her Jewish heritage, she had married a German
officer, had changed her name and suchlike. However, despite her attempts to
assimilate herself, she never succeeded fully in avoiding the disdain by the anti-
Semitic society (Arendt, 2000).

All her life Rahel was a Parvenu, who tried to adapt, pass for/as and pretend
to be someone she was not. She tried to take over the values that were not her

---

10   Interestingly enough, part of the gay and lesbian movement, as Duggan shows in
her analysis of gay and lesbian politics in the USA, sees such normalisation as the goal of
its politics. In such a way, as Duggan suggests, the 'New Homonegativity' came into being,
redefining the key concepts of the gay and lesbian politics: '"Equality" becomes narrow,
formal access to a few conservatizing institutions, "freedom" becomes impunity for bigotry
and vast inequalities in commercial life and civil society, the "right to privacy" becomes
domestic confinement, and democratic politics itself becomes something to be escaped'
(Duggan 2002: 190).

own, the values that were destroying her personality and self-respect. It seems that there is a clear parallel between the effects of the anti-Semitic society on Rahel's life and the effects of the heteronormative society on the lives of gays and lesbians; by adapting to the heteronormativity of everyday life, gays and lesbians are often pushed into mimicry and into denying their own identity. Or, in the words of a gay man, contemplating the effects of heteronormativity on his life: 'I have realised that censoring oneself, one's homosexuality results in censoring oneself in all other aspects of life. At the end you can censor yourself so much that you lose yourself' (quoted in Kuhar 2001). Rahel came to the same conclusion at the end of her life. She realised that the price she had been paying to be accepted was simply too high. She then became a Pariah. It is a position of a 'conscious outsider'. It is a political position which first of all draws attention to the marginalisation of certain individuals or groups in society; and second, it represents a rebellion against social norms and the power relations which make the marginalised position of certain individuals or groups possible in the first place (Arendt 2000).

Privacy (private intimate relations) can enter the public sphere in two ways: either as the 'social' in the sense of Parvenus, where the 'private' is robbed of its political potential, or as the 'political' in the sense of Pariahs. This can also be applied to two possible ways of coming out in the public sphere: the 'social' coming out is the one where a homosexual person does not challenge heteronormative social relations. The person enters the public sphere through the door of tolerance, which ensures them 'their place under the sun' as long as they 'normalise' their homosexuality. It means, among other things, that they will not flaunt their homosexuality in public. Coming out as a 'social' behaviour is actually a form of a kind request by a gay Parvenu to be assimilated into a broader society. It means that coming out as a 'political' act is only possible in the form of a Pariah. The Pariah is the one challenging the heteronormativity of the public sphere and refusing to subordinate oneself to heterosexual normalisation. Coming out as a political act is therefore a praxis of continuously challenging heterosexism, homophobia and power relations. Here it becomes clear how the social enables the political: social norms prevent coming out or limit it to the transparent closet, discussed below. Social norms therefore tend continuously to re-establish themselves by trying to abolish the 'political'. Following Arendt's distinction between the social and the political, one might suggest that coming out as social behaviour is typical of mainstream gay and lesbian identity politics, while coming out as political behaviour is part of the queer movement. However, having in mind Butler's (1991: 14) observation that every act of coming out of the closet reproduces the closet itself (as closet has no meaning without the act of coming out), the queer approach might organise its political potential beyond coming out. Still, it needs to be stressed that the distinction between the social and political dimension of coming out, introduced above, is an artificial one. It means that in the praxis of everyday life we continuously negotiate the spectrum of our actions which might be social in one context and political in another. In other words: there is a (potential) Parvenu and Pariah in each non-heterosexual individual.[11]

Conclusion: Extending the Transparent Closet

Eve Kosofsky Sedgwick (1993) understands coming out as a contagion which is transmitted to those to whom one has come out: when a child comes out to their parents, they become parents of a 'gay child' and are therefore pushed into the closet of the heteronormative society, already confronted by the child who has come out. This, however, suggests that coming out automatically establishes a new reality – that of living outside or beyond the closet. 'Coming out', which is used in gay and lesbian slang in Slovenia in its original English version, is understood as a self-contained act, reliant on the sole will of the person who comes out. Similar understanding of coming out is suggested also in the Western literature on homosexual identity formation (cf. Dank 1971; Cass 1979; Troiden 1988; Plummer 1996). Although coming out is also explained as a process – as a link of never-ending acts of coming out – a single act is understood as finished simply by one's decision to come out. It is suggested that coming out is a one-off act, after which everything changes.

According to the research on the everyday life of gays and lesbians in Slovenia, this is not necessarily the case.[12] People who do come out are sometimes expected to step back into the closet in order to ease the discomfort of those to whom one has come out. The concept of the 'transparent closet' has therefore been suggested to describe the phenomenon of 'unfinished coming out'. In family contexts, gays and lesbians are often pushed back into the closet after they come out. Their homosexuality is noted, but refused to be discussed and considered:

> The transparent closet thus refers to the situation, mostly in the family context, when coming-out to parents results in an annoying outcome of partial outing; parents know that their child is homosexual, but they are not willing to acknowledge it. The child steps out of the closet, but parental reactions and expectations push him/her back into the closet, which is now a transparent one as parents have noted the 'new identity', but refuse to accept it. (Kuhar 2007: 43)

Although I have used the concept of the transparent closet in the past to point at coming out as a relational process rather than as a one-sided act in the family context, the same concept can be applied to the public sphere as well: the Pride parades and similar activities organised by LGBT non-governmental organisations

---

11   I am grateful to the editors of this book for bringing this point out.

12   Although I have juxtaposed the Western concept of 'coming out' with 'Eastern European' experiences with it, I do not believe the 'transparent closet' is a specific experience limited to the gays and lesbians of Eastern Europe.

represent the coming out of the community in the city. Yet the violent reactions push gays and lesbians back into the closet – the transparent closet. In spite of this, the transparent closet should not necessarily always be understood as inevitably negative. As it is relational, coming out creates a possibility for a positive/ subversive use by gays and lesbians if they do not necessarily aim at acceptance, but rather at the 'disturbance of' (or, in Foucauldian terms, 'resistance to') the heteronormative system.[13] Nonetheless, such action (resistance) creates a reaction: possibly a violent one. If they step out, gays and lesbians risk violent reaction. Therefore, as least in the Slovenian context, the majority prefer to stay in – except for one day in a year, when some gays and lesbians proudly march through the city, loosening the heteronormative structure of the public space.[14] However, the experiences of Pride parades in Eastern Europe, if such events are allowed by local governments at all, and the story of Mitja Blažič from the beginning of this article, show that they do pay a price for this. A very painful one.

References

Arendt, H. 1996. *Vita Activa*. Ljubljana: Krt.
———. 2000. *Rahel Varnhagen: The Life of a Jewess*. Baltimore: The Johns Hopkins University Press.
———. 2003. *Izvori totalitarizma*. Ljubljana: Študentska založba.
Bauman, Z. 1991. *Modernity and Ambivalence*. Cambridge: Polity Press.
———. 1997. *Postmodernity and its Discontents*. Cambridge: Polity Press.
Butler, J. 1991. 'Imitation and Gender Insubordination'. In *Inside/Out: Lesbian Theories, Gay Theories*, ed. D. Fuss. New York and London: Routledge.
Cass, V. 1979. 'Homosexual Identity Formation: A Theoretical Model', *Journal of Homosexuality* 4(3): 219–35.
Dank, B.M. 1971. 'Coming Out in the Gay World', *Psychiatry* 34(2): 180–97.

---

13   One such action, organised a few times in the centre of Ljubljana, was a mass kissing of gay and lesbian couples. The action did not aim at acceptance, but rather at visibility as a precondition for resistance.

14   The first Pride parade in Slovenia was organised in 2001 as a reaction to an incident which occurred in front of the allegedly gay-friendly bar Café Galerija. The bouncer at the door refused to let in two gay men, saying that they should get used to the fact that it is not a bar for 'that kind of people'. Later Pride parades tended to become more mainstream and likeable, but still very political. However, part of the GLBT community refused to participate, claiming that Pride had lost its radical political edge. On the other hand (reading the GLBT internet forums), most gays and lesbians would not participate at Pride parades, fearing public disclosure, interpreting Pride as an unnecessary provocation or as a manifestation which disturbs the general population and consequently sheds bad light on the GLBT community as such. Interestingly enough, the majority of participants at the parades (approximately 300 to 500 people each year), as reported by the organisers, are straight people.

Duggan, L. 2002. 'The New Heteronormativity: The Sexual Politics of Neoliberalism'. In *Materializing Democracy: Toward a Revitalized Cultural Politics*, eds R. Castronovo and D. Nelson. Durham, NC: Duke University Press.

Duncan, N. 1996. 'Renegotiating Gender and Sexuality in Public and Private Space'. In *Body Space: Destabilizing Geographies of Gender and Sexuality*, ed. N. Duncan. London and New York: Routledge.

Foucault, M. 1980. *Power/Knowledge: Selected Interviews and Other Writings 1972–1977*, ed. C. Gordon. London: Harvester Press.

———. 1984. *Nadzorovanje in kaznovanje*. Ljubljana: Delavska enotnost.

———. 2000. *Zgodovina seksualnosti (Volja do znanja)*. Ljubljana: Škuc.

Gordon, N. 2002. On Visibility and Power: An Arendtian Corrective of Foucault, *Human Studies* 25(2): 125–45.

Hennessy, R. 1995. 'Queer Visibility in Commodity Culture'. In *Social Postmodernism: Beyond Identity Politics*, eds L. Nicholson and S. Seidman. New York: Cambridge University Press.

Isin, E.F. and Wood, P.K. 1999. *Citizenship and Identity*. London: Sage.

Kuhar, R. 2001. *Mi, drugi: oblikovanje in razkritje homoseksualne identitete* [*We, the Others: The Formation and Disclosure of Homosexual Identity*]. Ljubljana: Škuc-Lambda.

Kuhar, R. 2005. Intimno državljanstvo: zasebne izbire, javne politike ter vsakdanje življenje lezbijk in gejev (PhD dissertation). Ljubljana: Fakulteta za družbene vede.

———. 2007. 'The Family Secret: Parents of Homosexual Sons and Daughters'. In *Beyond the Pink Curtain: Everyday Life of LGBT People in Eastern Europe*, eds R. Kuhar and J. Takács. Ljubljana: Peace Institute, 35–47; also available at: http://www.mirovni-institut.si/Publikacija/Detail/en/publikacija/Beyond-the-Pink-Curtain-Everyday-Life-of-LGBT-People-in-Eastern-Europe.

Kuhar, R. and Magić, J. 2008. *Experiences and Perceptions of Homophobic Violence and Discrimination* (Research Report). Ljubljana: Legebitra.

Kuhar, R. and Švab, A. 2008. 'Homophobia and Violence against Gays and Lesbians in Slovenia', *Revija za sociologiju*, 39(4): 267–81.

Kuhar, R. and Takács, J. 2007. 'Introduction: What is Beyond The Pink Curtain?'. In *Beyond the Pink Curtain: Everyday Life of LGBT People in Eastern Europe*, eds R. Kuhar and J. Takács. Ljubljana: Peace Institute, 11–12; also available at: http://www.mirovni-institut.si/Publikacija/Detail/en/publikacija/Beyond-the-Pink-Curtain-Everyday-Life-of-LGBT-People-in-Eastern-Europe.

Kuhar, R., Maljevac S., Koletnik A. and Magić J. 2008. *Vsakdanje življenje istospolno usmerjenih v Sloveniji* (Research Report). Ljubljana: Legebitra.

Kuzmanić, A.T. 1994. 'Postsocializem in toleranca ali toleranca je toleranca tistih, ki tolerirajo – ali pa ne'. *Časopis za kritiko znanosti*, 22(164/5): 165–83.

Morgan, W. 2000. 'Queering International Human Rights Law'. In *Law and Sexuality: The Global Arena*, eds C. Stychin and H. Didi. Minneapolis: University of Minnesota Press.

Plummer, K. 1996. 'Symbolic Interactionism and the Forms of Homosexuality'. In *Queer Theory/Sociology*, ed. S. Seidman. Oxford: Blackwell.

Richardson, D. 1998. 'Sexuality and Citizenship'. *Sociology*, 32(1): 83–100.

Sedgwick, E.K. 1993. 'Epistemology of the Closet'. In *The Lesbian and Gay Studies Reader*, eds H. Abelove, M.A. Barale and D.M. Halperin. New York: Routledge.

Seidman, S. 2002. *Beyond The Closet: The Transformation of Gay and Lesbian Life*. New York: Routledge.

Simmel, G. 1950. 'The Stranger'. In *The Sociology of George Simmel*, ed. K.H. Wolff. New York: Free Press.

Švab, A. and Kuhar, R. 2005. *The Unbearable Comfort of Privacy: Everyday Life of Gays and Lesbians*. Ljubljana: Peace Institute; also available at: http://www.mirovni-institut.si/Publikacija/Detail/en/publikacija/The-Unbearable-Confort-of-Privacy-The-Everyday-Life-of-Gays-and-Lesbians.

Švab, A., Žakelj, T., Kuhar R., Bajt, V. Sedmak, M., Kralj A., Humer, Ž. and Boškić R. 2008. *Posledice diskriminacije na družbeno, politično in socialno vključenost mladih v Sloveniji: analiza glede na spol, spolno usmerjenost ter etnično pripadnost* (Research Report). Ljubljana: Fakulteta za družbene vede.

Troiden, R. 1988. 'A Model of Homosexual Identity Formation'. In *Social Perspectives in Lesbian and Gay Studies*, eds P.M. Nardi and B.E. Schneider. London: Routledge.

Valentine, G. 1996. '(Re)negotiating the "Heterosexual Street": Lesbian Production of Space'. In *Body Space: Destabilizing Geographies of Gender and Sexuality*, ed. N. Duncan. London and New York: Routledge.

Walby, S. 1994. Is Citizenship Gendered?, *Sociology*, 28(2): 379–95.

Warner, M. 1999. *The Trouble with Normal: Sex, Politics, and the Ethics of Queer Life*. Cambridge, MA: Harvard University Press.

Young, I. 1991. *Justice and the Politics of Difference*. Princeton: Princeton University Press.

Chapter 9

Heteronormativity, Intimate Citizenship and the Regulation of Same-Sex Sexualities in Bulgaria

Sasha Roseneil and Mariya Stoilova

Introduction

To the growing body of work on sexualities in Central and Eastern Europe, this chapter contributes a substantive focus on Bulgaria, a nation-state that has rarely been studied in anglophone literature on the post-communist condition and the history and sociology of sexuality.[1] We offer an historical discussion of the ways in which same-sex sexualities have been regulated in Bulgaria, which traces the major shifts that have taken place in law and policy. In so doing, we make an argument about how the regulation of same-sex sexualities might be understood as part of the wider regulatory practice of the Bulgarian state's 'intimate citizenship regime' (Roseneil 2010b). We suggest that the institutionalisation and regulation of intimacy in Bulgaria has been both implicitly and explicitly heteronormative, radically privileging the conjugal, procreative heterosexual couple, and variously, actively oppressing, excluding, and marginalising those who have acted on, and sought to live out, their same-sex desires and attachments. However, we also point to the ways in which this heteronormativity has, in recent years, been challenged as the intimate citizenship regime is reconfigured in the context of processes of globalisation from above and below – related to the country's accession to the European Union (EU) and the emergence of transnationally networked lesbian and gay activism.

---

1 The growing literature on sexuality in Bulgaria has been mainly a result of the efforts of lesbian and gay activists and experts from human rights organisations, and to a lesser extent of scholars and academics from various disciplines. A significant part of this literature focuses on historical and socio-legal analyses of sexuality (for example, Gruev 2006; Dimitrova 2008; Kukova 2008; Meshkova and Sharlanov 1994; Mihajlova 2006; Pisankaneva 2003; Popova 2004, 2009), as well as on recent LGBT activism (Atanasov and Dobrev 2008; Genova 2008; Pisankaneva 2002, 2009; Pisankaneva and Panaiotov 2005) and finally on cultural attitudes and representations of same-sex sexuality (Angelova and Liakova 2005; Atanasov 2008, 2009; Panaiotov 2009).

The research on which this chapter is based was undertaken as part of a larger comparative study of intimate citizenship in Europe.[2] Our use of the notion of 'intimate citizenship' draws on the work of Ken Plummer (1995, 2003), who has articulated the concept, in preference to the rather narrower one of 'sexual citizenship' (Evans 1993; Weeks 1998; Bell and Binnie 2000; Richardson 2000), as encompassing 'the decisions people have to make over *the control (or not) over* one's body, feelings, relationships; *access (or not) to* representations, relationships, public spaces, etc; and *socially grounded choices (or not) about* identities, gender experience; erotic experiences' (Plummer 1995: 151, original emphasis). From this starting point we carried out a three-pronged study of intimate citizenship across four countries, which involved historical analysis of the claims and demands of a range of social movements in relation to intimate life; a policy analysis of law and policy in relation to intimate life; and a socio-biographical study of the life and relationship stories of people from majority and racialised/minoritised groups living outside conventional heterosexual couples and families. Out of this research Roseneil has developed a normative understanding of *full* intimate citizenship as involving 'the freedom and ability to construct and live selfhood and a wide range of close relationships – sexual/love relationships, friendships, parental and kin relations – safely, securely and according to personal choice, in their dynamic and changing forms, with respect, recognition and support from state and civil society' (Roseneil 2010a: 82). The (far from fully realised) conditions of intimate citizenship that prevail in any particular nation-state at any particular time might be understood as that country's *intimate citizenship regime* (Roseneil 2010b). Intimate citizenship regimes develop historically, in path-dependent ways, and comprise the laws, policies and cultures that regulate and construct everyday lived practices of intimate life in ways that are more or less patriarchal or gender-equal, more or less heteronormative or sexuality-equal and more or less racist/ethnic majoritarian or multicultural.

In this chapter we begin by outlining the main characteristics of the Bulgarian intimate citizenship regime and the landscape of social movement activism around issues of intimate citizenship during the communist and post-communist eras. In this context we then go on to discuss the ways in which the regulation of same-sex sexualities has shifted over time, and how these changes might be understood in relation to the wider process of social transformation. Our discussion centres on two areas of law and policy regulating same-sex sexualities where there has been significant normative change: in moves to legitimate same-sex sexual practices and to protect lesbian, gay and bisexual people from discrimination; and on one

---

2   The study focused on Bulgaria, Norway, Portugal and the UK, and was a component of the EU-funded Framework 6 Integrated Project, FEMCIT: Gendered Citizenship in Multicultural Europe: The Impact of Contemporary Women's Movements. The research was directed by Sasha Roseneil, with Mariya Stoilova responsible for the Bulgarian element of the project. For more information see http://www.femcit.org and Roseneil (2008, 2009).

area of law and policy which has thus far proved resistant to change – that of same-sex relationship recognition.

The Bulgarian Intimate Citizenship Regime

The Bulgarian intimate citizenship regime has historically tended towards a more gender-equal form of familialism, at the same time as being strongly pronatalist and heteronormative. In his analysis of family systems across time and space, Goran Therborn (2004) points to the distinctive hue of the Bulgarian Orthodox patriarchy prior to communism, which was notable for granting married women the right to own property and to transact business independently, as well as equal access to divorce. Gender equality became state policy in 1944 with the Fatherland Front's seizure of power, and was instantiated in the communist Bulgarian Constitution of 1947, which also secularised marriage and equalised the status of children born within and outside marriage. Under the rule of the Bulgarian Communist Party there was a strong expectation that women should engage in paid labour, and levels of female employment were high (Petrova 1993; Panova et al. 1993; Koeva and Bould 2007). This was not, however, accompanied by any challenge to the domestic division of labour: women were to combine the roles of worker, mother and housewife. Early marriage was almost universal, as was child-bearing (Philipov and Kohler 2001; Frejka et al. 2008), and there was a limited 'range of available options for self-realisation outside the family' (Frejka et al. 2008: 8).

Under communism 'only reproductive sexual acts between spouses were considered legitimate sexual practices' (Popova 2004: 1, our translation). Sexual pleasure as an end in itself was disapproved of, even within marriage, and abortion was increasingly restricted.[3] The state's pronatalism reached its apotheosis in the 1951 Bachelor Tax (Decree for the Stimulation of Birth Rates). This penalised women aged between 21 and 45 and men aged between 21 and 50 who did not have children, requiring them to pay 5 per cent of taxable income at the age of 21, rising to 15 per cent at 35 (Ministry of Labour and Social Policy 2006). The law

---

3   Abortion first became available in 1956, but was later progressively restricted as part of the pronatalist policy. In 1968 abortion was prohibited for childless women; only women above the age of 45 or who had more than three children could have an abortion. A special medical board had the authority to approve abortions in 'special' circumstances, such as women under the age of 16, women who had one or two children, and in cases of rape or for medical reasons. Further restrictions on abortion were introduced in 1972, when abortion was prohibited for women with one child. These changes met with strong disapproval by the public and were revoked one year later (1973), when all women were allowed to present their case to the medical board and permissions were granted more easily. All restrictions were removed in 1989.

enabled public reprobation[4] and imprisonment for infidelity[5] (Penal Code 1956) and 'Comrade Courts', established in 1961, were public forums at which local Communist Party activists and members of the community discussed individuals' intimate lives – particularly issues of extramarital sex, domestic violence and alchoholism – and offered advice on how to preserve marriages (Popova 2004; Brunnbauer 2008). The attempt to confine sexuality to the marital relationship was further pursued through the arrest and imprisonment of prostitutes (Meshkova and Sharlanov 1994; Popova 2004, 2009), and of men who engaged in same-sex sex (Pisankaneva 2002; Popova 2009), which we discuss below. This often forced people with same-sex desires to enter marriages and to lead double lives (Pisankaneva 2009).

The criminalisation of same-sex sexual acts between men dates back to the rule of Simeon at the turn of the tenth century (893–927), when the death penalty was introduced (Bulgarian Helsinki Committee 2001). In 1896, in the post-independence era, the penalty was reduced to 'confinement to a dark cell for 6 months' (Penal Code, Art. 216 cited in Bulgarian Helsinki Committee 2001); but under communism, after a wave of conservative, pronatalist legal changes in the early 1950s, the punishment for homosexuality was increased to three years' imprisonment (Penal Code 1951). This new legislation penalised both acts of 'sexual intercourse' and acts of 'sexual satisfaction' between people of the same sex, with the latter encompassing, for the first time, sexual acts between women (Bulgarian Helsinki Committee 2001). It might be possible that a communist ideology of egalitarianism that expected an equal contribution from women in employment and promoted a culture of 'low gender polarisation' (Lofstrom 1998) was able to imagine women engaging in sexual activities and giving and receiving sexual pleasure in ways that were unthinkable in other contexts.[6] However, whilst there was a state campaign against 'intellectual homosexuals', who were sent to corrective labour camps by the communist regime, it seems that no women were sentenced for same-sex sexual acts (Gruev 2006; Pisankaneva 2002).

The post-communist era saw a general relaxation in the policing of heterosexual intimate lives. The Bachelor Tax was repealed and the 1991 Constitution stated that:

---

4   'Public reprobation' was the announcement of the sentence in public places, for example in front of the people with whom the accused worked or at an organisation of which s/he was a member (Law on the Administrative Punishments and Violations, SG 92/28.11.1969).

5   In 1956 changes in the Penal Code introduced imprisonment for up to six months or a fine of up to 1,000 Bulgarian leva and public reprobation for a spouse who left his/her family and was living with another person. The same punishment was stipulated for the person with whom the spouse lived. In the case of a second offence, the punishment was imprisonment for up to three years.

6   Our argument here has parallels with Lofstrom's (1998) discussion of why homosexual acts between women were criminalised in the 1889 Finnish Penal Code.

> The privacy of citizens shall be inviolable. Everyone shall be entitled to protection against any unlawful interference in his private or family affairs and against encroachments on his honour, dignity and reputation. (Art. 32:1)

The emphasis on supporting heterosexual reproduction has continued, albeit within the new globally sanctioned discursive framework of the rights and interests of the child (Protection of the Child Act 2000; The Family Code 2009). With rising levels of divorce and an increasing proportion of (a declining number of) children born outside marriage – reaching over 50 per cent in recent years (National Statistical Institute 2009) – there have been moves towards the legal recognition of heterosexual cohabitation;[7] but full recognition in the Family Code has recently been rejected (Family Code 2009) and access to partner-related benefits is limited to heterosexual married couples.[8] Alongside marriage, biological relations are privileged in a wide range of intimate citizenship rights and obligations – particularly in relation to issues of care, such as recognition as a care-giver and as 'next of kin' by hospitals, and in relation to inheritance.

The Landscape of Intimate Citizenship Activism in Bulgaria

During the one-party communist era there were no independent social movements organising around issues of intimate citizenship (or indeed around any issue). In the early years the various women's organisations which had existed prior to the coup in 1944 were unified into a single organisation, the Bulgarian Public's Women's Union (Български народен женски съюз). In 1950 this Union was merged into the Fatherland Front (Bulgarian Public's Women's Union 1950; Bulgarian Association of University Women 2008). 1968 saw the formation of the Committee of Bulgarian Women (Комитет на българските жени), still under the auspices of the Fatherland Front (Central Committee of the Bulgarian Communist Party 1968). This granted a highly circumscribed form of autonomy to 'organised women', rather than constituting an independent 'women's movement'. The issues taken up by organised women under communism included labour force participation and work–life balance, equality in family and partnership relations, women's living standards and education, and, most of all, childcare (Committee of the Movement of Bulgarian Women 1980). Whilst demands during this period were mostly addressed at the state and had a protectionist tinge, a wider range of intimate citizenship issues emerged into the

---

7 Changes to the Transplantation of Organs, Tissue, and Cells Act (2003) in 2007 allow cohabiting partners of more than two years to become living donors to their partners (Art. 26), when previously living donors could only be those related by marriage, origin or adoption. The 2009 Labour Code (Art. 163:7) allows both married and cohabiting fathers to take 15 days' paid leave on the birth of their child.

8 For instance, inheritance rights, survivor's benefits and adoption as a couple.

public sphere in the pages of the Movement of Bulgarian Women's magazine *Today's Woman* (Жената днес), including gender and domestic violence, women's reproductive rights, sexual pleasure and sexual objectification of women.[9]

It was only after 1989 that independent women's organisations began to emerge, with a significant spurt in the development of non-governmental organisation (NGO)-led feminism (largely funded from outside Bulgaria) from the late 1990s onwards (Daskalova 2000) as part of the development of what Steven Sampson (2002) calls 'project life' across the former communist states. Women's NGOs addressed a range of social issues that concerned women, including education and culture, political decision-making, employment, healthcare and the environment (Daskalova 2000; Daskalova and Filipova 2003). More recently, the focus of women's organisations has been on gender equality in economic, social and political citizenship, and, to a lesser extent, on issues related to intimate citizenship (Stoilova 2009). There has been little attention on issues of same-sex sexuality among women's organisations.

The first gay non-governmental organisation, the Bulgarian Gay Organisation 'Gemini', was established in 1992, focusing in its early years mainly on HIV prevention (BGO 'Gemini' 2007). In 2001, supported by the Open Society Institute – and later working in transnational coalition with the Dutch gay organisation COC and ACCEPT Romania – BGO 'Gemini' extended its aims to include wider campaigning around LGBT issues and community-building activities (such as the creation of a 'safe house', a library, a monthly bulletin, socio-cultural activities and self-help groups of lesbians and gay men). The first legal campaign by BGO 'Gemini' was directed at the criminalisation of sexual acts in public places, and it was involved in drafting the Law on Protection against Discrimination, which was passed in 2004. In 2004 BGO 'Gemini' hosted the first international conference on LGBT issues in Bulgaria and launched the first gay radio broadcast in 2006 (BGO 'Gemini' 2007).

Since the mid-2000s the range of actors on the lesbian and gay scene in Bulgaria has expanded to include youth, queer, lesbian and bisexual women's organisations and groups, such as LGBT Action, Gay-Straight Alliance, LGBT Idea, Queer Bulgaria and Bilitis. The choice of the name 'Bilitis' for a resource centre for lesbians and bisexual women references the earliest lesbian rights organisation in the United States – Daughters of Bilitis, founded in 1955 – whilst the use of the abbreviation 'LGBT' and of the concept of 'queer' clearly draws on more recent traditions of activism in the anglophone world. The emergence of these groups has contributed to the greater visibility of the lesbian and gay community in Bulgaria, and to the articulation of demands for legal protection and political representation. The focus has largely been on campaigning for legal recognition of same-sex partnering and parenting, action against discrimination, and HIV prevention. There have been annual Gay and Lesbian Fests since 2005, organised by Bilitis; three LGBT Prides (in 2008, 2009 and 2010), organised in Sofia; and

---

9   For more details about publications in *Today's Woman* see Stoilova (2009).

various street demonstrations, for example an anti-homophobic 'Free Gay Hugs' campaign (January 2010, Sofia) and an anti-death penalty in Uganda demonstration (January 2010, Sofia). In spite of these developments, activism in Bulgaria has been rather uneven and volatile as even the largest organisations, such as BGO 'Gemini' and Queer Bulgaria, have experienced long periods of organisational instability and inactivity. Furthermore, the activities and visibility of the gay and lesbian community are mostly concentrated in the capital (Pisankaneva 2009) and a few large Bulgarian cities.

In addition to this there have been various issues which have not been addressed, for example domestic violence, bisexuality and transgender identity.[10] The first sex-reassignment surgery in Bulgaria was performed in 1993, but the procedure for the recognition of the 'new' gender is still not regulated and there is only one piece of legislation that mentions sex-reassignment, according to which a person who has changed their gender has to apply for new documents within 30 days (Law for Bulgarian Identification Documents 2007, Art. 9). Furthermore, a regulation issued by the Ministry of Defence identifies transsexuality as a sexual disorder, thus making trans individuals unfit for military service (Dimitrova 2008: 11). These issues, however, have remained outside the activist agenda.

The Legitimation of Same-Sex Sexual Practices

After the intensification of anti-homosexual laws during the pronatalist 1950s, the first move towards the legitimation of same-sex sexual practice was decriminalisation in 1968. A number of other Soviet bloc countries had already decriminalised sexual acts between men (Hungary and Czechoslovakia, in 1961), with pressure for change coming from the medical profession – particularly 'the flourishing field of sexology' (Long 1999: 247) – and Bulgaria seems to have followed this liberalisation process.[11] The impact of decriminalisation was limited, however, both because it was not accompanied by the emergence of a lesbian or gay movement, subculture or community (Pisankaneva 2003) within which those with same-sex desires could organise, socialise and construct individual and collective identities, and because the decriminalisation was only partial. From 1968 until it was equalised in 1986, the age of consent for homosexual acts was four years older than for heterosexual sex (18 as opposed to 14). Same-sex relationships remained largely invisible culturally, and the law continued to discriminate between homosexual and heterosexual behaviour, and to regard same-sex sexual practices as deviant and disorderly. Art. 157:4 of the Penal Code (1968) rendered criminal homosexual acts in public places and homosexual acts performed in a

---

10 Despite the fact that some organisations state a concern with issues of bisexuality and transgender, and/or use the term 'queer' in their names (for example, LGBT Action, Bilitis, Queer Bulgaria), in practice these issues are largely missing from activist agendas.

11 A number of sexology clinics and a research institute existed under communism, but were closed in 1999 (Okoliyski and Velichkov 2004).

'scandalous manner' or 'in a manner that may incite others to follow a path of perversion'; and Art. 157: 5 made homosexual prostitution punishable.[12] In the 1970s and 1980s two new pieces of legislation, The People's Militia Act (1976) and its Supplementation (1983), further emphasised the communist regime's distaste for same-sex sexuality, allowing for the arrest and forceful resettlement of people committing 'anti-social acts' – amongst which was the 'public display of homosexuality'.[13] Culturally, homosexuality continued, throughout the communist era, to be seen as 'an unhealthy sexual and moral practice that reveals an admiration of Western lifestyles, and could be "cured" by corrective labor or public censure' (Pisankaneva 2003: 1). In 1986 the age of consent was equalised again without any public discussion or wider commitment to non-discrimination towards homosexuals.

The liberalisation of the intimate citizenship regime in relation to heterosexual intimate lives that accompanied the end of communism took well over a decade to begin to impact upon non-heterosexuals. The new post-communist right to an intimate life unhindered by the state, articulated in the 1991 Constitution, implicitly applied only to heterosexuals, and in 1997 conditions worsened for lesbians and gay men, with the raising of the age of consent for same-sex sex to 16. This move once again explicitly linked homosexuality with criminality, coming as it did as part of a wider set of amendments to the Penal Code aimed at reducing criminality during the economic and political transition (Kostov 1999). This occurred against the background of a cultural backlash of patriarchalism and conservatism (Daskalova 2000; Pisankaneva 2009) and growing negative publicity around issues related to homosexuality in the media (Atanasov 2009).[14] Ironically these anti-corruption moves were an important part of the process of preparation for accession to the EU, but the introduction of an unequal age of consent fell foul of the *acquis communitaire*.[15]

In the early 2000s both lesbian and gay and human rights NGOs (BGO 'Gemini' and the Bulgarian Helsinki Committee) and, most significantly, the European Commissioners investigating the country's preparedness for EU accession brought the issue of the inequalities relating to same-sex sexuality on to the political agenda for the first time (European Commission/EC 2002). The Regular Report on Bulgaria's Progress towards Accession in 2001 noted that

---

12   Art. 155:1 of the 1968 Penal Code penalised the persuasion of a woman to prostitution, but not the act of prostitution itself, while Art. 157 penalised both the prostitute and the client in the case of homosexual prostitution.

13   It seems, however, that no one was prosecuted under either of these articles (Bulgarian Helsinki Committee 2001: 7).

14   The public silence around homosexuality under communism was replaced by growing media attention, , which overwhelmingly represented same-sex sexuality as scandalous and deviant, and which used homophobic language (Atanasov 2009: 1).

15   The Copenhagen criteria set out in 1993 require candidate countries to adopt the acquis communitaire, the total body of EU laws and regulations.

'Bulgarian law currently discriminates against homosexuals. Discriminatory provisions in the Penal Code need to be removed to avoid discrimination' (EC 2001: 22). So it was that as part of accepting the anti-discrimination elements of the *acquis communitaire*, in order to be able to accede to the EU, Bulgaria revoked the various discriminatory paragraphs discussed above, including the unequal age of consent (SG/92/2002). Keen to speed the process towards accession, all groups in Parliament agreed to these changes within a year of the report, adopting the terms of the EU's modernising, anti-discrimination agenda in their reference to 'archaic formulations' that treat 'homosexual acts as perversions', and thereby 'support a discriminatory regime towards homosexuality' (Draft Law on Alteration and Supplementation of the Penal Code 2002: 2, our translation). The draft law went on to specify that 'the existence of the mentioned texts contradicts the regulations of European legislation, breaks international contracts and puts under question Bulgaria's accomplishment of the political criteria for EU membership' (Draft Law on Alteration and Supplementation of the Penal Code 2002: 2, our translation).

The final explicitly discriminatory provision in Bulgarian law relating to same-sex sexual acts was repealed in 2006. Art. 157 of the Penal Code stated that same-sex sexual acts (both 'sexual intercourse' and acts of 'sexual satisfaction') that used force or threat, or the abuse of a state of dependence or supervision, or which involved a person unable to defend him/herself were criminal offences, the punishment for which was to include public reprobation, which was not provided for heterosexual acts of the same nature.[16] With the revoking of this Article, equal punishment was established for sexual assault whatever the gender of the victim or aggressor, and 'homosexual intent' was no longer regarded an an aggravating factor.

So in an exceptionally short space of time, between 2002 and 2006, a number of legal changes were enacted that fully equalised the law surrounding same-sex sexual practice. However, the fact that these changes were top down rather than bottom up – brought about by the transposition of EU policies to Bulgaria rather than as a result of changing attitudes and social pressure and mobilisation within the country is – we would suggest, of lasting significance in terms of their impact on the everyday lives of people in Bulgaria.

The Protection of Lesbian, Gay and Bisexual People from Discrimination and Violence

The development of positive legislation in Bulgaria to protect lesbian, gay and bisexual people from discrimination and violence has been directly related to EU accession. The moves towards the legitimation of same-sex sexual practice which took place under communism were not accompanied by any overt condemnation

---

16   Public reprobation is still used, for instance, announcing the non-payment of child maintenance on local radio (Darik News 2007) or announcing a conviction for drink-driving by a minor on the municipality notice board (Darik News 2010).

of the oppression of homosexuals or any acknowledgement of an entitlement to protection against discrimination. The introduction of anti-discrimination legislation which included explicit mention of sexual orientation was a response to the demands of the EU. The EU Employment Equality Directive of 2000[17] banned discrimination based on religion and belief, age, disability and sexual orientation; in employment and occupation (access to employment and pay and conditions), vocational training and membership of employer and employee organisations, identifying four types of discrimination: direct, indirect, harassment and instruction to discriminate. The Directive also shifted the burden of proof from the employee to the employer in cases of alleged discrimination, and allowed organisations or associations to act with or for a complainant, both radical moves which serve to recognise the relative powerlessness of an individual worker-complainant, when facing the resources of their employer.

The Protection against Discrimination Act (PADA) (2004), which was regarded as 'revolutionary for the Bulgarian judicial system' (Mihajlova 2006: 1), enacted the Employment Equality Directive, targeting both direct and indirect discrimination, as well as shifting the burden of the proof in favour of the victim and allowing legal non-profit entities to initiate court cases and to act as plaintiffs on behalf of the victims. The law included all aspects of discrimination, direct and indirect, which are recognised in both international and Bulgarian law, explicitly including sexual orientation, and applies to the exercise of all rights recognised by law, thereby following the European Convention on Human Rights (Kukova 2008).[18] It also moved beyond the requirements of the Employment Equality Directive to address equal treatment and equal opportunities 'in principle in every part of the social sphere' (Kukova 2008: 3), offering protection in the areas of employment, education and training, as well as in the provision of goods and services, which is not yet addressed by EU law. It also provided for the establishment of a statutory commission against discrimination to deal with the implementation of the Act and cases of discrimination, the Protection against Discrimination Commission (PADC).

The lesbian and gay organisations which had been formed from the early 1990s had not addressed the issue of anti-discrimination legislation in advance of the issue being brought on to the political agenda by the accession negotiations. Lacking experience of lobbying and campaigning, and political capital and credibility – and less well supported and funded by international agencies than the women's NGOs – they were relatively marginal actors in the public consultation and discussions about the anti-discrimination proposals, in contrast to the women's

---

17   Directive n. 2000/78/EC, 20 November. Available at: http://ec.europa.eu/employment_social/news/2001/jul/directive78ec_en.pdf.

18   The Bulgarian Constitution outlaws discrimination on grounds of sex, race, nationality, ethnic origin, origin, religion or belief, education, opinions, political belonging, personal or public status, property status. PADA introduces a number of 'new' grounds: citizenship, disability, age, marital status and also sexual orientation.

organisations, which were active in the drafting of the proposals. However, after the Protection against Discrimination Act (PADA) was passed, lesbian and gay organisations have been involved in testing its implementation.

The first and most widely discussed such case was in 2004–2005, when Sofia University was successfully charged with sexual orientation discrimination for banning a group of gay men from using its saunas.[19] In 2009 a bisexual woman prisoner, supported by the Bulgarian Helsinki Committee, won a case against the Prosecutor's Office of Bulgaria for direct discrimination. She was awarded non-pecuniary damages because a prosecutor had turned down her request to be put forward for early release on the basis that she 'had "a clear and stable homosexual orientation" and her "way of life" and "emotional state, thinking and behaviour" were problematic' (Bulgarian Helsinki Committee 2009: 1). The case revealed how the authorities had collected detailed information about the woman's intimate life – with reports addressing her 'accommodation', 'family relations', 'lifestyle and contacts', 'emotional status' and 'mindset and behaviour' – in a manner reminiscent of the communist regime. She was described as having a 'masculine behavioural pattern' and 'masculine appearance' (Fundamental Rights Agency/ FRA 2008: 138–9).

Alongside PADA, a number of other legislative changes mainstreamed anti-sexual orientation discrimination provision across the Bulgarian welfare state. The Health Law (SG 70/10.08/2004), which lays out the principles governing the provision of healthcare, now includes sexual orientation in the list of grounds which cannot be used in the assessment of a patient's health condition; and the Judicial Ethics Code (SG 60/22.07.2005) includes sexual orientation in the grounds on which lawyers may not discriminate. The Social Security Act (SG 12/13.02.2004) has provisions that do not allow insurance companies to refuse additional voluntary insurance to individuals based on numerous grounds, among which are sex and sexual orientation (Art. 283); and sexual orientation is mentioned as grounds on which discrimination or privilege is not allowed by the Regulation of the Procedures for Selection of State Servants (SG 6/23.01.2004).

Whilst there is inconsistency in the incorporation of protection against sexual orientation discrimination into Bulgarian law, and there are areas where it is not included in the list of illegal forms of discrimination, the direction of legal and policy change is clear: the Bulgarian state has been taking on board the new European norms about sexual orientation discrimination. Indeed, revisions to the Constitution of 1991 have been considered by the Ministry of Justice (Temporary

---

19   This was the first case of sexual discrimination won by one of the biggest lesbian and gay organisations, Queer Bulgaria, on behalf of the victims. The Sofia University 'St Kliment Ohridski' was found guilty of direct discrimination against a group of four young men who were denied access to the sauna and verbally assaulted by the security guards in January 2004 due to their sexual orientation. The court found that the victims suffered non-pecuniary damages and each of them was offered compensation of 500 Bulgarian leva. In addition to this the university had to grant them access to the sauna.

Commission for Preparation of Proposals for Changes in the Constitution 2004) in order to bring the Constitution into line with the EU Charter of Fundamental Rights, which would include constitutional protection against sexual orientation discrimination.

However, when it comes to homophobic speech and violence – against which there have been European Parliament resolutions and Fundamental Rights Agency pronouncements, but no legally binding directives requiring member states to institute criminal law sanctions – the Bulgarian state has not acted. Homophobic speech is banned as harassment on the grounds of sexual orientation by PADA (Kukova 2008), and one case has been brought, unsuccessfully, to court and another to the PADC; but there have been no policy initiatives to combat homophobic violence. The Bulgarian Helsinki Committee (2001) points to police violence against homosexuals, the collection of personal information from homosexual victims of violence that does not relate to the case and refusal to register acts of homophobic violence. BGO 'Gemini' (2004: 1) has stated that lesbian and gay people 'very often' say that they 'prefer' 'becoming reconciled [to violence] to defending their rights and seeking legal protection'. And despite campaigning by lesbian and gay activists, homophobic intent was not included as an aggravating factor in hate crimes or hate speech in the 2009 revised Penal Code, even though its extension included as aggravating factors race, ethnicity, nationality, religion and political views.

Another demonstration of the inconsistency in the development of anti-discrimination protection was the recent case of a Bulgarian municipality passing a Public Order Regulation (Art. 14/12.11.2009, Pazarjik) forbidding 'the public demonstration and expression of sexual and other orientation' (LGBT Action 2010a), thereby recalling the revoked provisions of the Penal Code (1968) which banned the public display of homosexuality. The youth organisation 'LGBT Action' organised a protest against the regulation which was subject to violent homophobic attacks and resulted in the arrests of five anti-gay demonstrators (Standart 2010). The regulation was pronounced unconstitutional and was found to violate basic human rights by the Ombudsman of the Republic of Bulgaria, who also pointed out that the formulation is 'unclear, unpredictable and creates the risk of arbitrary judgements by local authorities' (Statement of the Ombudsman cited in LGBT Action 2010b: 1, our translation). A ruling from the PADC revoked the regulation.

Gaps in protection and inconsistencies in implementation notwithstanding, public debates about changes in the law concerning sexual orientation discrimination, and publicity about cases taken under the law, have provided an agenda around which to organise, and a space for lesbian and gay activists to speak publicly about the discrimination and violence they face in their daily lives. In addition, they provide the normative grounds from which claims for the recognition of same-sex relationships proceed.

The Recognition of Same-Sex Relationships

The ongoing heteronormativity of the intimate citizenship regime in Bulgaria is underlined by the absence of any legal recognition of same-sex relationships in law and policy, and of any signs that such recognition is on the agendas of the political parties. The 1991 Constitution, adopted after the fall of the communist regime, defined marriage for the first time – and in advance of the trend that developed in the early years of the twenty-first century in the wake of demands for same-sex marriage – as 'a voluntary union between a man and a woman' (Art. 46: 1). More recently, in 2008–2009 debates about the formal legal recognition of cohabitation – which have been posed in terms of the need to acknowledge social transformation, the emergence of a 'new value system' and 'basic civil rights, mobility, and freedom of personal life' (Council of Ministers 2008b: 61) – have continued to explicitly define cohabitation as 'between a man and a woman' (Family Code Proposal, Art. 13, Council of Ministers 2008a). There has been much debate about marriage 'dying out', as more and more people cohabit and have children outside marriage, and there has also been strong resistance to legal change that might downgrade the value of marriage. The 'gold standard' status of heterosexual marriage has been defended on the basis that it represents the ideal for national public morality, whatever the reality of people's everyday family practices (Council of Ministers 2008b).

So, despite the wide-ranging anti-discrimination legislation enacted in the first decade of the twenty-first century, and the 2009 Family Code stating that 'every person has the right to marry and to found a family' (Family Code 2009, SG 47/23.07.2009), same-sex partners remain, in every respect, legal strangers. There is no provision for the recognition of same-sex partners in relation to any rights or obligations, or any fiscal and social benefits. Same-sex partners have no rights to inheritance, to a share in a pension or a 'family name'; to be given information about or to be involved in decision-making about their partner's health. They have no care entitlements, tax relief or survivor's benefit. They are not allowed to refuse to testify against each other in court, as married heterosexual couples may; and they cannot adopt children together, or access reproductive technologies.

Whilst the EU has, thus far, not intervened in the field of family law, and there are no directives relating to same-sex partnership recognition and hence no pressure on the Bulgarian state to enact legal change in this area, EU regulations on movement, residence, asylum and family reunification require member states to recognise partnerships that are recognised in a couple's state of origin.[20] This means that same-sex married/partnered or cohabiting couples from another EU member state are, in principle, allowed to enter and reside in Bulgaria as a couple if they provide a formal certificate delivered by the authorities of the state of origin testifying to

---

20 Entry, Residence and Exit of EU Citizens and Accompanying Members of Their Families Act, 2007.

their relationship.[21] For nationals of non-EU countries, however, the regulations are different and the notion of 'family members' is restricted to opposite-sex spouses or partners (Act on Foreigners in the Republic of Bulgaria 2007).[22]

The recognition of same-sex relationships has been one of the main goals of lesbian and gay activism in Bulgaria in recent years. The earliest initiatives were undertaken in 2004 and 2005 by BGO 'Gemini' and Queer Bulgaria. During the pre-election campaign these groups sought support from various political parties for the representation of gay rights in parliament, and for the pursuit of legal recognition of same-sex relationships. These demands, however, have remained largely ignored by politicians, and Bulgarian Socialist Youth is the only political group to have openly declared its support for these quests for sexual orientation equality.

BGO 'Gemini' also played an active role in the heated public debate that surrounded the process of revising the Family Code, between 2006 and 2009, to which a range of religious groups, conservative, pro-family and nationalist organisations replied with homophobic campaigns. BGO 'Gemini' demanded that the amendments to the Family Code should include the legal recognition of same-sex cohabitation and parenting (BGO 'Gemini' 2008c). In support of these claims it organised the first Gay Pride in Bulgaria, under the slogan 'Me and My Family' (June 2008). Public reaction was polarised, but homophobic responses were more visible, and there were violent outbursts against the 200 participants in the parade. Firecrackers, Molotov cocktails and stones were thrown at the marchers. More than 80 people were arrested for violence, including the leader of a Bulgarian nationalist organisation. The parade was accompanied by about 100 police officers and no participants in the march were injured. However, the organisers of the parade received numerous threats to their lives, both before and after the march (source: personal meetings with BGO 'Gemini'). Popular responses to the march saw the participants as demanding 'special' rights that were regarded as endangering public morality, and as putting children at risk of 'becoming homosexual'.

BGO 'Gemini' also sent an open letter to the chairs of the National Assembly and the Judicial Committee on the subject of partnership recognition, referring to the illegitimacy of sexual orientation discrimination, and to the respectable, law-abiding status of homosexual citizens:

> From judicial and moral points of view such limitation is unjust, and represents discrimination against Bulgarian citizens based on their sexual orientation ... Homosexual Bulgarian citizens are part of the public, they are tax-payers and

---

21   There are no data on the actual implementation of the free movement of same-sex couples within the EU in general, or on the granting or refusal of visas or residence permits in Bulgaria in particular (Kukova 2008: 5).

22   Dimitrova (2008) gives as an example how a civil partner of a Bulgarian citizen was denied the right to residence because the couple had entered a civil partnership in Iceland.

voters, and have the right to demand to be granted equality. (BGO 'Gemini' 2008b: 1, our translation)

An article published on the website of BGO 'Gemini' (2008a) analysed the main arguments advanced in public discussions of the Family Code to deny legal recognition to same-sex relationships. The most common argument was that marriage is a union between a man and a woman, as the Constitution and the Family Code explicitly state. Other arguments focused on the idea that a same-sex family was an inappropriate environment for raising children, suggested the immorality of same-sex relationships, and expressed concerns that such changes would undermine the institution of marriage and its procreative functions. It was also very common that legal recognition of same-sex relationships was seen as giving special rights to people in such relationships.

The statement of the former Head of Parliament, Ognyan Gerjikov, is typical of the way in which same-sex relationships have been discussed in the political sphere:

> With all my respect for the different, I cannot accept that gay marriages should be made legal in Bulgaria. We are a patriarchal society and this would 'detonate' public opinion. So may those who find it necessary to be together in a same-sex [relationship] not want the official recognition of the state for this. (Nova Television 2009, our translation)

This reluctant-realist acceptance of the existence of same-sex relationships, and the nod to 'respect for the different' alongside a refusal of state recognition for such relationships, is a global contemporary discursive response to the demands of lesbians and gay men for equal intimate citizenship rights. Writing in the UK prior to the introduction of civil partnerships for same-sex couples in 2005, Richardson suggests that lesbian and gay men 'are granted the right to be tolerated as long as they stay within the boundaries of that tolerance, whose borders are maintained through a heterosexist public/ private divide' (Richardson 1998: 90). And Cooper (2001: 86) points out that notions of 'proper place' and the public/private divide both contribute to the preservation of inequality because they create exclusions. Furthermore, gay demands for equal rights in terms of opportunities, recognition, freedom or satisfaction (Cooper 2001: 76) are often constructed as seeking special rights or protecting special interests, and are presented as 'promoting' a single minority viewpoint (Duggan 1994; Brickel 2000). A distinctively traditionalist, and Bulgarian-nationalist, hue is added to this position by Gerjikov in his reference to Bulgaria as a 'patriarchal society'– a performative reassertion of the historical power of the Orthodox Church, which brushes aside the twentieth-century communist commitment to gender equality in work and family, and the reality of the long-standing relative lack of cultural authority of the Church.

Conclusion

According to the 2008 Eurobarometer study on discrimination in the EU, people in Bulgaria have the lowest levels of comfort with the idea of having a homosexual person as a neighbour,[23] and with the idea of having a homosexual person in the highest political office of all EU member states.[24] Bulgaria also has the lowest proportion of people knowing their rights, should they be a victim of discrimination or harassment (17 per cent) (EC 2008: 22), and the lowest level of awareness of discrimination against LGBT people: only 20 per cent saw discrimination on the basis of sexual orientation as widespread (EC 2008: 52), against an EU average of 51 per cent, and only 1 per cent said that they had witnessed discrimination on the grounds of sexuality, against an EU average of 6 per cent (EC 2008: 57). The research also found that Bulgaria had the lowest proportion of respondents who reported having friends who are homosexual – at 7 per cent, against an EU average of 34 per cent. The 2006 Eurobarometer study reported that 15 per cent of Bulgarians were in favour of same-sex marriage, against an EU average of 42 per cent, and 12 per cent thought that same-sex couples should be allowed to adopt, against an EU average of 31 per cent (EC 2006).

We do not cite these statistics to draw conclusions about the quality of life of lesbians, gay men and all of those with same-sex desires in Bulgaria, which would be much better researched through in-depth qualitative and ethnographic studies (a task to which we have begun to make a small contribution). It would be all too easy to read these data as suggesting that Bulgaria is exceptional in its levels of homophobia and intolerance of lesbians and gay men, and we certainly do not wish to encourage such readings. The 2008 Eurobarometer report itself notes the high proportion of respondents in Bulgaria who gave the spontaneous answer that they would be indifferent to having a homosexual neighbour,[25] and points to the 12 per cent who answered that they 'do not know', or who refused to answer (against an EU average of 1 per cent) (EC 2008: 57). These results suggest that there are considerable numbers of people in Bulgaria who are either completely uninterested in the issue, or unable to conceive of the situation or to formulate a position on it. This, together with the low levels of reported awareness of sexual orientation discrimination and of anti-discrimination legislation in general, and the low levels of personal acquaintance with lesbians and gay men, all combine to

---

23   An average 'comfort level' of 5.3 on a 10-point 'comfort scale', with Latvia at 5.5 and Lithuania at 6.1 in the lowest grouping, and Sweden at 9.5 and the Netherlands and Denmark at 9.3 in the highest grouping, against an EU average of 7.9 (EC 2008: 57).

24   An average 'comfort level' of 3.5 on a 10-point 'comfort scale' along with Cyprus (also 3.5) and Romania (3.9), against Sweden (9.1), Denmark (9.0), the Netherlands (8.8) and an EU average of 7.0 (EC 2008: 58).

25   In Bulgaria, Latvia and Luxembourg 25 per cent, and in the Czech Republic 27 per cent (EC 2008: 57).

suggest that issues surrounding sexual orientation and lesbian and gay rights have largely failed to be registered by the Bulgarian population at large.

Rather than *revealing* high levels of homophobia in Bulgaria, the Eurobarometer data are suggestive of the novelty of the *idea* of homophobia and of attention to sexual orientation discrimination within a country which lacks the history of social movement mobilisation that created these notions, and that propelled them on to the European political agenda and into the biopolitical technologies of European surveys, with their rankings of member states according to levels of conformity with emerging European norms of anti-homophobia and sexual orientation equality. EU research on discrimination against, and attitudes towards, homosexuals has emerged in the context of the regulatory framework which has been developed since the 1997 Treaty of Amsterdam created an explicit legal competence for the EU to combat discrimination based on sexual orientation. After meeting the requirements of the *acquis communitaire* to fully decriminalise same-sex sexual practice, and then enacting the EU directives which incorporate sexual orientation discrimination into a comprehensive anti-discrimination framework, Bulgaria – along with other new member states that evince low levels of conformity with new European norms on homosexuality[26] – is faced with the political-cultural challenge of rising up the league tables that measure the changing norms and ethics of the European community of nations.

In contrast to many Western European and Nordic countries – where there has been over half a century of lesbian and gay activism which built on a longer history of sub-cultural community life, of bars and clubs, and literary and artistic production – self-organising, self-identifying communities of lesbian and gay men are a recent development in Bulgaria. Much lesbian and gay life takes place in what Melucci (1995) calls 'submerged networks', informal groupings of people who gather in clubs and bars, and through online forums, and who are largely invisible to the heterosexual world. Even public figures who are known to be gay rarely 'come out' explicitly and declare their sexual identity publicly (Pisankaneva and Panaiotov 2005). The cultural normalisation, and indeed valorisation, of same-sex relationships and desires that has proceeded through pop music, television and film, and the coming out of key figures in the entertainment industries in the UK over the past 20 years (Roseneil 2000) has barely begun in Bulgaria. The Eurobarometer surveys might be seen as measuring, in one rather crude quantitative way, the level of 'normalisation' of lesbian and gay lifestyles and identities across European civil societies. Whilst there is considerable evidence that a process of normalisation is well underway in many countries – as discussed by Bech (1999), Seidman et al. (1999) and Roseneil (2000) in relation to Denmark, the United States and the UK respectively – there is little evidence of such a process in Bulgaria.

---

26   Notably Romania and Poland, which have lower levels of acceptance of same-sex marriage and adoption than Bulgaria – with only 11 per cent of Romanians supporting same-sex marriage and only 7 per cent of Poles supporting adoption by same-sex couples, according to the 2006 Eurobarometer survey (EC 2006).

However, there are real signs of change. Lesbian and gay groups have begun to challenge the heteronormativity of the national intimate citizenship regime, in the context of an opening up of the issues around homosexuality in the wake of accession to the EU. The full decriminalisation of same-sex sexuality and the creation of a comprehensive anti-discrimination framework which includes sexual orientation discrimination constitute important shifts in the landscape of heteronormativity in Bulgaria. Whilst these changes have undoubtedly been imposed on Bulgaria from outside, as part of the wider process of rapid Europeanisation that is affecting much of contemporary Europe, rather than emerging from the country's own internal struggles and political compromises, they open up possibilities for those living non-normative sexualities to find a public voice and begin to occupy public space. Whilst marriage remains defined as exclusively heterosexual and is posited as the ideal moral accomplishment, from which, along with blood ties, all intimate rights and responsibilities are derived, its popularity is declining, and more and more people are living, loving and having children outside its boundaries, implicitly challenging the social and moral centrality of marriage. The contiguity of such changing everyday practices of intimate life with transformations in law and policy governing same-sex sexualities might, we suggest, prefigure the possibility of further shifts in the Bulgarian regime of intimate citizenship in years to come.

References

Angelova, V. and Liakova, M. 2005. Сексуалното различие като проблем пред българските печатни медии ['The Issue of Sexual Diversity as Dealt with in Bulgarian Newspapers'], *Sociological Problems* 2–3: 165–86.

Atanasov, N. 2008. Защо ме е страх да се прибера в България ['Why I'm Afraid to Go Back to Bulgaria'], *Altera*, vol. 3.

———. 2009. Медийната видимост на хомосексуалността като парадокс ['Paradoxes of the Media Visibility of Homosexuality'], *Liberalen Pregled*, vol. 11. Available at: http://librev.com/ [accessed: 14 April 2010].

Atanasov, N. and Dobrev, D. 2008. Гей парадът в България. Равносметката ['The Gay Pride in Bulgaria. The End-Balance'], *Kultura* 27: 2510.

Bech, H. 1999. 'Commentaries on Seidman, Meeks and Traschen: "Beyond the Closet?": After the Closet'. *Sexualities* 2: 343–6.

Bell, D. and Binnie, J. 2000. *The Sexual Citizen: Queer Politics and Beyond*. Cambridge: Polity Press.

Brickel, C. 2000. 'Heroes and Invaders: Gay and Lesbian Pride Parades and the Public/Private Distinction in New Zealand Media Accounts'. *Gender, Place and Culture* 7(2): 163–78.

———. 2005. 'The Transformation of Heterosexism and Its Paradoxes'. In *Thinking Straight: the Power, the Promise, and the Paradox of Heterosexuality*, ed. C. Ingraham. New York and London: Routledge.

Brunnbauer, U. 2008. 'Making Bulgarians Socialist: The Fatherland Front in Communist Bulgaria (1944–1989)', *East European Politics and Societies* 22(1): 44–79.

Bulgarian Association of University Women (BAUW). 2008. 'Who Are We?' Available at: http://bauw-bg.com/en/who_are_we.html (accessed: 29 June 2008).

Bulgarian Gay Organisation (BGO) 'Gemini'. 2004. Джемини в Бургас, Русе и Варна ['Gemini' in Burgas, Ruse and Varna]. Available at: http://www.bgogemini.org/bg/page.php?id=7 (accessed: 13 April 2010).

———. 2007. History of the Bulgarian Gay Organisation 'Gemini', Available at: http://www.bgogemini.org/eng/page.php?id=78 (accessed: 13 April 2010).

———. 2008a. Новият семеен кодекс: Не става само с преписване, трябва и акъл! ['The New Family Code: Only Copying Won't Do, You Need Savvy!']. Available at: http://www.bgogemini.org/bg/page.php?id=345 (accessed: 14 April 2010).

———. 2008b. Отворено писмо до Комисия по правни въпроси в НС за измененията в Семейния кодекс ['Open Letter to the Judicial Committee at the National Assembly on the Family Code Changes']. Available at: http://www.bgogemini.org/bg/page.php?id=346 (accessed: 14 April 2010).

———. 2008c. Предложение за промени в Семейния кодекс ['Proposal for Family Code Changes']. Available at: http://www.bgogemini.org/bg/page.php?id=314 (accessed: 14 April 2010).

Bulgarian Helsinki Committee. 2001. *Bulgarian Legislation about Homosexuals*, Special Thematic Reports. Available at: http://www.bghelsinki.org/index.php?module=resources&lg=en&id=77#1b (accessed: 4 January 2010).

———. 2009. 'BHC Wins a Case against Prosecutor's Office for Discrimination of a Bisexual Inmate'. Available at: http://www.bghelsinki.org/index.php?module=news&lg=en&id=2095 (accessed: 13 April 2010).

Bulgarian Public's Women's Union (BPWU). 1950. State Archive, Fund 7, Opis 1.

Central Committee of the Bulgarian Communist Party (CC of BCP). 1968. Minutes from the Meeting on 21 May 1968. Available at: http://www.nbu.bg/historyproject/index.html (accessed: 14 April 2010).

Committee of the Movement of Bulgarian Women (CMBW). 1980. За по-активното участие на българските жени във всенародната борба за изпълнение плана за социално-икономическото развитие ['For More Active Participation of Bulgarian Women in the People's Fight for Accomplishment of the Plan for Socio-Economic Development']. *State Archive*, Fund 417, Opis 5–7.

Cooper, D. 2001. 'Like Counting Stars? Re-Structuring Equality and the Socio-Legal Space of Same-Sex Marriage'. In *The Legal Recognition of Same-Sex Partnerships*, eds R. Wintemute and M. Andenæs. Oxford: Hart Publishing.

Council of Ministers. 2008a. Проект за Семеен кодекс ['Proposal for Family Code'], Judicial Commission, Session 8, 1 April 2008, Number 802-01-37.

Available at: http://www.parliament.bg/bills/40/802-01-37.pdf (accessed: 13 April 2010).

———. 2008b. Minutes from Parliamentary Sittings on 2 October 2008. Available at: http://www.parliament.bg/?page=plSt&lng=bg (accessed: 14 April 2010).

Darik News. 2007. Осъдиха габровец на обществено порицание ['A Man from Gabrovo is Sentenced to Public Reprobation'], 2 November. Available at: http://dariknews.bg/view_article.php?article_id=194484 (accessed: 14 April 2010).

———. 2010. 'Обществено порицание' за непълнолетна пияна шофьорка ['Public Reprobation for a Minor Drink-Driver'], 27 January.

Daskalova, K. 2000. 'Women's Problems, Women's Discourses in Bulgaria'. In *Reproducing Gender*, eds S. Gal and G. Kligman. Princeton: Princeton University Press.

Daskalova, K. and Filipova, P. 2003. *Citizenship and Women's Political Participation in Bulgaria. Network for European Women's Rights*, Country Reports. Available at: http://www.newr.bham.ac.uk/topics/Political/political_reports.htm (accessed: 21 March 2008).

Dimitrova, M. 2008. *The Social Situation Concerning Homophobia and Discrimination on Grounds of Sexual Orientation in Bulgaria*, Fundamental Rights Agency. Available at: http://fra.europa.eu/fraWebsite/attachments/FRA-hdgso-part2-NR_BG.pdf (accessed: 14 April 2010).

Duggan, L. 1994. 'Queering the State', *Social Text* 39: 1–14.

European Commission (EC). 2001. *Regular Report on Bulgaria's Progress towards Accession,* Available at: http://ec.europa.eu/enlargement/archives/pdf/key_documents/2001/bu_en.pdf (accessed: 12 April 2010).

———. 2002. *Road Map for Bulgaria and Romania*. Available at: http://ec.europa.eu/bulgaria/documents/abc/roadmap-br-ro-2002_en.pdf (accessed: 11 August 2009).

———. 2006. *Standard Eurobarometer 66*. Available at: http://ec.europa.eu/public_opinion/archives/eb/eb66/eb66_en.htm (accessed: 14 April 2010).

———. 2008. *Special Eurobarometer 296: Discrimination in the European Union. Perceptions, Experiences and Attitudes*. Available at: http://ec.europa.eu/public_opinion/archives/ebs/ebs_296_en.pdf (accessed: 10 April 2010).

Evans, D. 1993. *Sexual Citizenship*. London: Routledge.

Frejka, T., Sobotka, T., Hoem, J.M. and Toulemon, L. 2008. 'Summary and General Conclusions: Childbearing Trends and Policies in Europe'. *Demographic Research* 19(2): 5–14.

Fundamental Rights Agency of the European Union (FRA). 2008. *Homophobia and Discrimination on the Grounds of Sexual Orientation and Gender Identity in the EU Member States: Part I – Legal Analysis*. Available at: http://fra.europa.eu/fraWebsite/material/pub/comparativestudy/FRA_hdgso_part1_en.pdf (accessed: 14 April 2010).

———. 2009. *Homophobia and Discrimination on the Grounds of Sexual Orientation and Gender Identity in the EU Member States: Part II – The*

Social Situation. Available at: http://fra.europa.eu/fraWebsite/attachments/ FRA_hdgso_report-part2_en.pdf (accessed: 14 April 2010).

Genova, Y. 2008. За тибетците и лесбийките ['For Tibetans and Lesbians']. *Altera*, vols 8–9.

Gruev, M. 2006. Комунизъм и хомосексуализъм в България (1944– 1989) ['Communism and Homosexuality in Bulgaria (1944–1989)']. *Anamnesis* vol. 1. Available at: http://www.anamnesis.info/Komunizam_ Homoseksualizam_doktor_Mihail_Gruev.pdf (accessed: 14 April 2010).

Koeva, S. and Bould, S. 2007. 'Women as Workers and as Carers under Communism and After: The Case of Bulgaria'. *International Review of Sociology* 17(2): 303–18.

Kostov, I. 1999. Изказване на министър-председателя Иван Костов пред Народното събрание, 11 юни 1999 [Speech by Prime Minister Ivan Kostov before the National Assembly, 11 June 1999]. Available at: http://sun450. government.bg/old/bg/prime_minister/statements/NS-Kostov_prestapnost_ 06_11.html (accessed: 12 April 2010).

Kukova, S. 2008. *Legal Study on Homophobia and Discrimination on Grounds of Sexual Orientation in Bulgaria,* European Union Agency for Fundamental Rights (FRA). Available at: http://fra.europa.eu/fraWebsite/attachments/FRA-hdgso-NR_BG.pdf (accessed: 4 April 2020).

LGBT Action. 2010a. Казусът 'Пазарджик' [The 'Pazarjik' Case]. Available at: http://freepazardjik.wordpress.com/about/ (accessed: 14 April 2010).

———. 2010b. Омбудсманът призова общинските съветници да не злоупотребяват с правомощията си ['The Ombudsman Urged Aldermen to Not Abuse Their Powers']. Available at: <http://freepazardjik.wordpress. com/2010/03/24/ombudsman-reshenie/> [accessed: 14 April 2010].

Lofstrom, J. 1998. 'A Pre-Modern Legacy: The Easy Criminalisation of Homosexual Acts between Women in the Finish Penal Code of 1889'. In *Scandinavian Homosexualities: Essays on Gay and Lesbian Studies*, ed. J. Lofstrom. New York: Howarth Press.

Long, S. 1999. 'Gay and Lesbian Movements in Eastern Europe: Romania, Hungary and the Czech Republic'. In *The Global Emergence of Gay and Lesbian Politics: National Imprints of a Worldwide Movement*, eds B.D. Adam, J.W. Duyvendak and A. Krouwel. Philadelphia: Temple University Press.

Melucci, A. 1995. *Nomads of the Present: Social Movements and Individual Needs in Contemporary Society*. London: Century Hutchinson.

Meshkova, P. and Sharlanov, D. 1994. *Българската гилотина: тайните механизми на народния съд* [Bulgarian Guillotine: Secret Mechanisms of the People's Court]. Sofia: Agencia Demokracia.

Mihajlova, D. 2006. *Законът за зашита срещу дискриминацията като инструмент за заита на жертвите на неравно третиране, основано на признака сексуална ориентация* [The Law against Discrimination as an Instrument for Protection of Victims of Unequal Treatment Based on Sexuality].

National Anti-Discrimination Campaign, European Institute. Available at: http://diversity.europe.bg/ (accessed: 14 April 2010).

Ministry of Labour and Social Policy. 2006. *National Strategy for Demographic Development of the Republic of Bulgaria 2006–2020*. Available at: <http://www.mlsp.government.bg/bg/docs/demography/STRATEGY-%20FINAL.pdf (accessed: 14 April 2010).

National Statistical Institute (NSI). 2009. *Main Demographic Indicators*. Available at: http://www.nsi.bg/Population_e/Population_e.htm [accessed: 14 April 2010].

Nova Television. 2009. Всичко за майката ['Everything about the Mother']. Temata na Nova, broadcast 27 March.

Okoliyski, M. and Velichkov, P. 2004. 'Bulgaria'. In *International Encyclopaedia of Sexuality*, eds R. Francoeur and R. Noonan, R. London: The Continuum International Publishing Group.

Panaiotov, S. 2009. Политиката и горделивата нетолерантност ['Politics and Haughty Intolerance']. *Liberalen Pregled*, April. Available at: http://www.librev.com/index.php?option=com_content&task=view&id=539&Itemid=26 (accessed: 9 April 2009).

Panova, R., Gavrilova, R. and Merdzanska, C. 1993. 'Thinking Gender: Bulgarian Women's Im/Possibilities'. In *Gender Politics and Post-Communism: Reflections from Eastern Europe and the Former Soviet Union*, eds N. Funk and M. Mueller. London: Routledge.

Petrova, D. 1993. 'The Winding Road to Emancipation in Bulgaria'. In *Gender Politics and Post-Communism: Reflections from Eastern Europe and the Former Soviet Union*, eds N. Funk and M. Mueller. London: Routledge.

Philipov, D. and Kohler, H.-P. 2001. 'Tempo Effects in the Fertility Decline in Eastern Europe: Evidence from Bulgaria, the Czech Republic, Hungary, Poland, and Russia'. *European Journal of Population*. 17(1): 37–60.

Pisankaneva, M. 2002. 'Reflections on the Butch-Femme and the Emerging Lesbian Community in Bulgaria'. In *Femme-Butch: New Considerations of the Way We Want to Go*, eds M. Gibson and D. Meem. Binghampton, New York: Harrington Park Press.

———. 2003. The Forbidden Fruit: Sexuality in Communist Bulgaria, Conference 'Past and Present of Radical Sexual Politics', 'Socialism and Sexuality' Fifth Annual Meeting, University of Amsterdam, 3–4 October. Available at: http://www.iisg.nl/womhist/pisankaneva.doc (accessed: 14 April 2010).

———. 2009. Bulgaria. In *The Greenwood Encyclopaedia of LGBT Issues Worldwide*, ed. C. Stewart. Santa Barbara, CA: Greenwood Press.

Pisankaneva, M. and Panaiotov, S. 2005. 2004-та през призмата на гей активизма ['2004 through the Prism of Gay Activism'], *LiterNet* 5(66), 14 May. Available at: http://liternet.bg/publish14/m_pisankyneva/2004.htm (accessed: 14 April 2010).

Plummer, K. 1995. *Telling Sexual Stories: Power, Change, and Social Worlds*. London: Routledge.

————. 2003. *Intimate Citizenship: Private Decisions and Public Dialogues.* Seattle and London: Washington University Press.

Popova, G. 2004. Обезтелесеното тяло на социализма [The Bodiless Body of Socialism]. In *Култура и критика* [*Culture and Critique*] vol. 4, eds A. Vacheva, J. Eftimov and G. Chobanov. Available at: http://liternet.bg/publish7/ gpopova/tialo.htm [accessed: 14 April 2010].

————. 2009. Забраненият език – от дискурсивното обезличаване до фактическата асимилация на хомосексуалните в България в периода 1945–1989 ['The Forbidden Language – from Discursive Depersonalisation to Factual Assimilation of Homosexual People in Bulgaria between 1945 and 1989'], *NotaBene,* vol. 2. Available at: http://notabene-bg.org/ (accessed: 14 April 2010).

Richardson, D. 1998. 'Sexuality and Citizenship', *Sociology* 32(1): 83–100.

————. 2000. 'Constructing Sexual Citizenship: Theorizing Sexual Rights', *Critical Social Policy* 20(1): 105–35.

Roseneil, S. 2000. 'Queer Frameworks and Queer Tendencies: Towards an Understanding of Postmodern Transformations of Sexuality', *Sociological Research Online* 5(3): 1–19. Available at: http://www.socresonline.org.uk/5/3/ roseneil.html.

————. 2002. 'The Heterosexual/ Homosexual Binary: Past, Present and Future'. In *Handbook of Lesbian and Gay Studies*, eds D. Richardson and S. Seidman. London: Sage.

————. 2008. (ed.) 'Policy Contexts and Responses to Changes in Intimate Life', pp. 396. FEMCIT WP 6 Working Paper 1. Available at: http://www.femcit. org/files/WP6_WorkingpaperNo1.pdf.

————. 2009. (ed.) 'Changing Cultural Discourses about Intimate Life: The Demands and Actions of Women's Movements and Other Movements for Gender and Sexual Equality and Change', pp. 398. FEMCIT WP6 Working Paper 2. Available at: http://www.femcit.org/files/WP6_WorkingpaperNo2.

————. 2010a. 'Intimate Citizenship: A Pragmatic, Yet Radical, Proposal for a Politics of Personal Life'. *European Journal of Women's Studies* 17: 77–82.

————. 2010b. *Intimate Citizenship Regimes In Multicultural Europe: The Tenacity of the Couple Norm.* Sub-plenary Paper presented at the British Sociological Association conference, Glasgow Caledonian University, April 2010.

Sampson, S. 2002. 'Weak States, Uncivil Societies and Thousands of NGOs: Benevolent Colonialism in the Balkans'. Available at: http://www.anthrobase. com/Txt/S/Sampson_S_01.htm [accessed: 23 April 2010].

Seidman, S.; Meeks, C. and Traschen, F. 1999. 'Beyond the Closet? The Changing Social Meaning of Homosexuality in the United States'. *Sexualities* 2(1): 9–34.

Standart. 2010. Бой и арести на гей протест ['Fight and Arrests at a Gay Protest'], 20 March.

Stoilova, M. 2008. 'Policy Contexts and Responses to Changes in Intimate Life in Bulgaria'. In *Contexts and Responses to Changes in Intimate Life*. FEMCIT,

Work Package Intimate Citizenship, Working Paper No. 1. Available at: http://www.femcit.org/files/WP6_WorkingpaperNo1.pdf [accessed: 14 April 2010].

———. 2009. 'Changing Cultural Discourses about Intimate Life: The Demands and Actions of Women's Movements and Other Movements for Gender and Sexual Equality and Change in Bulgaria'. In *Changing Cultural Discourses about Intimate Life: The Demands and Actions of Women's Movements and Other Movements for Gender and Sexual Equality and Change.* FEMCIT, Work Package Intimate Citizenship, Working Paper No. 1. Available at: http://www.femcit.org/files/WP6_WorkingpaperNo2 [accessed: 14 April 2010].

Therborn, G. 2004. *Between Sex and Power: Family in the World, 1900–2000.* London: Routledge.

Weeks, J. 1998. 'The Sexual Citizen'. *Theory, Culture and Society* 15(3): 35–52.

Chapter 10

Situating Intimate Citizenship in Macedonia: Emotional Navigation and Everyday Queer/*Kvar* Grounded Moralities[1]

Alexander Lambevski

Emilija's Fall from Traditional Heterosexual Grace[2]

Strong-willed, incredibly smart, ambitious, highly successful in a prestigious profession, unconventionally sexy and fiercely independent, Emilija is a cosmopolitan woman (*gradska žena*) in her early forties, filled with a seductive mix of sophistication, intellect, charm and *joie de vivre*. She was, for most of her life, very close to both her loving, upper middle-class parents. While part of the former communist ruling elite, her parents were dissidents of sorts, both persistently refusing to become members of the Union of Communists. Highly educated workaholics, professionally highly acclaimed, law-abiding, extroverted and committed to personal integrity and modern parenting, Emilija's parents were true believers in meritocracy and raised their single daughter to seek ultimate validation in her own achievements. Outwardly, her parents always presented an image of an ideal heterosexual marriage and a modern family filled with love, egalitarianism, fidelity, sacrifice, emotional restraint, mutual understanding and support for the differing needs of each member of the family. In terms of their

---

1   I use the terms 'Macedonia' and 'Macedonian' to refer to the territory, people and language of the largest ethnic group in the sovereign state officially recognised by 129 countries in the world as the 'Republic of Macedonia', but also referred to by the United Nations, the European Union (EU) and many other countries by that necrophilic reference 'the former Yugoslav Republic of Macedonia'. I fully acknowledge that references to 'Macedonia' and 'Macedonian' 'also cover ... many [other] places, identities, and ideas attached to people from different political, ethnic, and religious groups over many centuries' (van Selm 2007: 1; also on this see Cowan 2000).

2   The names of all protagonists in this true story have been changed to protect their privacy. Any other identifying information has been omitted or changed, again to protect the protagonists in the story. I have known 'Emilija' and her parents for 20 years now. The story I present here is my own reconstruction of things that they have shared with me over many years, although I had many informal interviews with Emilija in 2007 and 2008 in which she clarified many intimate details. I have tried to be true, as much as I could, to the spirit of the story as Emilija told it to me.

sexual mores though, her parents were very conservative. Emilija's sexuality had to be under constant vigilant parental surveillance in order to assure that were no 'costly mistakes' like early or unwanted pregnancies, and that she married an appropriate man who would preserve or even enhance their family's already high standing in Macedonian society.

Emilija's boyfriends had to be vetted by her parents as soon as she started dating someone more seriously. Adultery, extramarital sex, promiscuity and divorce were the most shameful things, apart from the unthinkable and unmentionable homosexuality, that could happen to a girl from a good family, blighting the reputation of the whole family. While not exactly daddy's good girl, Emilija indeed pleased her parents by marrying a somewhat bohemian man from a highly prestigious background during the collapse of Yugoslavia in 1992. Her retired parents had some misgivings about Emilija's choice of a struggling artist for a husband, but they were in such awe of her husband's parents that they eventually relaxed, congratulating themselves on completing their parental duties. However, life had some bitter surprises in store for the whole family.

A few years into her childless marriage, Emilija deeply fell in love with a not so happily married male colleague, who had three children. She had a long, tempestuous and clandestine intimate relationship with this man in hotel rooms, rented holiday villas and apartments. One day, sick and tired of all the lies and deception involved in keeping her secret in the closet, she came out with the truth to her husband and parents. She quickly divorced her husband in a relatively amicable fashion, and moved out of her husband's home to live on her own in a rented apartment, sending her parents into despair and rage. The façade of their, and their daughter's, upper middle-class respectability and success, in which her parents had so emotionally invested, was shattered. For a while, Emilija had to endure her parents' regular barrages of insults, recriminations and declarations of her *persona non grata* status. One night in a particularly frenzied rage, her father – usually a very mild-mannered man, who despised any displays of violence – shouted 'You, rotten (queer) whore, whore [*pokvarena kurva*]. Get out of my sight!' repeatedly, while throwing an empty bottle of brandy at Emilija. After that incident, he cut all ties to his daughter, expressly forbidding his wife to see her, and took to the bottle, increasingly becoming unmanageable in his drunken fury. Her mother, a sworn atheist, turned to New Age spirituality, castigating herself for her *permissiveness* in raising Emilija, trying to cope with the new situation and seeking solace in the company of accepting and friendly New Age people. She continued to secretly see and support her daughter whenever she could, while at the same time trying to repair the bond between her husband and her daughter.

The emotional vacuum left by Emilija's parents was filled by her closest five or six friends, some of whom she had known since her high school and university days, while others were work colleagues or people she had met in the vibrant scene of cafes, taverns, restaurants, hotels and nightclubs epitomising Skopje's *good life*. The bleak transitional post-socialist political and economic landscape of Macedonia, marked by an extremely badly managed and corrupt privatisation of the whole economy and endless cycles of job losses and liquidation of state companies, seemed to intensify Emilija's relationship with her friends and their desire to enjoy life as fully as they could under these very difficult circumstances. Emilija was lucky that her employment was so secure, since there were shortages of highly qualified and experienced people in her well-regarded profession. This security made her determined that any possible *rapprochement* with her beloved father would be on terms acceptable to her.

Emilija continued her relationship with her married male colleague, feeling relieved that at least she had removed some layers of deception while still keeping the affair secret at work. She, at least for a while, loved the freedom of being able to enjoy the company of her lover in the privacy of her own home. Although she never asked her lover to leave his wife and children, she was haunted by guilt for being *the other woman* and struggled to imagine a satisfactory solution to her situation, that now loomed large as an ethical conundrum: while she did not want to be a *home wrecker*, she felt like a thief, stealing moments of affection and attention from the man she loved so much.

Tanja, another woman very similar to Emilija, was in Emilija's innermost sanctum of trust. While Tanja was the only person with whom Emilija would share her most intimate thoughts and feelings about her love life, Tanja kept some big secrets about the true nature of the arrangements in her own marriage. Fearing Emilija's reaction, particularly Emilija's possible suspicion that Tanja may have been harbouring an erotic desire for her under the pretext of close friendship, Tanja finally plucked up the courage to disclose to Emilija that both she and her husband, Zoran, were bisexuals in an open marriage. Emilija was initially shocked, then intrigued, and finally quite angry that her best friend would hide such a big thing from her all these years. Having been through a hell of deceptions, lies and concealments herself, Emilija intuitively and quickly grasped the logic behind Tanja's concealment of her bisexuality. Within a few weeks, Emilija's anger gave way to creating even a deeper bond between the two women struggling to live honestly with their most intimate desires.

Like plants drawn to sunlight, Emilija was always attracted to unconventional men. Trendy, arty, intelligent, soft-spoken, loyal, good-looking, quietly subversive, with an ambiguous sexuality, softer masculine edge and a wickedly sharp sense of humour used to mock the *seljaci* (peasants) and the *malogragjani* (petty bourgeois), seen as enemies of cosmopolitans (*gradski lugje*), these dandies provided the soothing cocoon of trust, safety, confidence, understanding and fun that Emilija needed to unwind from the emotional demands of her work, her relationship with her lover and the grief of being treated as a pariah by her parents, particularly her father.

One snowy winter night in a Mavrovo villa owned by the father of one of the dandies, and used regularly by Emilija to rendezvous with her male lover in the early days of their clandestine relationship, all her friends were gathered in the warm family room after a long day of skiing. After some glasses of *rakija* (brandy) and shiraz, something within Emilija just broke and she collapsed in an outpouring of pain, guilt, shame and self-recrimination. 'I didn't want this. I didn't plan it at all. It just happened,' cried Emilija cryptically. Once she had composed herself a bit, she announced that she was pregnant, in a voice that had so much anguish that her friends almost immediately understood the multitude of difficult scenarios, choices and decisions she had to work through. They listened carefully and probed Emilija gently about how she felt about it, professing that they would support her unconditionally whatever she decided to do.

Emilija's outpouring of emotions and ethical dilemmas was contagious, reaching into the deepest emotional recesses of all her friends. The door to the emotional safe where big intimate secrets were carefully guarded opened, and a flood of cathartic confessions from others in the circle filled the room with the incredible bonding power of trust. It was a long and extraordinary night. Tanja and Zoran talked about their bisexuality and open marriage, while Goran and Mile opened up about their secret gay lives and long-distance transnational relationships with boyfriends in the near abroad. There was so much information divulged that evening – so many revelations and discoveries, so many suspicions dispelled – that most of what happened that night was slowly digested during the group's numerous friendship rituals over the next few months. The most surprising revelation for all of them was the clear realisation that they were, despite their very privileged lives, social pariahs in the eyes of 'respectable' people due to their erotic desires and intimate choices. What was even more surprising, uncanny even, was that they all felt so drawn to each other well before they knew that they were embarking on such non-traditional life journeys.

With her friends' help, Emilija decided that she wanted a child and continued her pregnancy. Goran, her gay friend, even offered to marry her in order to *legitimise* the child in the eyes of her parents and the world, and pledged financial and other support to help her raise the child. Emilija was deeply touched by this gesture, but still felt uncomfortable with yet more deception. She was very excited about the baby, while at the same time worried to death about how she was going to reconcile her mothering with the demands of her career. She informed her lover that she was pregnant with his child, to which he responded that she was using 'cheap tricks to get him to leave his wife', suggesting that she should terminate the pregnancy and expect no help from him in raising the child. Disappointed beyond belief, extremely furious and sad at the same time, Emilija broke it off with her lover there and then.

Emilija was now desperate to patch things up with her parents, feeling that she needed their help, particularly her mother's, to raise the child. She was dreading how they would react to the news about her pregnancy, given her father's view on legitimate and 'illegitimate' ways of having children. She invited them to her place for dinner, and broke the news. There was initial tense silence, but then, to Emilija's utter astonishment, her parents started crying: 'Oh, dear daughter, thank you. That's wonderful.' Her parents had suffered miserably; they missed their daughter, while at the same time were wrecked by shame and what other people might think about them and their daughter. This suffering made them think very hard about the nature of their daughter's infraction, coming to the realisation that Emilija was just being true to herself. They greeted Emilija and the news with long hugs, kisses and cries of joy and all-round forgiveness. Her parents were ecstatic that they would finally be grandparents, despite the fact that they had reached this stage of their lives in such an unexpected, and 'illegitimate', fashion.

Emilija's parents invited her to move back to their home so they could start making the necessary preparations for the child. Emilija was so relieved that her retired parents had embraced this new project of helping her raise the child with such enthusiasm. She moved back to her parents in her last trimester, and with her she brought all her closest friends, who visited her on a daily basis and filled her parents' home with their life stories and experiences. What was unimaginable only a few years ago now became ordinary. Rather than seeing social freaks, her parents finally saw people who tried to find happiness on their own terms.

Emilija gave birth to a healthy girl who is now lavished with affection by her, her grandparents and her friends. After the expiry of paid maternity leave, she reluctantly returned to work. While her little girl is the centre of her universe, and despite the demands of her career, Emilija still regularly finds time to be with her friends. Still heartbroken from her last relationship, she has just started to date men again. Her mother, now well into her late seventies and fearing that there will be no one there to look after her daughter and granddaughter, still nudges Emilija to find a 'good husband' so both she and her father can die in peace. Emilija defiantly responds to these nudges that she neither wants nor needs a husband.

Postscript

Eighteen months after our interviews in 2008, Emilija sent me an email informing me that her ex-lover, the father of her daughter, was now regularly involved in her daughter's life. Through a series of very difficult conversations, emotional breakdowns and threats of relationship breakups, Emilija, her ex-lover, his wife and Emilija's parents came up with a new arrangement for raising Emilija's daughter. While Emilija and her parents would still perform the lion's share of the parenting, it was agreed that her ex-lover would contribute financially and would do some of the parenting by spending one day a fortnight with his daughter at Emilija's parents' place, with plans to introduce her to the other three children from his marriage as soon as they were all old enough to understand their relationship to each other and the complexities of their parents' stories.

Contextualising Intimate Citizenship in Macedonia

In the next few sections, I want to link the microsocial and macrosocial, connect 'the relevant ... parts in [Emilija's and her friends'] experience[s] to the relevant' theories and practices of intimate citizenship in a manner sensitive to the Macedonian context (Lambevski 2009: 3). Here, I just want to give a brief scan of recent developments in the area of regulation of sexualities in Macedonia in order to background Emilija's story.

On a difficult journey to becoming a fully integrated part of the political, economic and cultural 'Western' alliance of countries of the 'free world' (the European Union, NATO and its allies), Macedonia is in the midst of tectonic ideological reconfigurations shifting the country from the hegemony of communist orthodoxy to the domination of a new ideological order blending economic liberalism, masculinist Macedonian nationalism, heterosexism and patriarchal Orthodox Christianity. The main political forces behind this conservative push are the powerful Internal Macedonian Revolutionary Organisation-Democratic Party for Macedonian National Unity (IMRO-DPMNU) and the Macedonian Orthodox Church.

As a candidate-country, Macedonia's integration into the EU requires that its government actively combats discrimination based on sexual orientation, by synchronising all relevant legislation and policies with those of the EU (i.e. Article 13 of the Treaty of Amsterdam 1997 and the Treaty of Lisbon 2007). Both treaties are seen as a 'means of enriching European citizenship more broadly' (Stychin 2001: 294); and with respect to sexuality in the Central and Eastern European context, claims to rights 'which might originally appear to be passive, private and even disciplined have come to possess an active, public, political and even democratic component as they emerge in the political space of the EU' (Stychin 2001: 294) and its candidate-countries (Turkey, Croatia and Macedonia).

The Macedonian government and parliament dominated by the IMRO-DPMNU have been particularly resistant to passing a number of legislative reforms that would firmly enshrine the principle of non-discrimination of lesbian, gay, bisexual and transsexual/transgendered (LGBT) people in Macedonian society. The passing of a non-discrimination law explicitly prohibiting discrimination on all the bases mentioned in Article 5b of the Treaty of Lisbon 2007 has been one of the main conditions imposed by the EU, along with resolving its fundamental differences over its name with Greece, for Macedonia to start official negotiations to finalise its integration into the EU (*The Former Yugoslav Republic of Macedonia 2009 Progress Report*: 19, 54; Trajanoski 2010; Stojančevska 2010; Čomovski 2010). The recent public debate in Macedonia on the government's proposal for a law on non-discrimination has exposed a long series of exclusions through which Macedonia is imagined and performed as a (patriarchal and hetero) normative nation (Bhabha 1991; Watt 2005).

Despite enormous pressure coming from the European Union, the Macedonian government in its law on non-discrimination excluded sexual orientation under the pretext that the Macedonian constitution does not recognise sexual orientation as a valid basis of discrimination. The real motive behind the IMRO-DPMNU led coalition government's opposition to including sexual orientation in its law on non-discrimination was recently publicly expressed by the leader of the conservative Women's Union of IMRO (Unija na ženite na VMRO), Kosana Nikolić-Mazneva. She said that the inclusion of sexual orientation in the proposed law would open the door to homosexual marriages – despite the fact that the gay and lesbian movement in Macedonia is advocating only for civil unions or registered partnerships for gay and lesbian couples – and adoption of children by gay people, which 'must be stopped at all cost' (Stojančevska 2010). Around the same time, the incumbent Macedonian president, Gjorgje Ivanov, also from the IMRO-DPMNU, said that homosexuals 'are stigmatised by Life itself' (Čomovski 2010), causing outrage in the more progressive media and non-governmental sector in Macedonia.

As a performance, normative 'nations are always in the making' (Watt 2005: 162; also see Bhabha 1991). Macedonian citizenship, as a set of heterogeneous normative discourses and practices of including and excluding, is continuously 'revealed [and remade] through encounters with social [and sexual] difference' (Watt 2005: 162). Macedonian nationalists problematically and controversially articulate modern Macedonia as the continuation of the 'glorious' ancient Macedonia of Phillip II and Alexander the Great[3]. In this nationalist re-articulation, Macedonia is imagined as a 'pure' and 'healthy' Orthodox Christian national community, free from 'vices and sins' (Trajanoski 2010), 'deviants', 'perverts' and 'criminals'. In the name of 'health' and 'morality', the IMRO-DPMNU led government, the media controlled by people and companies close to the ruling party (particularly the tabloid daily *Večer* and the TV station SITEL), and the Orthodox Church in the last three to four years have engaged in quick-fix populism. They are all now publicly stigmatising, bullying and harassing 'Others'. The list is long: homeless people, beggars, female sex workers, single parents (particularly single mothers), childless heterosexual married couples, 'baby killers' (*čedomorki*) and doctors who perform abortions, HIV-positive people, homosexuals, young heterosexuals engaging in sex in parks at night and drug users (Trajanoski 2010). With its fixation on origins, 'health' and 'purity', the current IMRO-DPMNU led coalition government has only 'heightened ... [the] sense of ethnic, gendered and sexed nationalism' (Watt 2005: 161) in this multiethnic, multiconfessional and multicultural country.

In response to the rapid social, economic, political, cultural and legal transformations associated with the fall of communism, globalisation and European integration, the Macedonian IMRO-DPMNU led coalition government has elevated sexuality as one of its core concerns for policy and legal regulation. Like in many post-socialist Central and Eastern European countries, the local regulation of sexualities has become the imaginary 'red zone'. There, the Macedonian government has decided to exercise 'the sovereign will of the people' by refusing to 'bow' to dictates from Brussels and other 'meddling' foreigners on the issue (Kligman 1998; Roman 2001; Stychin 2003; Watt 2005; Dioli 2009;

---

3 As exemplified by its proposed project to completely architecturally revamp the central district of the capital so it contains symbolically the 'whole history' of masculinised Macedonia from its 'founding' to today as seen by the male, ethnically Macedonian, heterosexual ideologues of the ruling party (see the government video clip showing the government's vision for the centre of Skopje on http://www.youtube.com/watch?v=F6xrYguH68M).

Woodcock 2009). Instead of the sexual 'chaos' and 'moral uncertainty' brought by globalisation (Altman 2001) and EUropeanisation (Woodcock 2009; see also Woodcock in this volume), the IMRO-DPMNU and the Macedonian Orthodox Church promise the 'soothing certainty' of a 'return' to traditional patriarchal and homophobic 'family' values (Stulhofer and Sandfort 2005; Iveković 1996, 2002; Wait 2005; Dioli 2009: 2–7).

There are several, seemingly disparate, political developments that revolve around the Macedonian nationalists' concern about issues of the 'reproduction' of the (ideal form of) the Macedonian nation. Discouraging non-normative sexualities by refusing to guarantee legal protection from discrimination for LGBT people is just one method. This is to force Macedonian men and women to 'correctly orientate' (ILGA-Europe 2001: 40; Watt 2005: 168) towards producing children in a 'proper' environment that ensures the making of future obedient soldiers and taxpayers of the nation (McClintock 1993; Grewal 1996; Ahmed 2004: 144–5), and blindly loyal servants to the national (Orthodox) Church. The IMRO-DPMNU also revamped the Family Law (*Zakon za semejstvoto 2008*)[4] in order to ensure that the legally privileged form of intimate partnership is a gendered, different-sexed marriage (Jones 2009: 12). It is defined as a 'legally regulated union between a man and woman through which the interests of the married partners, the family and society are fulfilled' (Article 6, *Zakon za semejstvoto 2008*; for a comparative analysis of European marriage and partnership legislation, see Jones 2009).

The Macedonian government launched in 2008 a public policy campaign titled 'Everyone with Three Children' (*'Sekoj treba da ima treto dete'*) aimed at increasing the low birthrate among ethnic Macedonians (State Statistical Office of the Republic of Macedonia 2009). Fearing that if the current comparative birthrates in the two largest ethnic communities in Macedonia continue to fall, ethnic Albanians would, in the not so distant future, outnumber ethnic Macedonians. The government, goaded by the Orthodox Church, is also proposing another measure to 'fix' the low birthrate among ethnic Macedonians by flagging its intention to ban abortions. To the Macedonian Coalition of Marginalized Communities, the IMRO-DPMNU led government is now responding with its own conservative 'alliance to ban abortions and defend marriage' (Čomovski 2010), aimed at firmly delineating the boundaries of the 'normal', 'pure' and 'healthy' Macedonian nation.

Bearing in mind this larger social and political context of the debates on Macedonian citizenship, I will now return to Emilija's story. I will use her story as an indicative case study of some of the connections between various, relatively new, turn-of-the-century social practices, public and not-so-public discourses and stories in Macedonia '*about how to live the personal life in a late modern world where we are confronted by an escalating series of choices and difficulties around intimacies*' (Plummer 2001: 238, emphasis in original). Following Plummer, I will organise these 'somewhat disparate concerns around the personal life'

---

4   I thank Prof. Mirjana Najčevska from the SS Cyril and Methodius University in Skopje for helping me find the relevant Macedonian legislation.

(Plummer 2001: 238) and their wider political implications by using the concept of intimate citizenship (Plummer 1995, 2001). Intimate citizenship is a sensitising concept which 'suggests directions along which to look' (Blumer 1969: 148) for new appropriate ways of 'living lives with others' (Plummer 2001: 238) in late modernity and fostering 'a new climate of emerging moralities and ethics' (Plummer 2001: 238) in the intimate sphere.

Conceptualising Intimate Citizenship

For my purposes here I will define intimate citizenship as a set of heterogeneous social, cultural, economic, political and legal practices that have the human 'body, its possibilities, needs and pleasures' (Weeks 1998: 37) as its main concern. The aim of intimate citizenship is to extend the definition of citizenship and belonging, and help create a more inclusive democratic polity that is committed to the full, free and consensual development of alternative sexual identities and forms of intimate lives (Evans 1993, Turner 1993a: 2, Waites 1996, Richardson 1998, Weeks 1998: 38). Intimate citizenship is about 'the *control (or not) over* one's [sexualised and gendered] body, [intimate] feelings, [erotic and other] relationships: *access (or not) to* representations, relationships, public spaces, etc, and *socially grounded choices (or not)*' (Plummer 1995: 151, emphasis in original) about erotic and intimate identities and experiences.

Practicing intimate citizenship happens through telling new sexual and intimate stories in the plurality of late modernity (Plummer 2001: 242, 249; Fraser 1997), or making sexual choices that are different from the norm and constructing new political identities around these choices, or through struggling to remove 'large stretches of sexual intimate life from institutional control' (Seidman 2001: 326). Intimate citizenship is also about rearranging the current and sexual intimate regime of norms in order to make it more liveable, or generating explicit political claims to 'equal protection of the law, to equal rights in employment, parenting, social status, access to welfare provision, and partnership [and marriage] rights (Weeks 1998: 37). In combination with other difference-centred citizenship discourses (Pateman 1988; Lister 1997; Yuval-Davis and Werbner 1990; Kymlicka 1995; Flores and Benmayor 1997; Nash 2001; Kabir 2005; Weeks 1998; Richardson 2000; Stychin 2001; Plummer 2001, 2003; Oleksy 2009), intimate citizenship offers both an implicit and explicit critique of the masculinist, racist, classist, nationalist and heterosexist biases, occlusions and hesitations (Weeks 1998: 38) in traditional liberal, republican and communitarian discourses on, and practices of, citizenship (Marshall 1950; Benhabib 1992; Moynagh 1997; Weeks 1998; Balibar 1990; Avineri and de-Shalit 1992; Daly 1993; Lister and Pia 2008: 8–22).

'Western' 'LGBT' vs 'Queer' Debates on Intimate Citizenship

While much of the literature on sexual or intimate citizenship has focused on the globalised articulation of new sexual health rights, sexual rights and sexual justice

(Kaplan 1997; Weeks 1998; Parker et al. 2004; Cowan 2005), intimate citizenship, as Plummer (2001) and Weeks (1998) point out, is also about a set of mutual *'rights, obligations, recognitions and respect around those most intimate spheres of life* – who to live with, how to raise children, how to handle one's body, how to relate as a gendered being, how to be an erotic person' (Plummer 2001: 238, emphasis in original). This aspect of intimate citizenship has been a particularly sticky issue for some queer theorists, who worry that in the process of seeking recognition one has to renounce the very specificity of one's more radical, erotic and intimate existence for which one is seeking recognition and respect from others. This recognition may normalise and discipline one's public expression of this specificity, confine it to its 'proper' expression in the privacy of one's 'home', and forced one to be publicly exactly the same as the 'good heterosexual' citizen (Bell and Binnie 2000; Aizura 2006; Langdridge 2006; Schippert 2006).

Queer politics and theory coming from the US have been particularly wary about the dangers of privatisation, de-radicalisation, de-eroticisation, sanitisation, normalisation, disciplining and confinement of non-normative sexualities and intimacies lurking in the background of the pursuit of citizenship rights (Warner 1999; Seidman 2001; Schippert 2006). As Seidman observes, 'queers are not against identity politics [of citizenship rights for sexual minorities *per se*] but deflate its emancipatory narrative by exposing its exclusionary and disciplinary effects' (Seidman 2001: 326). It is so because gay and lesbian identity-based politics of citizenship rights (as practised in the US and many other parts of the 'Western' world), leaves in place moralising and oppressive norms 'that sustain sexual hierarchies unrelated to gender preference' (Seidman 2001: 326).

Some North American, Western European and Australian queer scholars (Bell and Binnie 2000, Aizura 2006, Langdridge 2006, Schippert 2006) have criticized Weeks' seminal essay 'The Sexual Citizen' (1998) for its construction of a political teleology that leads in a linear fashion from the 'moment of transgression', 'characterized by the constant invention and reinvention [and public and not-so-public expression] of new senses of the [sexual or intimate] self, and new challenges to the inherited [hegemonic patriarchal heterosexual] institutions and traditions that hitherto had excluded these new [selves]' (Weeks 1998: 36), like the moment when Tanja and Zoran or Goran and Mile in the story above came out to Emilija and her parents as bisexuals in an open marriage and gays respectively, to the 'moment of citizenship' when one as a citizen makes explicit political claims to rights and entitlements, and also accepts the potentially normalising and disciplining 'responsibilities to fellow citizens, and to the community which defines citizenship' (Weeks 1998: 36).

While I agree with Weeks's assertion that (intimate) citizenship in order to mean anything 'must be about involvement in a wider society' (Weeks 1998: 36), this involvement does not necessarily take the shape of his transgression-to-citizenship teleology. As Stychin (2001), Cossman (2002) and Jones (2009) show, 'things are not [as I am hoping to show below] so clear cut as [intimate] "citizenship is never wholly disciplined" and there are often transgressive moments with claims to citizenship and moments of citizenship with acts of transgression' (Langdridge 2006: 379).

Fraser (1989) and Stychin (2001) argue for a more balanced appraisal of the discourse, practice and politics of sexual or intimate citizenship and rights. Accordingly, we could appreciate that 'their [polyvalent] capacity to generate critical leverage and escape co-optation [into the normative heterosexist and patriarchal regime] is entirely relative to' (Fraser 1989: 63) how they are actually deployed and practised in specific contexts. As Escoffier notes, 'only the active exercise of democratic rights [in a context-sensitive manner] allows a group to resist, modify, or restructure the forms of domination operating through discipline and normalization' (1998: 226).

As I already indicated above, intimate citizenship is a discourse inevitably bound with the vexing issue of values and ethics about how to live and love in a globalised world simultaneously comprised of tradition, modernity and postmodernity through which we all move at 'different paces and to differing degrees' (Plummer 2001: 239) – a world that is 'no longer guided by a few universally applicable sets of norms, but have become unstable, fluctuating, and in some ways confusing' (Schippert 2006: 291; also see Giddens 1992; Beck and Beck-Gernsheim 1995). Like Emilija and her friends show, 'traditional ways of life are no longer viable or meaningful for very many people, who have no choice but to choose' (Weeks 1998: 45) a different way to live. For many in the conservative (rural and petty bourgeois) support base of the IMRO-DPMNU and the Macedonian Orthodox Church, this is a 'profoundly frightening threat' (Weeks 1998: 45); for others, like Emilija, her parents, her friends and their parents and friends, this is an 'opportunity for inventing themselves afresh' (Weeks 1998: 45).

Jeffrey Weeks *Invented Moralities: Sexual Values in an Age of Uncertainty* (1995) and his subsequent work (1998) provide 'an excellent example of a serious effort to wrestle with some foundational challenges at the lgbt/queer border – and are exemplary for current ['Western'] debates of sexual citizenship' (Schippert 2006: 288). His book (1995) is a brave attempt to develop a philosophical framework for thinking about sexuality, intimacy and ethics in an age of uncertainty. Weeks does not want to cede any moral ground to 'the moralist [anti-sex, conservative, fundamentalist religious] right wing or unprincipled libertarianism' (Schippert 2006: 291). He aims to develop a framework for thinking of answers to 'the question of 'how shall I/we live?' in a way that are morally responsible and can enter into conversation with other claims, meanings, and lives for the purpose of exchange, communication, and democratic process' (Schippert 2006: 291). Only if we can answer this crucial question for ourselves, 'only then can we communicate with each other about our choices … only then can we clarify, think through, evaluate which choices we want to make' (Schippert 2006: 293). Weeks's ultimate goal is an ethics 'that emerges out of a struggle with uncertainty yet does not need to embrace universal doctrine and does not need to prescribe or dictate what shall constitute moral value for others or all' (Schippert 2006: 291).

Although Weeks does not position himself as an 'LGBT' scholar or a 'queer' theorist, Schippert is right in pointing out that the reception of Weeks's work is 'symptomatic for the different directions and strategies "LBGT" and "queer" might stand for' (2006: 288) in a 'Western' context. While LGBT politics wholeheartedly embraces the politics of intimate or sexual citizenship, queer politics is ambivalent about it, seeing in it a potential for a 'robust defense of a private sphere that is juridically and socially protected from interference by the state and other citizens' (Seidman 2001: 327; also see Weeks 1998: 37); but it wants to 'radicalize the idea of privacy to defend an idea of ... [intimate] citizenship that includes an expansive concept of sexual intimate choice and variation' (Seidman 2001: 327).

As the editors of this volume point out in their introduction, it is difficult, if not impossible, to say with certainty what 'LGBT' and 'queer' might stand for in the context of Central, Eastern and South-Eastern European debates on sexual and intimate citizenship. It is difficult to insert recent developments in the area of feminist, lesbian and gay activism in Central and Eastern Europe, with its strong focus on the 'assimilationist' or 'mainstreaming' aspects of sexual citizenship, into Western narrative, which, as the editors of this volume argue, is already in its 'queer' stage, with 'long history and plurality of models, forms of engagement, goals and structures' (Mizielińska and Kulpa in this volume; see also Mizielińska 2006, 2009).

Grounding Intimate Citizenship

My intention here is not to enter these ('Western') academic debates on intimate citizenship in an abstract way. Much of the debate on the value of the concept of intimate or sexual citizenship in the 'West' has been highly theoretical and abstract, with staking of different political and academic positions that make sense in the 'West' (like *LGBT versus queer*) and delineating finer and 'pure' philosophical differences. Here, following Plummer, I will take a different route into the debate about sexuality, intimacy, ethics and citizenship. While many of the principled discussions and concerns expressed in more theoretical LGBT and queer debates on intimate citizenship, as I sketched them briefly above, are undeniably useful and will inform my analysis here, intimate citizenship 'does not readily lend itself to this mode of analysis' (Plummer 2001: 248).

In taking a 'grounded everyday moralities' approach (Plummer 2001: 248), I want to draw attention to the importance of the local and the situational in the debates on intimate citizenship. Emilija's and her friends' stories show the ways 'in which moral life is rarely abstract and usually bound up' with an escalating series of immediate crises (Plummer 2001: 248). For example from Emilija's 'adultery', issues of disclosure, secrecy and integrity and feelings of moral failure, to her unplanned pregnancy and concerns about how she was going to raise her child given her particular situation. And further from issues of Tanja's and Zoran's disclosure of their bisexuality and open marriage, to Goran's and Mile's disclosure of their homosexuality and their battle with intense fears of social rejection and ostracism from their closest friends.

I think telling Emilija's life story is a powerful way to concretely represent the significant shifts in attitudes, beliefs and practices around intimacies in particular, still relatively small segments of Macedonian society in the last 20 years. Her story shows how many women occupying similar intersections of privileged social locations (Anthias and Yuval-Davis 1992; Yuval-Davis 2006: 199–202) in Macedonia (upper middle-class, heterosexual, ethnic Macedonian, highly educated, stably employed, in her mid-40s) 'get through their days making [difficult] decisions about what can be done [in their intimate lives] through telling stories of their moral choices which are embedded in their lives and their environments' (Plummer 2001: 248). For Rorty (TV, novel, film or even ethnographic) stories are the 'principal vehicles of moral change and progress' (1989: xvi) in late modernity. For Plummer, 'the development of ideas of intimate citizenship may well depend upon proliferating communities of such stories' (2001: 248) as Emilija's.

Emotions and Heteronormativity

My intention here is to use Emilija's story to focus precisely on the emotional aspects of the politics of intimate citizenship. I will situate these between the political and cultural work emotions do in sustaining particular dominant regimes of sexual and intimate norms. They play a crucial role in creating and sustaining places, spaces, private understandings and arrangements; rituals and practices that act as emotional refuges (Reddy 2001: 128); that provide 'safe release from prevailing emotional norms and allow ... relaxation of emotional effort, with or without an ideological justification [of an explicit 'queer', 'LGBT' or 'feminist' theory and politics] (Reddy 2001: 129), and that make intimate lives more liveable.

In order to make this argument, here I will need to briefly engage with the political relevance of emotions. Emotions are goal-oriented thoughts (Reddy 2001), signals (Kring 2000) and clues (Hochschild 2003) about where we stand at any moment in relation to others, the world, the environment and the cosmos; that initially lie outside language in visual, aural, visceral, musculoskeletal or gestural form (Reddy 2001: 88); and that exceed our capacity to translate into talk or bodily action within a very short time span (Reddy 2001: 94). Emotions are always about something: they have a relational intent, 'they involve a direction or orientation toward an object' (Ahmed 2004: 7; see also Reddy 2001: 102). As such, emotions are 'the most immediate, the most self-evident, and the most relevant of our orientations toward life' (Reddy 2001: 3), and 'they involve a stance on the world, or a way of apprehending the world' (Ahmed 2004: 7; see also Hochschild 2003: 29). The translation of these goal-oriented thoughts into words or bodily action requires the use of the cultural stocks of knowledge, discourses (Foucault 1980), theories (Quine 1969) or narratives of our societies.

This translation is filled with indeterminacy, 'limitations, incompleteness, and imprecision' (Reddy 2001: 80; Alcoff 1996), since signals or messages from the environment 'arrive in many different languages, [discourses, narratives] or codes, and where some of the messages are successfully translated into other codes, while others are not' (Reddy 2001: 80). To put it in other words, emotions are like provisional hypotheses that use the 'theories' or 'discourses' of our societies to filter out 'evidence about the self-relevance of what we see, recall or fantasize' (Hochschild 2003: 28). Taking our emotions as clues, and then 'correcting for them may be our best shot at' (Hochschild 2003: 31) testing what is real.

Reddy considers the act of translation of emotions into words and bodily actions using the cultural stocks of knowledge of our societies to be a peculiar type of a speech act, 'different from both performative and constative utterances, which both describes (like constative utterances) and changes (like performatives) the world, because emotional expression has an exploratory and a self-altering effect on activated' emotions (Reddy 2001: 128). He calls these speech acts *emotives* (Reddy 2001). We not only feel emotions, but when we express them verbally or corporeally we also 'work to create, intensify, suppress, and transform them' (Gordon 1990: 163) to achieve a number of, often painfully contradictory, goals – from the cultural requirement to present a socially acceptable face to the world in the guise of the 'good heterosexual' citizen, to overcoming shame, self-loathing and guilt to satisfy our deepest non-normative sexual needs. Wikan (1990) and Hochschild (2003) call this process *emotional management*, while Reddy (2001) calls it *emotional navigation*. Both metaphors imply purposive, intentional action, while in reality much of the transformational work emotives do is highly unintentional and unpredictable (Reddy 2001: 122). There is an emergent quality to emotional navigation, since it 'does not produce an object which is a finished emotion ... [r]ather, it generates a stage in process ... one emotion leads to another' (Barbalet 2001: 181). As Barbalet notes, 'endeavors to manage an emotion lead to emotions which are reactions to the ... [initially] managed emotion' (2001: 181). This opens the ground for having new thoughts and new feelings about oneself, familiar people, events, objects, places, narratives, relationships and discourses of domination and exploitation – an emotional transformation that leads from the catatonia of the searing shame that dominated groups of people feel (Scheff 1990; Warner 1999) to action demanding social redress coming from feeling justified anger (Barbalet 2001: 126–48).

Emotions also have a valence or a hedonic tone, which means the inherent pleasantness or unpleasantness 'of emotional reactions to [norms], things, [people], events, or situations' (Reddy 2001: 22) and intensity, which refers to the ease or difficulty in overriding them (Reddy 2001; 21). Because of their valence and intensity, emotions strongly incline human behaviour (Barbalet 2002: 2) and it is precisely because of this that 'emotions become politically relevant, because they are capable of guiding action long after explicit threats or explicit rules [laws and policies] have been forgotten' (Reddy 2001: 119). Every stable political regime relies on a set of 'normative emotions and ... official rituals, practices and emotives that express them and inculcate them' (Reddy 2001: 129) that Reddy calls *emotional regime*. Heteronormativity is such an emotional regime, aimed at orienting thoughts, words, emotions and bodily actions by proscribing that the desire to be a 'normal' (heterosexual) should be a high-priority goal for everyone. However, as many anthropologists of emotions have now amply demonstrated, arriving at the normatively 'prescribed feelings is unpredictable and involves planning and effort' (Reddy 2001: 59) or emotional management through ongoing repetition of rituals and customs (see Appadurai 1990: 92–111; Lutz and Abu-Lughod 1990; Wikan 1990; Reddy 2001: 59).

Compulsory heterosexuality or heteronormativity is the 'accumulative [emotional] effect of the [ongoing] repetition, [through familial, communal and state rituals and customs,] of the [highly idealised] narrative of [a particular type] of heterosexuality as an ideal [morally superior] coupling' (Ahmed 2004: 145; also see Loutzenheiser and MacIntosh 2004: 152). Often the concept of heteronormativity (Warner 1999) has been used to equate official and prevailing sexual norms with some imaginary homogenous heterosexuality. However, as Smith (2001) and Emilija's story show, 'heterosexuality is a highly differentiated phenomenon' (Smith 2001: 305). In the Macedonian context, many heterosexual practices have been subjected to intense social stigma and/or legal and policy regulation.

Heteronormativity is 'more than simply the presumption that it is normal to be heterosexual' (Ahmed 2004: 148). As Ahmed points out, the 'norm' is regulative and 'supported by an ideal that associates sexual conduct with other forms of conduct' (Ahmed 2004: 149). In Emilija's case this is reflected in her parents' insistence that her husband should be a 'good match' in ethnic and class terms; someone who would preserve or even enhance Emilija's and her parents' social status and material well-being; and that she should be 'faithful and monogamous' in her marriage – a patriarchal idealisation of female monogamy and faithfulness that 'often equates intimacy with [men's] property rights or rights to the intimate [female] other as property' (Ahmed 2004: 149). To be divorced in a country with the third lowest crude divorce rate in Europe – 0.7 per 1,000 (Marcu 2009: 8) – and to give birth and raise a child out of wedlock in a society that severely stigmatises both single mothers and 'illegitimate' children means to fail to reproduce the norm of the 'good heterosexual' citizen. In this way, Emilija and many other Macedonian heterosexuals like her become failed, *queer*; or, to use a term that has local resonance in the Skopje dialect of the Macedonian language and is phonetically and semantically close to the term *queer* as it used in English, *(po)kvar(eni)*, heterosexuals. Her failure to reproduce this norm becomes a *kvar*, a malfunction in the operation of the heteronormative machine.[5]

---

5 The Queer Beograd Collective found in the Serbian, Croatian and Slovenian word *kvar*, literally meaning malfunction, a brilliant way to translate and localise the English-language *queer*. Etymologically *kvar* is the root of many nouns (*pokvarenjak, pokvarenjača/pokvarenjačka, pokvarenost* – a male queer, female queer, queerness) and adjectives (*pokvaren, pokvarena* – male and female versions of the adjective queer) that

Heteronormativity is enforced through strategies of emotional shaming, deviance hunting, 'cultural pollution and censorship, criminalization and civic disenfranchisement, sequestration and violence' (Seidman 2001: 322). Emilija's story demonstrates how her own family, particularly her father, assumes the role of a major enforcer of heteronormativity, employing many of the above-mentioned strategies. In this way, her family functions both as a repressive and ideological state apparatus (ISA) (Althusser 1984), where the heterosexist and patriarchal ideology of Macedonian 'good' citizenship is maintained through family discourses, emotionally charged rituals and practices, segregation/banishment and physical and symbolic violence.

The emotional utterance or emotive 'you queer whore', when it was uttered by her father, was a first-person present tense claim to patriarchal fury at Emilija's 'immorality' and failure to be a 'good wife' and a 'good citizen'. The emotive reveals his new orientation or relation to her, apprehending his daughter's illicit affair with a married colleague and divorce through the discourses, narratives, scripts and rituals of normative (compulsory) heterosexuality that imbibe his own sense of upper middle-class worth. The utterance both described Emilija's 'shameful' failure to reproduce the form of the 'good' or 'ideal' heterosexual citizen and drastically changed her parents' and her world for many years, by banishing the 'polluted' or 'rotten' (*pokvarena*) Emilija from the 'pure' parental home. At the time he uttered this emotive, neither Emilija nor her father could have possibly predicted the astonishingly powerful effect it would have on both of them for many years – not seeing or talking to each other for years, although they lived only a few blocks apart. With the emotive her father acted out, what Goffman calls, a line – 'a pattern of verbal and nonverbal acts by which he expresse[d] his view of … [Emilija's] situation and through this his evaluation' of Emilija and himself (1967: 5). The next few years Emilija's father dedicated enormous emotional effort (Reddy 2001: 129) to maintain his heteronormative (and patriarchal) *face* (Goffman 1967: 5), an image of normative social values 'a person effectively claims for himself by the line others [particularly his wife and daughter in this case] assume he has taken during' encounters with them (Goffman 1967: 5). Emilija's father's emotional suffering (Reddy 2001: 129) resulting from the acute goal conflict between (needing to) love his daughter and maintaining his heteronormative *face*, as I point out below, is resolved by his taking another *line* on his daughter, a *line* arising out of his love for his daughter.

The very anticipation of her father's intensely negative emotional reaction to her relationship with her work colleague helped Emilija hone her emotional management skills peculiar to the 'repressive social logic … that we've come to call the closet – a[n intense] pressure individuals feel to compulsively project a public heterosexual identity [only of the good kind] by confining [not only

---

have similar pejorative connotations as the English *queer* (see Dioli 2009: 10–12). These words, although not part of standard Macedonian, are widely used in the everyday speech of Macedonian-speaking people born and raised in Skopje.

homosexuality but all other non-normative sexualities and intimacies] to a[n often extremely claustrophobic and narrow] private world' (Seidman 2001: 322). As Emilija and her friends know very well, living in the closet 'entails such intensive and extensive daily efforts at [emotional] self-management' (Seidman 2001: 322) that the need to hide one's non-normative intimate life becomes 'the basis for a primary self-identity and a distinct way of life' (Seidman 2001: 323).

Being symbolically degraded as a 'whore' contributed to Emilija having a dominated heterosexual, *queer/kvar* identity, a person 'for whom shame and guilt are at the core of ... [her] sense of self; public invisibility becomes in part self-enforced' (Seidman 2001: 322). From her own experience, Emilija learned what it must feel like to be in her bisexual and gay friends' skins, although she acknowledged in one of our interviews that her friends' closet was much tighter than hers: in Emilija's case 'to be confronted with such stark choices, to be presented with the tools of [emotional] self-management represented by the searing shame [and guilt] of' the public and not-so-public breach of heteronormativity (Reddy 2001: 137) means to experience political oppression.

However, unlike many other more disadvantaged people, Emilija also has other tools for emotionally navigating the perilous waters of the highly differentiated emotional regime of heteronormativity. Norms are applied, and felt, with differing degrees of (emotional) intensity, depending on the different intersections of social positions or locations (class, ethnicity, religion, sexuality, age etc.) different people occupy (Stoetzler and Yuval-Davis 2002).

Due to her postgraduate education, prestigious occupation, stable employment and high enough income, Emilija was able to live on her own with no one's support and thus built a stable emotional refuge where she could safely retreat from the 'repetitive strain injuries' (Ahmed 2004: 145), and where she could safely emotionally explore the fallout from her fall from traditional heterosexual grace. As Reddy notes, 'those who depend on a single contractual relationship for their income and social identity [like] (married women under certain legal regimes) ... are, in practice, severely limited in the types of emotional management strategies they may adopt' (Reddy 2001: 127).

Since Emilija is not dependent for her income, or social identity, on her father (or her ex-husband, or her male lover, for that matter), her father's heteronormative fury is not the end of the world for her. Instead of sincere or less sincere expressions of shame, guilt and contrition to her parents (especially to her father) – grovelling and assurances that she would 'right the wrong' – she adopts a more defiant 'wait and see' approach mixed with anger, disappointment, sadness, pride, and determination. While she admitted to me that she felt initially immensely ashamed and guilty that she had kept her intimate relationship with her male colleague from her (now ex) husband and parents for years, once she came out to them she felt 'strangely liberated', as she put it (again an effect of the powerful self-altering effects of emotives). She felt sorry for her lover's wife, and extremely frustrated with his inability or unwillingness to confront his wife about the truth of their relationship; but eventually she stopped feeling ashamed and guilty for falling in love with her married colleague. To feel 'strangely liberated' from the tight grip of norms, to feel less than searing shame and guilt, is to feel a *deviant emotion* (Thoits 1990). Genet beautifully captured this emotional transformation when he epigrammatically said: 'My pride takes its royal hue from the purple of my shame' (*Mon orgueil s'est colore avec la pourpre de ma honte*) (1949: 237, quoted in Halperin 2007: 79).

There is no question that Emilija endured terrible emotional suffering, which Reddy defines as 'an acute form of goal conflict, especially brought on by emotional thought activations' (2001: 129). For many years she sacrificed the love, respect and support of her beloved parents in the vain hope that she would openly and happily live with her work colleague. She sought her loved one in order to realise a high-priority desire to be with him, and yet she exposed herself to rejection since she knew that in order to truly love her male work colleague she had to embrace his own high-priority goal – that is that he did not want to put his very young children through the turmoil of an acrimonious divorce, which prevented him from leaving his wife. The extraordinary emotional effort involved in concealing her relationship with her male colleague from anyone but a few of her closest friends was at deep odds with Emilija's need to live with integrity. This suffering was/is both a tragedy and an injustice. It is a tragedy because in the black-and-white heteronormative world it is 'tragic' for an already married woman to fall in love with, and be loved by, a man married to another woman (we have heard, read and seen too many cautionary tales of this in our novels, movies and TV dramas). However, to be symbolically degraded to a 'rotten whore', to be threatened with physical violence and to be turned into an 'evil and bad person' over her tragic love is an injustice inflicted by the repressive regime of heteronormativity.

Emilija is spared the worst excesses often committed in the name of heteronormativity because she lives and moves in an upper middle-class milieu, in which extreme displays of violent anger are seen as gauche. Her parents, when everything is said and done, still genuinely and deeply love her. A working-class, rural or a lower middle-class woman in Macedonia could have been killed, or physically and psychologically maimed (WAVE 2008: 105–9).[6]

---

6   'According to the study "Life in a Shadow" conducted by the Association ESE in 2007 every 2nd woman [in Macedonia] is affected by some form of psychological violence. 36.5% of the women state control of movement and contacts by their partner. The most common forms of physical violence are slaps (87.5%), threats of use of force (70.1%), grabbing and shoving (63.9%). The most severe forms of physical violence are most rarely used – burning or scalding (2.5%) or the use of a knife or a gun (9.9%). Every 4th woman reported having been physically attacked within her family. It is indicated that almost every 5th woman (18.9%) has reported recurrence of physical violence over 20 times. 10% of women have experienced the dominant form of sexual violence such as unwanted sexual intercourse (85.5% of the reported sexual violence), humiliating sexual intercourse, forced watching of pornographic films and pimping are represented to a far lesser extent' (WAVE 2008: 105).

Ahmed notes that '[f]amily love may be conditional upon how one lives one's life in relation to social ideals' and points out 'the role of [our] loving of others in enforcing social ideals'. Ahmed argues that in order to re-enter one's family and one's community, one's shameful failure to live up to the social ideals of those one loves must be 'witnessed, as well as be seen as temporary'. 'The relationship to others who witness my shame is anxious; shame both confirms and negates the love that sticks us together' (all quotes Ahmed 2004: 107).

While this is undeniably true in many cases of *queer shame*, Emilija's story shows another emotional dynamic through which the heteronormative ideals of her own parents are reworked. As already indicated, on the eve of the birth of Emilija's child, her parents, particularly her father, are presented with a stark, intensely emotional choice of their own, a logical outgrowth of their own heteronormative thinking and actions: either continue with Emilija's excommunication in order to prove a heteronormative point and risk being complete strangers to their long awaited grandchild, or re-evaluate not only Emilija's 'shameful' life but also their own 'family' values and have both their daughter and grandchild firmly back into their lives. In the end, her father's love (her mother's love was never in question) for Emilija negates, or significantly modifies the intensity of, the shame and confirms the 'love that sticks [them] together' (Ahmed 2004: 107). Another family located at a similar or other intersection of social locations could easily have taken a very different *line* on their *deviant* children (Goffman 1967).

Emilija re-enters her parents' home, which again becomes her family home, on her own terms. She is not contrite for what she has done; she does not follow Mummy and Daddy's ways; she has a houseful of 'sexual deviants' visiting her every day; she is happy to raise her daughter without a husband; and she dates without marriage and long commitment agendas.

Emotional Refuges and Intimate Citizenship

By way of conclusion I want to argue here that, although Emilija and her friends do not formulate explicit political grievances (the 'moment of citizenship' in Weeks's teleology) and in no way occupy clearly expressed and consciously politicised ('feminist', 'LGBT' or 'queer') stands, they nonetheless struggle 'to find a better way or to improvise a personal variation on prescribing [sexual and intimate] norms' (Reddy 2001: 137).

To arrive eventually at such an original arrangement, within a Macedonian context, for raising Emilija's daughter is a testament to the skills of Emilija, her parents, her ex-lover and his wife in navigating heteronormativity in a fairer and more honest way. This way takes account of the competing and contradictory goals, needs and desires of all the involved parties, a way that does not require the emotionally manipulative *either/or* logic of heteronormativity. The journey to creating this more complicated intimacy group around Emilija's daughter, as we saw, was, and is still, filled with conflict, tension and intense emotions.

Emilija's story, however, is far from an isolated case. There are many heterosexual women and men in Macedonia who have similarly struggled to rework Macedonian sexual and intimate norms. They work in academia, the government, the media, the non-governmental sector and the professions, and in such a small country many of them know each other personally. The circulation of their stories taking place in the emotional refuges these heterosexual men and women have created help develop alternative positive, subaltern and not entirely visible cultures around issues of intimacy and sexuality that 'leak into the wider public sphere and cultures', thus shifting 'the margins and the boundaries of the wider society' (Plummer 2001: 245; also see Plummer 1995). These intimate not-so-public spheres act as repositories of social capital, where the development of trusting relationships between friends, family members, work colleagues and sometimes even strangers (Phelan 2001) create the necessary 'featherbed (or warm bath)' (Collins 2004: 166) of trust, solidarity, sympathy and loyalty. From there the citizenship claims for recognition and respect for one's intimate choices from the wider, and more explicitly political and far less friendly, public spheres may (or may not) be launched.

Many of these, more queer, heterosexuals have gay, lesbian or bisexual friends,[7] and their own inability or unwillingness to live up to traditional sexual and intimate values makes them more sympathetic to the more explicit citizenship claims, as understood by Weeks (1998), made by the Macedonian lesbian, gay, bisexual and transgendered movement. Making explicit citizenship claims in the wider public spheres usually requires not only getting sympathy from the dominant majority (Turner 1993b; also see Clark 1997) but also mobilisation of justified and righteous anger. The conditions of possibility for queer, gay and lesbian or women's anger to get a just hearing from the wider society are not of their making (Ahmed 2004: 177). Although heterosexuals like Emilija still enjoy many comforts of heterosexuality (Ahmed 2004: 147), like the legal recognition of de facto or cohabiting relationships (*vonbračni zaednici*) between unmarried men and women (Article 13, *Zakon za semejstvoto* 2008) not extended to gays and lesbians, the affinity between queer heterosexuals and lesbians and gays resulting from their jointly feeling, albeit with differing intensities, the grip of heteronormativity makes the conditions for hearing the gay and lesbian grievances in some Macedonian public spheres, like the one consisting of progressive media outlets, non-governmental organizations, academics and centre left and left-wing political parties a bit more receptive.

In creating a new type of intimacy and support group comprising her traditional heterosexual parents, her queer friends, her heterosexual ex-lover and her daughter, Emilija has not only created an emotional refuge from dominant Macedonian

---

7   In a recent survey by Eurobarometer, only 6 per cent of interviewed Macedonian citizens reported that they have LGBT friends, as opposed to the 38 per cent average for the whole EU and 68 per cent of interviewed Dutch citizens reporting that they had LGBT friends (Eurobarometer 2009: 85–91; also see *Dnevnik*, 10 November 2009, and Jovanovska 2009).

norms, but has also made a successful citizenship claim for respect and recognition in how to conduct her intimate life and how to raise her daughter. The same goes for the recognition and respect for their sexual and intimate choices won by Emilija's friends from her parents. Phelan (2001) is right when she points out that 'important as state institutions are, they are not the sole arbiters of citizenship' (Langdridge 2006: 376). Thus, it 'is important to recognize the ways in which citizenship' (Langdridge 2006: 376) involves recognition and participation as a valued member/citizen in the social and political life of any unit of the social and political community (families, schools, neighbourhoods, workplaces, civil society organisations, the state etc.). If the nuclear (and extended) family is an ideological state apparatus (Althusser 1984), then to be recognised by it 'not in spite of one's unusual or minority characteristics, but with those characteristics understood as part of a valid possibility for the conduct of life' (Phelan 2001: 15) represents an important microscopic reordering of (Macedonian) state and society.

References

Ahmed, S. 2004. *The Cultural Politics of Emotions*. New York: Routledge.

Aizura, A.Z. 2006. 'Of Borders and Homes: The Imaginary Community of (Trans)sexual Citizenship'. *Inter-Asia Cultural Studies* 7(2): 289–309.

Alcoff, L.M. 1996. *Real Knowing: New Versions of the Coherence Theory*. Ithaca: Cornell University Press.

Althusser, L. 1984. *Essays on Ideology*. London: Verso.

Altman, D. 2001. *Global Sex*. Crows Nest, NSW: Allen and Unwin.

Anthias, F. and Yuval-Davis, N. 1992. *Racialized Boundaries: Race, Nation, Gender, Colour and Class and the Anti-Racist Struggle*. London and New York: Routledge.

Appadurai, A. 1990. 'Topografies of the Self: Praise and Emotion in Hindu India'. In *Language and the Politics of Emotion*, eds C.A. Lutz and L. Abu-Lughod. Cambridge: Cambridge University Press.

Avineri, S. and de-Shalit, A. (eds) 1992. *Communitarianism and Individualism*. Oxford: Oxford University Press.

Balibar, E. 1990. 'Paradoxes of Universality'. In *Anatomy of Racism*, ed. D.T. Goldberg. Minneapolis: University of Minnesota.

Barbalet, J. 2001. *Emotion, Social Theory and Social Structure: A Macrosociological Approach*. Cambridge: Cambridge University Press.

———. 2002. 'Introduction: Why Emotions are Crucial'. In *Emotions and Sociology*, ed. J. Barbalet. Oxford: Blackwell Publishing.

Beck, U. and Beck-Gernsheim, E. 1995. *The Normal Chaos of Love*. Cambridge: Polity Press.

Bell, D. and Binnie, J. 2000. *The Sexual Citizen: Queer Politics and Beyond*. Cambridge: Polity Press.

Benhabib, S. 1992. *Situating the Self*. Cambridge: Polity.

Bhabha, H.K. (ed.). 1991. *Nation and Narration*. New York and London: Routledge.

Blumer, H. 1969. *Symbolic Interactionism*. Upper Saddle River, NJ: Prentice Hall.

Brown, K.S. 2000. 'In the Realm of the Double-Headed Eagle: Parapolitics in Macedonia'. In *Macedonia: The Politics of Identity and Difference*, ed. J.K. Cowan. London: Pluto Press.

Clark, C. 1997. *Misery and Company: Sympathy in Everyday Life*. Chicago: University of Chicago Press.

Collins, R. 2004. *Interaction Ritual Chains*. Princeton: Princeton University Press.

Cossman, B. 2002. 'Sexing Citizenship, Privatizing Sex'. *Citizenship Studies* 6(4): 483–506.

Cowan, J.K. (ed.) 2000. *Macedonia: The Politics of Identity and Difference*. London: Pluto Press.

Cowan, S. 2005. '"Gender is No Substitute for Sex": A Comparative Human Rights Analysis of the Legal Regulation of Sexual Identity'. *Feminist Legal Studies* 13: 67–96.

Čomovski, G. 2010. 'Vladata nema razbiranje za homoseksualcite?' *Radio Slobodna Evropa* (online: 7 February). Available at: http://www.time.mk/read/NONE/5d496e9b2e/index.html (accessed: 7 February 2010).

Daly, M. 1993. *Communitarianism: Belonging and Commitment in a Pluralist Democracy*. Belmont: Wadsworth Publishing Company.

Dioli, I. 2009. 'Back to a Nostalgic Future: The Queeroslav Utopia'. *Sextures* (online) 1(1): 1–21. Available at: http://sextures.net/dioli-queeroslav-utopia (accessed: 21 February 2010).

Dnevnik, 2009. Makedoncite ne se družat so homoseksualci (online: 10 November). Available at: http://www.dnevnik.com.mk/default-mk.asp?ItemID=017CC4E 8B801E240A43A5AD6765BC92D&arc=1 [accessed: 10 November 2009].

Escoffier, J. 1998. *American Homo: Community and Perversity*. Berkeley: University of California Press.

Eurobarometer. 2009. *Discrimination in the EU in 2009*. Brussels: European Commission.

Evans, D. 1993. *Sexual Citizenship: The Material Construction of Sexualities*. London: Routledge.

Flores, W. and Benmayor, R. (eds) 1997. *Latino Cultural Citizenship: Claiming Identity, Space and Rights*. Boston, MA: Beacon Press.

Foucault, M. 1980. 'Two Lectures'. In *Power/Knowledge: Selected Interviews and Other Writings*, ed. C. Gordon. New York: Pantheon Books.

Fraser, N. 1989. *Unruly Practices: Power, Discourse and Gender in Contemporary Social Theory*. Cambridge: Polity.

———. 1997. *Justice Interruptus: Critical Reflections on the Postsocialist Condition*. London: Routledge.

Genet, J. 1949. *Journal du voleur*. Paris: Gallimard.

Giddens, A. 1992. *The Transformation of Intimacy: Sexuality, Love and Eroticism in Modern Societies*. Cambridge: Polity Press.

Goffman, E. 1967. *Interaction Ritual: Essays on Face-to-Face Behavior*. New York: Pantheon Books.

Gordon, S. 1990. 'Social Structural Effects on Emotions'. In *Research Agendas in the Sociology of Emotions*, ed. T. Kemper. Albany: State University of New York Press.

Grewal, I. 1996. *Home and Harem: Nation, Gender, Empire and the Culture of Travel*. Durham, NC: Duke University Press.

Halperin, D. 2007. *What Do Gay Men Want?: An Essay on Sex, Risk and Subjectivity*. Ann Arbor: The University of Michigan Press.

Hochschild, A. 2003. *The Managed Heart: Commercialization of Human Feeling*. Berkeley: University of California Press.

International Lesbian and Gay Association (ILGA). 2001. Equality for Lesbian and Gay Men: A Relevant Issue in the EU Accession Process [online, ILGA]. Available at: http://www.ilga-europe.org [accessed: 17 November 2009].

Iveković, R. 1996. *Le pouvoir nationaliste et les femmes*. Bologna: Europe and the Balkans International Network and Ravenna: Longo Editore.

Iveković, R. and Mostov, J. (eds) 2002. *From Gender to Nation*. Ravenna: Longo Editore.

Jones, T. 2009. 'The Queer Joys of Sexless Marriage: Coupled Citizenship's Hot Bed!' *Sextures* [online] 1(1): 1–25. Available at: http://sextures.net/jones-sexless-marriage [accessed: 17 January 2010].

Jovanovska, S. 2009. 'Makedoncite ne sakaat rozov lider' [online: 10 November]. Available at: http://www.time.mk/read/NONE/7252b5417f/index.html [accessed: 10 November 2009].

Kabir, N. (ed.) 2005. *Inclusive Citizenship*. London: Zed Books.

Kaplan, M.B. 1997. *Sexual Justice: Democratic Citizenship and the Politics of Desire*. New York and London: Routledge.

Kligman, G. 1998. *The Politics of Duplicity: Controlling Reproduction in Ceausescu's Romania*. Berkeley and Los Angeles: University of California Press.

Kring, A. 2000. 'Gender and Anger'. In *Gender and Emotion: Social Psychological Perspectives*, ed. A. Fischer. Cambridge: Cambridge University Press.

Kymlicka, W. 1995. *Multicultural Citizenship*. Oxford: Clarendon Press.

Lambevski, S.A. 1999. 'Suck My Nation: Masculinity, Ethnicity and the Politics of (Homo)Sex'. *Sexualities* (2)4: 397–419.

———. 2003. 'Feeling the Paranoiac, The Schizzo and the Depressive: A Semiotic Analysis of Macedonia's Emotional Architecture. In *Before the Rain. Social Semiotics* 13(2): 161–78.

———. 2009. 'Emotions, Belonging and the Microsociology of Venal Border Crossings: Encountering the Macedonian State as a Flexible Queer Citizen-Cowboy'. *Sextures* [online] 1(1): 1–43. Available at: http://sextures.net/lambevski-emotions-and-belonging [accessed: 21 February 2010].

Langdridge, D. 2006. 'Voices From the Margins: Sadomasochism and Sexual Citizenship'. *Citizenship Studies* 10(4): 373–89.

Lister, M. and Pia, E. 2008. *Citizenship in Contemporary Europe*. Edinburgh: Edinburgh University Press.

Lister, R. 1997. *Citizenship: Feminist Perspectives*. Basingstoke: Macmillan.

Loutzenheiser, L.W. and MacIntosh, L.B. 2004. 'Citizenships, Sexualities, and Education'. *Theory into Practice* 43(2): 151–8.

Lutz, C. and Abu-Lughod, L. 1990. *Language and the Politics of Emotion*. Cambridge: Cambridge University Press.

Marcu, M. 2009. *The EU-27 Population Continues to Grow (31/2009)*. Brussels: Eurostat.

Marshall, T.H. 1950. *Citizenship and Social Class*. Cambridge: Cambridge University Press.

McClintock, A. 1993. *Imperial Leather: Race, Gender and Sexuality in the Colonial Contest*. New York and London: Routledge.

Mizielińska, J. 2006. 'Queering Moominland: The Problems of Translating Queer Theory into a Non-American Context'. *SQS Journal of Queer Studies* 1: 87–104.

———. 2009. *Queer Theory in Poland: On Some Problems with Translation*. Advanced Seminar Presentation given at the Centre for Baltic and East European Studies, Soedertoerns University, 7 September.

Moynagh, P. 1997. 'A Politics of Enlarged Mentality: Hannah Arendt, Citizenship Responsibility, and Feminism'. *Hypatia* 12: 27–53.

Nash, K. 2001. 'Feminism and Contemporary Liberal Citizenship: The Undecidability of "Women"'. *Citizenship Studies* 5(3): 255–68.

Oleksy, E. (ed.) 2009. *Intimate Citizenships: Gender, Sexualities, Politics*. London: Routledge.

Parker, R., di Mauro, D., Filiano, B., Garcia, J., Munoz-Laboy, M. and Sember, R. 2004. 'Global Transformations and Intimate Relations in the 21st Century: Social Science Research on Sexuality and the Emergence of *Sexual Health* and *Sexual Rights* Frameworks'. *Annual Review of Sex Research* 15: 362–98.

Pateman, C. 1988. *The Sexual Contract*. Stanford: Stanford University Press.

Phelan, S. 2001. *Sexual Strangers: Gays, Lesbians and Dilemmas of Citizenship*. Philadelphia: Temple University Press.

Plummer, K. 1995. *Telling Sexual Stories: Power, Change and Social Worlds*. London: Routledge.

———. 2001. 'The Square of Intimate Citizenship: Some Preliminary Proposals'. *Citizenship Studies* 5(3): 237–53.

———. 2003. *Intimate Citizenship: Private Decisions and Public Dialogues*. Seattle: University of Washington Press.

Quine, W. 1969. *Ontological Relativity and Other Essays*. New York: Columbia University Press.

Reddy, W. 2001. *The Navigation of Feeling: A Framework for the History of Emotions*. Cambridge: Cambridge University Press.

Richardson, D. 1998. 'Sexuality and Citizenship'. *Sociology* 32(1): 83–100.
———. 2000. *Rethinking Sexuality*. London: Sage.
Rorty, R. 1989. *Contingency, Irony and Solidarity*. Cambridge: Cambridge University Press.
Roman, M. 2001. 'Gendering Eastern Europe: Pre-Feminism, Prejudiced and East-West Dialogues in Post-Communist Romania'. *Women's Studies International Forum* 24: 14–34.
Scheff, T. 1990. *Microsociology: Discourse, Emotion and Social Structure*. Chicago: Chicago University Press.
Schippert, C. 2006. 'Containing Uncertainty: Sexual Values and Citizenship'. *Journal of Homosexuality* 52(1–2): 285–307.
Seidman, S. 2001. 'From Identity to Queer Politics: Shifts in Normative Heterosexuality and the Meaning of Citizenship'. *Citizenship Studies* 5(3): 321–8.
Smith, A.M. 2001. 'The Politicization of Marriage in Contemporary American Public Policy: The Defense of Marriage Act and the Personal Responsibility Act'. *Citizenship Studies* 5(3): 303–20.
State Statistical Office of the Republic of Macedonia. 2009. News release, no. 2.1.9.14, 3 July 2009.
Stoetzler, M. and Yuval-Davis, N. 2002. 'Standpoint Theory, Situated Knowledge and the Situated Imagination'. *Feminist Theory* 3(3): 315–34.
Stojančevska, V. 2010. Dali e ustavna homofobijata? *Vreme* [online: 12 February]. Available at: http://www.time.mk/read/NONE/acfcb92d7e/index.html [accessed: 12 February 2010].
Stulhofer, A. and Sandfort, T. (eds) 2005. *Sexuality and Gender in Postcommunist Eastern Europe and Russia*. Binghamton, NY: The Haworth Press.
Stychin, C. 2001. 'Sexual Citizenship in the European Union'. *Citizenship Studies* 5(3): 285–301.
———. 2003. *Governing Sexuality*. Oxford and Portland, OR: Hart Publishing.
The Former Yugoslav Republic of Macedonia 2009 Progress Report. 2009. (SEC. 2009 1335). Brussels: Commission of the European Communities.
The Treaty of Amsterdam 1997 [online]. Available at: www.eurotreaties.com/amsterdamtreaty.pdf [accessed: 4 January 2010].
The Treaty of Lisbon 2007, Official Journal of the European Union, 50(C306), 17 December.
Thoits, P.A. 1990. 'Emotional Deviance: Research Agendas'. In *Research Agendas in the Sociology of Emotions*, ed. T. Kemper. Albany: State University of New York Press: 180–203.
Trajanoski, Ž. 2010. 'Lošo vino'. *Dnevnik* [online: 3 February]. Available at: http://www.dnevnik.com.mk/default-mk.asp?ItemID=317BC89520AA6342BC13C85D16854E95&arc=1 [accessed: 3 February 2010].
Turner, B. (ed.) 1993a. *Citizenship and Social Theory*. London: Sage.
———. 1993b. 'Outline of a Theory of Human Rights'. *Sociology* 27(3): 489–512.

Van Selm. J. 2007. *Macedonia: At a Quiet Crossroad* [online: Migration Policy Institute]. Available at: http://www.migrationinformation.org/Profiles/display.cfm?ID=68 [accessed: 8 October 2009].

Waites, M. 1996. 'Lesbian and Gay Theory, Sexuality and Citizenship: Review Article'. *Contemporary Politics* 2(3): 139–49.

Warner, M. 1999. *The Trouble with Normal: Sex, Politics and the Ethics of Queer Life*. New York: Free Press.

Watt, G. 2005. 'Sexual Citizenship in Latvia: Geographies of the Latvian Closet'. *Social and Cultural Geography* 6(2): 16181.

WAVE. 2008. *Country Report 2008: Reality Check for Women and Children Victims of Violence*. Vienna: WAVE.

Weeks, J. 1995. *Invented Moralities: Sexual Values in an Age of Uncertainty*. Cambridge: Polity Press.

———. 1998. 'The Sexual Citizen'. *Theory, Culture and Society* 15(3–4): 35–52.

Wikan, U. 1990. *Managing Turbulent Hearts: A Balinese Formula for Living*. Chicago: University of Chicago Press.

Woodcock, S. 2009. 'Gay Pride as a Violent Containment in Romania: A Brave New EUrope'. *Sextures* [online] 1(1): 1–17. Available at: http://sextures.net/woodcock-gay-pride-romania [accessed: 21 February 2010].

Yuval-Davis, N. 2006. 'Belonging and the Politics of Belonging'. *Patterns of Prejudice* 40(3): 197–214.

Yuval-Davis, N. and Werbner, P. (eds) 1990. *Women, Citizenship and Difference*. London: Zed Books.

Zakon za semejstvoto 2008, Prečisten tekst, 22 December [online: Gragjanska organizacija 'Most']. Available at: http://www.pravo.org.mk/documentDetail.php?id=500&gid=20&tid=1&page=documentlaws.php [accessed: 3 January 2010].

Zakon za volontersvo 2007. Služben vesnik na Republika Makedonija, no. 85, 9 February.

Zakon za zaštita na pravata na pacientite 2008. Služben vesnik na Republika Makedonija, no. 82/08, 8 July.

Index